M. Bossu, John Reinhold Forster

Travels Through that Part of North America Formerly Called

Louisiana.

Vol. I

M. Bossu, John Reinhold Forster

Travels Through that Part of North America Formerly Called Louisiana.
Vol. I

ISBN/EAN: 9783744755856

Printed in Europe, USA, Canada, Australia, Japan

Cover: Foto ©Andreas Hilbeck / pixelio.de

More available books at **www.hansebooks.com**

TRAVELS

THROUGH

LOUISIANA.

TRAVELS

THROUGH THAT PART OF

NORTH AMERICA

FORMERLY CALLED

LOUISIANA.

By Mr. BOSSU, Captain in the French Marines.

Translated from the FRENCH, By JOHN REINHOLD FORSTER, F.A.S.

Illustrated with NOTES relative chiefly to NATURAL HISTORY.

TO WHICH IS ADDED BY THE TRANSLATOR

A SYSTEMATIC CATALOGUE of all the known Plants of English North-America,

O R, A

FLORA AMERICÆ SEPTENTRIONALIS.

TOGETHER WITH

An ABSTRACT of the most useful and necessary articles contained in PETER LOEFLING's TRAVELS through Spain and Cumana in South America. Referred to the Pages of the original Swedish Edition.

VOL. I.

Ornari res ipfa negat, contenta doceri. *Horat.*

LONDON:
Printed for T. DAVIES in Ruffel-Street, Covent-Garden.
MDCCLXXI.

T O

WILLIAM CONSTABLE, Efq;

of BURTON-CONSTABLE.

S I R,

THE zeal with which you promote the
great caufe of learning, and efpecially that of Natural Hiftory, the Polite
Arts and Antiquities, intitle you to the
regard and homage of every one who is
converfant with Arts and Sciences : but
the favour you were fo kind to beftow upon me, before you proceeded on the tour
through the different parts of Europe, en-
courages me to take this early opportunity
to congratulate you on your return to your
philofophic retirement, and publicly to acknowledge the gratitude and attachment
which will ever prompt me to think myfelf happy in my weak endeavours to approve my conduct and fentiments to my
friends and benefactors.

May

May you always enjoy perfect health, and all the rational and moral bleffings of this life; and, after a long feries of years, diftinguifhed by actions of benevolence, friendfhip, and virtue, exchange thefe tranfitory enjoyments for everlafting felicity. Thefe are the fincere and invariable wifhes of him who fubfcribes himfelf, with the trueft regard,

S I R,

Your moft obliged

.LONDON, Oct. 5.
1771.

obedient humble fervant,

JOHN REINHOLD FORSTER.

PREFACE.

THE prefent publication appears with a view to fupply the English reader with a good account of a country, which now enjoys the happinefs to be under the mild influence and fway of the British fceptre ; and, if properly adminiftered and peopled, might in time become one of the great fupports of that power, which makes *Great Britain* refpected over all the globe. The country here defcribed is fufceptible of great improvements, capable to fupply the mother-country with immenfe ftores of raw materials for her manufactures, and to take in return the products of our induftry ; a commerce which, connected with religious and civil liberty, is the only bafis on which the grandeur of this nation can be laftingly founded with any degree of probability.

The Catalogue of North American plants is a mere attempt, to make the curious more attentive to the American fpontaneous products, and which will give a higher degree of certainty of fuccefs to the plantations of fuch plants as were recommended to the public, by the ingenious and great promoter of Natural Hiftory and Plantations *John Ellis*, Efq;· in a *Catalogue of fuch foreign plants as are worthy of being encouraged in our American colonies for the purpofes of medicine, agriculture, and commerce.*

The

The Englifh names affixed to the greater part of the plants, will make it more eafy to the common people to know and to ufe them, bring the fcience more down even to the loweft capacities, fix the hitherto vague and multifarious denominations of plants in various parts of America, and obviate that confufion and drynefs already too common in the ftudy of that ufeful branch of knowledge.

Loefling's defcriptions of the Spanifh and South American plants are the only things in his journal which deferve the attention of a curious reader; the letters publifhed along with them in the Swedifh, are compliments of a grateful pupil to his tutor, and queries and *dubia* relative to botany; and therefore not worth a tranflation. The Englifh public has now all the voyages and publications of the Linnæan fchool; *Haffelquift, Ofbeck, Toreen, Kalm,* and *Loefling* make the whole of them.

The French word *outarde* fignifies commonly a *buftard,* but in North America they give that name to a kind of geefe, which I therefore beg to correct, vol. i. p. 96.; having but lately got an information about it, from a gentleman who is juft returned from North America.

The *Sardines* mentioned vol. i. p. 2. are not, as I have fufpected in the note, the *pilchards,* fo common on our weftern coafts; but a kind of herring, not yet defcribed, peculiar to the neighbourhood of *Belle-Ifle,* and the coaft of French Bretany.

TRAVELS

THROUGH

LOUISIANA.

LETTER I.

To the Marquis de l'Estrade.

The Author's Departure for America; Defcription of the Town of Cape François; Cruelties of the Spaniards towards the Natives of the Ifle of St. Domingo; working of the Mines; true Origin of the Mal de Naples.

WHEN I had the honour of taking my leave of you, I was ordered to communicate to you every particular that fhould appear remarkable to me in this new world; you farther defired of me an account of all interefting fubjects which might happen on

Vol. I.   B   the

the paſſage. I am glad that my ſtay at *Cape François* affords me an opportunity of fulfilling an engagement which is dear to me, becauſe its execution may prove agreeable to you.

I was at *Belle-Iſle* in 1750, *M. Le Chevalier de Groſſoles* commanded at that place; he gave me a letter from the Count *d'Argenſon*, from which I learnt, that his Majeſty had made me Lieutenant in the Marines; this Miniſter gave me orders to ſet out immediately for *Rochefort*; accordingly I went on board the firſt fiſhing ſmack deſtined to carry the Anchovies * *(Sardines)* to *Rochelle*, which are caught on the Coaſt of *Bretany*, and which are the chief ſupport of the inhabitants of *Belle-Iſle*.

In

* The *true Anchovies* are caught in the Mediterranean; and thoſe few that now and then appear in the ſeas near *England* or *France,* are rather rare examples; they are certainly not ſo numerous that a profitable fiſhery of them could be inſtituted. The *Sardine* of our Author, therefore, ſeems to be the *Pilchard*, a fiſh that is very copiouſly caught on the coaſts of *Cornwall* and *French Bretany*. *Linnæus* has no peculiar ſpecific name for this fiſh, though the great *Engliſh* natural hiſtorian, *Ray*, in his Syn. piſc. 104, had pointed out the characters of this ſpecies; which now is done more fully by Mr. *Pennant*, in his Britiſh Zoology, III. p. 291. F.

In November we weighed anchor before the
Palace *, (which is the name of the town on this
ifland); and the very firft night of our voyage
we had fuch a violent ftorm on the coaft of *Poitou*, that our little veffel being beat about and
furrounded by the waves, we expected every
moment to go to the bottom : The crew confifted of a pilot, and three failors from Lower *Bretany*, who are commonly called *Sea-wolves* †;
and are fo well accuftomed to this element, that
they brave the hardeft weather. The wind having increafed, our captain was obliged to put in
at the *Ifle de Dieu*, fituated between *Poitou* and
the county *d'Aunis*. We ftaid there eight days ;
at the expiration of which, the fea being calmed,
we fet fail again, and continued our voyage to
the Ifle of *Rhé*; from whence I croffed a channel of the fea about three leagues broad, that
feparates the ifle from the continent, and arrived at *Rochelle*, and the day after 1 came to
Rochefort. I was directed to addrefs myfelf to
the intendant of the department of the marine,
who is M. *le Normant de Méfi*, a man of real
merit, and deferving of the place he occupies,
by his talents and the goodnefs of his heart : he
told me, that, as foon as I fhould have equipped
myfelf for my voyage, I was to go to *Rochelle*,

and

---

* Le Palais.　　　† *Loups de mer:*

and embark in the fhip called the *Pontchartrain*, of 400 tuns. M *le Normant* had freighted this fhip for the King's account, in order to tranf-port four companies of the marines, whom we took in at the citadel on the ifle of *Rhé:* they were deftined to reinforce the garrifon of *New Orleans.*

We fet fail from *Rochelle* the 26th of Decem-ber, and had contrary winds for above a fort-night on the coaft of Spain. We were already willing to put in at *Corunna,* in order to be fhel-tered from the violence of the winds; when happily the wind fhifted; and, towards the end of January, we were in fight of *Madeira,* an ifle belonging to *Portugal* *; it is called the queen of iflands, on account of its fertility and the excellence of its foil; it has near twenty leagues in circumference, produces good wines, and very fine fruits.

On the 15th of February we paffed the tropic of Cancer. The next day the failors fpent in ·fome

---

* It is an African ifland in the Atlantic ocean, and fitu-ated to the north of the Canary iflands; which latter were difcovered in 1417, by a Norman gentleman called *Jean Bethencourt,* who bore the title of King of the Canaries, and made the conqueft of them to the Spaniards, who poffefs them now.

fome ridiculous ceremonies, which they oblige thofe to undergo who never paffed the line before: they are baptifed with fea-water; but may avoid this too abundant afperfion by making a fmall prefent to the boatfwain.

Two months after leaving *Rochelle* we arrived at Cape *François*, in the ifle of *St. Domingo*; which is that part of *America* where the Spaniards have firft built towns and forts.

The town lies at the bottom of a promontory: it is defended by a fort cut·in the rock, at the entrance of the port. This fortrefs, which has a good ftore of artillery, projeƈts into the fea; and by that means forms a cape, from whence the town takes its name. Its inhabitants are European merchants, Creoles, and negroes; the laft being employed to cultivate fugar-canes, coffee, indigo, cacao, cotton, caffia, tobacco, and various other produƈts.

The French and Spaniards have divided the ifland between them; the latter poffefs the weftern part of it*. *San Domingo* is the capital of

B 3   the

---

* Since that time the Spaniards have given their fhare of this ifland to the French. F.

the ifland; it is the feat of a bifhop, whom the King of Spain appoints.

This ifland is celebrated by the origin of the *mal de Naples*, or venereal difeafe. Authors difagree fo much on this fubject, and have told the ftory in fo many different ways, that I think I fhall not do amifs to reprefent it in its true light.

Nicolas de Obando was governor of this ifle, towards the end of the fifteenth century, during the reign of King *Ferdinand* of *Arragon* and *Ifabella* of *Caftile:* he had ftrict orders to work at the converfion of the fubdued Indians; he diftributed them among the Spaniards, giving a hundred of them to one man, fifty to another; and calling this proceeding a *repartimiento*, (a divifion). I believe you will agree with me, Sir, that this is a very fingular method of making converts in *America*; fuch maxims are quite contrary to the true fpirit of the Chriftian religion *.

Thefe

---

* " The King Don *Ferdinand*, being informed of thefe
" diforders, had turned all his attention towards remedying
" them; and his care chiefly regarded the Indians, whom
" he wifhed to protect and convert, as it has always been the
" maxim of the Catholic kings. He gave feveral orders,
" and

Thefe Spaniards, greedy of gold, forced the wretched Indians to work in the mines, and kept them almoft buried in the earth for eight or nine months together. This hard labour, the fulphureous vapours which continually rofe from the mines, and the famine to which they were reduced by the impoffibility of cultivating their grounds, fo corrupted the mafs of their blood, that their faces became tinged with a faffron colour; a kind of puftules came out on every part of their body, and caufed them infupportable pains. They foon communicated this ficknefs to their wives, and fo of courfe to their enemies; and they all perifhed for want of a remedy.

The afflicted Spaniards hoped, that this kind of peft would not follow them to *Europe*, whither they went for the change of air; but they were deceived; and, on their return, they gave the Europeans the diftemper they got from the *Americans*.

How-

" and publifhed laws, that they fhould be inftructed with
" mildnefs, difintereftednefs, and by example: but as an
" arrow falls without force at the bottom of the aim, when
" it is beyond the reach of the arm that fhot it; fo, all the
" methods which he made ufe of to make his defigns fuc-
" ceed, loft their force as they got to a greater diftance."
Don Antonio de Solis.

However, Providence pitied thefe wretched iflanders : an Indian woman, the wife of a Spaniard, difcovered, fome time after, that a kind of wood called *guayacan*, was a fufficient cure for their diftemper *.

It is but too true, Sir, that evil produces evil. The Spaniards have facrificed millions of men in the new world; they have laid wafte countries of vaft extent, in order to ufurp the gold of the Indians.

Gold and filver give as much trouble and fatigue to thofe who work them out of the mines, as they afford contentment and eafe to their poffeffors. A Spanifh engineer told me, that twenty-nine years were fpent in fearching, in the mountains of *Potofi*, for the famous vein of *Crufero*, which is two hundred and fifty yards deep. Such is the hard and fupernatural labour which power and defire of riches exacts, and which is

executed

---

* Notwithftanding what our author fays concerning the origin of this difeafe, it is well known, that the inhabitants of South and North America had the difeafe when the Europeans came to them ; but they well knew how to cure it, though they carefully kept this knowledge from their European enemies ; and it has but lately been difcovered, that in the fouth the *Guayacum*, and in the north the *Stillingia fylvatica*, together with other plants, are the Indian fpecifics. F.

executed by neceſſity and ſervitude, in order to extract gold from the bowels of the earth. The wretched workmen who are employed there, enjoy neither the air of our atmoſphere, nor the light of the ſun, and bury themſelves in infectious and cold abyſſes; of which the exhalations are ſo unwholeſome, that they cauſe ſwoons and giddineſs to the workmen as ſoon as they offer to go in. They make uſe of candles to light them in theſe dark ſubterraneous places: the metal is generally hard in them; they break it in pieces with hammers, load it on their ſhoulders, and mount upwards oñ ladders made of twiſted hides of oxen, with wooden ſteps, contrived in ſuch a manner, that whilſt one goes up on one ſide, another may deſcend on the other: theſe ladders are divided into ten ſets. A man generally carries two *arobas* of metal on his back *, wrapped up in a piece of cloth: he that goes firſt has a candle faſtened to his thumb; and they all hold themſelves with both hands on the ladder, in order to be able to go upwards for the ſpace of 250 feet.

The general hiſtory of *America* tells us, that the nations of *Florida* took the ſacks with ſilver, and threw them far from themſelves as uſeleſs. The *Mexicans*, on the contrary, were fond of gold;

---

* An Aroba is 25 pounds, *poids de Marc.*

gold; though, as *Joseph d'Acosta* says, in his univerfal hiftory of the Indies, " it is true that " their avarice was not arrived to that pitch " where ours is; and that, notwithftanding " their being idolaters, they never have worfhip- " ped gold and filver fo much as fome bad " Chriftians have done, who have committed " the moft atrocious crimes for the fake of that " metal."

The fame author relates the following anec- dote, which perfectly characterizes man's ftupid defire after riches. " A Spanifh monk, confi- " dering the height of the famous volcano of " *Guatimala*, took it into his head, that that " which he faw inflamed muft needs be a mafs of " gold, fince it had burnt for many ages toge- " ther without being cohfumed. Mifled by this " falfe principle, he invented fome kettles, " chains, and other inftruments, with which " he intended to draw the liquid gold from this " kind of well: but the fire difappointed him; " for the chain and kettle were fcarce entered " into this infernal orifice, but they immediate- " ly melted down. However," fays our author, " this man perfifted in inventing new methods " for fetching up the gold after which he thirfted " fo much; but one day happening to come too " near the mouth of the volcano, the exhalations

" from

" from it killed him, when he expected to have
" fucceeded in his whimfical defign. Thus
" blind mortals haften their death by too great a
" purfuit after the luxuries of this life."

But to return to the Indians of *Saint Domingo*. The hiftory of that ifle informs us, that a *Cacique* * called *Poncra*, being haraffed by the Spaniards, refolved to flee from his village, which the enemies found abandoned, and where they took three thoufand marks of gold, which had been left there. *Vafco Nunez de Balboa*, the fucceffor of *Nicolas de Obando*, fent his people to the Cacique, with orders to affure him, that he fhould not fear to return, becaufe he fhould be his friend; but that if he did not come back, he fhould go and hunt for him, and caufe him to be devoured by his dogs †.

Poncra

---

* A cacique is a petty prince or king of the Indians.

† The Spaniards had brought over with them from *Europe* fome maftiffs, which they had taught to hunt the Indians; as foon as they were let loofe upon thefe wretches, they tore out their bowels, and devoured them. One of thefe dogs called *Barémel* was very much dreaded all over the ifland; and though he was guarded by a fhield againft the arrows of the Indians, they, it is faid, at laft killed him, by piercing his eyes with darts, which was a kind of triumph for them.

Antonio

Poncra was frightened by his threats, and did not venture to difobey. He brought with him three of his vaffals. *Nunez de Balboa* employed in vain all the cunning imaginable to bring him to difcover the place where they got the gold, which he had heard contained great quantities of that metal: good ufage and punifhments were equally infufficient to bring him to confefs what perhaps he did not know. As to the three thoufand *marks* of gold which had been found, *Poncra* faid, that thofe who had amaffed them died in the times of his fathers, and that he had not thought it worth while to fend people to fearch for more, having no need of it. This unhappy Cacique was given up to the fury of the dogs, that devoured him with his three companions.

Some time after, a Spaniard fell into the hands of the fubjects of the unhappy *Poncra*; they reproached him with the excèffive thirft of his countrymen after gold, and the injuftices it led

them

Antonio de Herrera, in his firft *Decas*, relates, that this fierce creature, whofe inftinct was fingular, guarded a narrow pafs in the ifle of *St. Domingo*; and that one day an Indian woman, being defirous of paffing by him, addreffed him in thefe words: *Signor Dog, do not hurt me; I carry this letter to the Chriftians:* he adds, that *the dog immediately fmelled at her, piffed at her,* (thofe are his very words) *and fuffered her to pafs without doing her any harm.*

them to commit; that this avidity alone forced
them from their country, and brought them
acrofs numberlefs perils to that ifland, to difturb
its inhabitants, who lived peaceably before in
their huts, under the protection of the *Great
Spirit* *.

After this fhort harangue, they melted fome
gold, and poured it into his mouth and ears,
faying, *Thou dog, fince thou art fo willing to poffefs it, glut thyfelf.*

It muft, however, be owned, Sir, that, if
the Mexican hiftory fhews us nothing but horror,
that of *St. Domingo*, on the other hand, furnifhes
us with inftances of generofity.

Don Pedro de Magaratit, formerly a commandant here for the King of Spain, was offered a
couple of living turtle - doves, by an Indian
in a great famine. The general took them,
paid the Indian handfomely for them, and begged part of the garrifon to go with him to the
higheft part of the town; where, being arrived,
he faid to them, holding the little creatures in
his hand, " Gentlemen, I am forry that people
" have

* Thus the Indians call the Supreme Being.

" have not brought me provisions sufficient to
" treat you all ; I cannot resolve to satisfy my ap-
" petite, whilst you are starving :" and as he
had spoke these words, he let the birds fly
away.

An infinite number of other instances may be
added to this, which do no less honour to the
inhabitants of this isle. There are several that
deserve to be recorded in history ; and among
those that I have been told, I cannot help thinking the following story worth your notice. An
old inhabitant of St. Domingo had acquired a
considerable fortune there by his labour, industry, and trade. His conduct and manners remained unaltered by prosperity ; and he only
valued his riches, because they enabled him to
serve others.

Whenever a ship arrived from France, he ran
to the coast to see the passengers land, and generally conducted them to his home. One day he
saw several young people, who expected to make
their fortune as soon as they arrived ; they had
letters of recommendation, on which they depended so much, that they took little notice of
the good planter, who accosted them ; he left
them, wishing them all kind of prosperity :
some

fome time after he met them again looking very fad and difcontented with the reception they had found. Gentlemen, fays he to them, you are not recommended to me, and you did not rely on me. I am your fellow-creature, and you want affiftance; come to my houfe, you will there find a table and a lodging at your fervice; and during that time perhaps fomething may offer, that will fuit your inclinations. The young people were enraptured, and accepted his offers; they followed him to his houfe, where they found a table fpread for twenty perfons, and ferved by as many Negro fervants. One of the new comers afked whether they were at a wedding, and was furprifed to hear that this was nothing extraordinary. The mafter of the houfe kept them in his houfe for fome time; his advices, and the pains he took about them, foon procured them very advantageous fituations.

You will eafily believe, Sir, that fo good a mafter was loved and refpected by all his flaves, who looked upon him as upon their father. This man was very far from being animated by the brutal avidity of fome planters, that force their wretched flaves to fuch hard labour, that they refufe to marry, in order to avoid generating flaves to fuch mafters, who treat them,

when

when old and infirm, worfe than their dogs and horfes*.

As to the inhabitants of the French iflands in the Weft Indies, I can affure you they are very generous towards ftrangers : a perfon may even travel in the interior parts of the country, without the leaft expence to himfelf; if his countenance be free and open, and his behaviour decent, he is fufficiently qualified for a favourable reception in every habitation.

It is with great juftice that we reckon the *Creoles* noble in France : their fentiments are fo noble and delicate in every ftation of life, that they perfectly deferve that appellation.

Man is every where the fame ; he is equally fufceptible of good and evil ; education corrects his vices, but does not give him virtue ; the fame

---

* I have feen a planter, whofe name was *Chaperon,* who forced one of his negroes to go into a heated oven, where the poor wretch expired ; and his jaws being fhrivelled up, the barbarous *Chaperon* faid, I believe the fellow laughs, and took a poker to ftir him up. Since that time he is grown the fcare-crow of all the flaves ; who, when they have done fomething amifs, are threatened by their mafters with, *I will fell thee to Chaperon.*

fame Being has created the civilized man and
the favage, and has endowed them with the
fame qualities, as you will find in the fequel of
my correfpondence. If I cannot amufe you
with my ftile, at leaft I fhall make my narrative
interefting, through the fingularity of the facts
I intend to relate.

I am, S I R, &c.

Cape François, the 15th
of February 1751.

L E T T E R II.

To the same.

The Author's Departure from Cape François *for* Louifiana. *Short Defcription of the Harbour of the* Havannah. *Of the famous Gulph of* Mexico; *and of* New Orleans,

S I R,

WE weighed anchor the 8th of March laft; and on the 15th we were in fight of *Cuba*, which is the moft temperate of all the *Antilles*. The *Havannah* is the ftore of all the riches of America, on account of its fituation, and the extent and convenience of its harbour, which can contain upwards of a thoufand fhips. It is the common *rendez-vous* of the Spanifh fleets returning to Europe; and it is defended by three forts. *Cuba* is two hundred leagues long, and between twenty-five and thirty broad; fixteen years have been fpent in difcoveries to afcertain whether it was an ifle or

continent:

continent: it lies under the tropic of Cancer, that is, in twenty-three degrees and a half north latitude. Near the middle of the ifland, to the fouthward, are a number of little ifles very clofe to each other, which are called the Garden of the Queen *.

During the equinox we fuffered a very violent ftorm between Cape *Catoche* and Cape *Antonio*; the latter, which we doubled on the twenty-third, is at the weftern point of the ifle of *Cuba*. I was very fea-fick, having never been at fea on fo long a voyage; but the defire of ferving my country in a new land, fufficiently compenfated all the hardfhips I underwent on my paffage. The winds changed, the fea became fmooth, and, a few days after, we entered into the famous gulph of *Mexico*, where we met with a prodigious quantity of floating timber, coming from *Louifiana* down the river *Miffifippi*: thefe logs of wood are feen for above two hundred leagues at fea, and ferve as guides to the entrance of the river in hazy and foggy weather; it being very difficult to get into it, on account of the rocks and fhoals in the neighbourhood of its entrance.

C 2

In

_____

* Jardin de la Reyna.

In the firſt days of April we perceived the fort *Baliſe* at the mouth of the *Miſſiſippi*. Mr. *le Moine d'Iberville*, a Canada gentleman, diſcovered, in 1698 *, this mouth of the river, which M. *de la Salle* miſſed in 1684. Our veſſel ſtruck upon the bar; we fired a gun to call the pilot, and at the ſame time the captain diſembarked the artillery of the ſhip, and the two hundred regular troops which were on board for the ſervice of the colony of *Louiſiana*; which made the veſſel ſo much lighter, that ſhe came afloat again.

On the 4th of April, we ſet on ſhore eighteen officers at Fort *Baliſe* †, where M. *de Santilly* commanded: this officer treated us to the beſt of his power, while we ſtayed at his poſt, which is entirely ſurrounded with marſhes full of ſerpents and crocodiles.

The *Marquis de Vaudreuil*, governor of *Louiſiana*, being informed of our arrival, ſent ſeveral

boats

---

* Mr. *d'Iberville*, governor of *Louiſiona*, conducted the firſt colony thither in 1699: after his death the country had no governor for a long while: the ſecond was M. *de la Motte Cadillac*; and the third, M. *de Bienville*, youngeſt brother of the firſt.

† They reckon thirty leagues from this place to *New Orleans*, on account of the bendings in the river.

boats to fetch us, and to bring us refreshments; we distributed our soldiers on board them, and, by sailing and rowing, we got to *New Orleans* on Easter-day. The Marquis *de Vaudreuil* is to receive twenty-four companies of marines, to augment the forces in *Louisiana*; these troops come on board of merchant-ships, freighted for the King's account; there are likewise some female recruits enlisted in *France*, who come to people these climates. Industrious soldiers, who chuse to marry these girls, get their dismission, and a certain number of acres of ground to cultivate: they get victuals from the King for three years together, and he makes them a present of half a pound of gun-powder, and two pounds of shot every month; of a gun, a hatchet, a pick-axe, and corn to sow their fields; with a cow, a calf, cocks and hens, &c.

The Marquis *de Vaudreuil* has distributed the twenty-four new companies in the different parts of the colony, without any regard to persons; so that every one may equally share the advantages and the disadvantages. As to the detachment near the *Illinois*, a post five hundred leagues distant from *New Orleans*, it has fallen to the share of the company to which I belong. I have the honour of being among the officers which M. *Rouillé*, the secretary of state for the marine,

C 3   has

has recommended to the Marquis *de Vaudreuil*; and I am made perfectly fenfible of the deference fhewn to fuch a recommendation. I can affure you, Sir, that the General's table is of great ufe to me, and to all thofe that are lately arrived, and have not had time to take any fixed lodgings. The affluence is very great; but the governor does the honours of his table in fo noble and generous a manner, that he acquires the efteem and friendfhip of all the officers, who juftly ftile him the father of the colony. M. *Michel de la Rouvilliere*, who fuperintends the markets *, likewife contributes to render life agreeable to us, by the juft prices he fixes upon the victuals of the country, and by every thing relative to his office.

We expect to fet out for the *Illinois* the 20th of Auguft next; Mr. de *Macarty*, who is to go with us, has been appointed commandant of the detachment by the court. The different nations which I fhall be obliged to vifit during this long voyage, will furnifh me amply with materials for a defcription of the fine river *Miffiffippi*, and the people on its banks.

In the mean while, I intend to give you a defcription of *Louifiana* in general; but I believe I do

---

* L'ordonnateur.

I do not need to be very prolix on this fubject, as you probably know moft of the plans and accounts that have been publifhed of it. Let me only obferve to you, that *New Orleans*, the ftreets of which run all in ftreight lines, is now much greater and more populous than formerly. There are inhabitants of four forts, *viz.* Europeans, Americans, Africans or negroes, and *Meftizos* *. The latter are thofe born of Europeans and the natives of this country, whom we call favages. The *Creoles* are thofe that are born here of a French man and French woman, or of European parents.

The Creoles in general are very brave, tall, and well made; they are well difpofed for cultivating the arts and fciences; but as they cannot make great progrefs therein for want of good mafters, the rich and well-meaning fathers fend their children to *France*, as to the beft fchool in the world, for all forts of acquirements.

As to the fair fex, whofe only art is that of pleafing, they are already born with that advantage here, and have no need to acquire it in Europe.

* Métifs,

New Orleans and *Mobile* are the only towns
where they fpeak the French pretty pure. The
negroes are brought thither from Africa, and
are employed in cultivating the grounds, which
are excellently adapted to the culture of indigo,
tobacco, rice, maize, or Indian corn, and fugar-canes, of which they have already made
plantations that have fucceeded very well. Thus
the merchants, tradefmen, and ftrangers, who
live here, enjoy as it were an enchanted abode,
rendered delicious by the purity of its air, the
fertility of its foil, and the beauty of its fituation.
New Orleans lies on the banks of the *Miffifippi*,
which is one of the greateft rivers in the world;
becaufe, for 800 leagues together, it paffes
through known countries. Its pure and delicious
water * runs for the fpace of forty leagues between a number of habitations, which form an
elegant fight on both its fhores; where the plea-
fures of hunting and fifhing, and all other enjoyments of life, are abundant.

The capuchins are the firft monks that went
over to *New Orleans* as miffionaries in 1723.
Their fuperior was the vicar of the parifh; thefe
good

---

* *M. le Normant de Méfi*, being *Intendant* of the marine
at *Rochefort*, always drank this water at his table. It has
the quality of contributing to the fecundity of women.

good friars only employ themfelves in affairs relative to their ftation in life.

Two years after, the Jefuits fettled in *Louifiana*. Thefe cunning politicians have found means to get the richeft fettlement in the whole colony, which they have obtained through their intrigues.

The Urfuline nuns were fent thither almoft at the fame time. The occupation of thefe pious girls, whofe zeal is truly laudable, is the education of young ladies; they likewife receive orphans into their community, for which the King pays them fifty *écus* a-head penfion. Thefe nuns are likewife charged with the care of the military hofpital.

My ftay here has as yet been fo fhort, that I have not been able to give you any account of the nations which inhabit the banks of the river; however, I will endeavour to give you an idea of the character and turn of the *Chitimachas*, who are fettled on a river or branch which bears their name, to the weftward of *New Orleans* : I believe the anecdote will prove interefting to you, though this nation is very near extinct.

In

In 1720, one of their nation, having hid himself in a lonely place on the banks of the *Miſſiſippi*, had murdered the *Abbé de St. Côme*, who was then the miſſionary of the colony. M. *de Bienville*, who was then governor, made the whole nation anſwerable for it; and, to ſpare his own people, he employed ſeveral nations of his allies to attack them.

Theſe Indians were worſted; the loſs of their beſt warriors forced them to aſk for peace : the governor having granted it them, on condition that they would bring the head of the murderer, they punctually executed that condition; and afterwards preſented the *calumet* or pipe of peace * to M. *de Bienville*.

The following is a relation of what I have heard concerning the ceremonies of this ſolemn embaſſy.

They arrived at *New Orleans*, ſinging the ſong of the calumet, which they diſplayed to the wind,

---

* The calumet is a long pipe, with a head of red, black, or white marble, and a pipe of a reed two and a half or three feet long. The Indians ſend it by deputies to thoſe nations with whom they will renew or treat of peace. It is adorned with the feathers of the white eagle; it is a ſymbol of peace and plenty amongſt them; and one may go every where without fear, with the calumet in hand, becauſe nothing is held more ſacred.

wind, and in a certain cadence, to announce their embaffy; and they were dreffed out with their beft ornaments, as is always ufual amongft them on fuch occafions. The chief of the deputation faid to the governor : *How happy am I to find my-felf in thy prefence; thou haft long been angry with our nation ; we have been informed of what thy heart has told thee, and we have heard with great joy, that it was willing to give us fine days.* They then fat down on the ground, leaning their faces on their hands, the fpeaker without doubt to recover his breath, and the others to keep filent. During this interval every body was ordered not to talk, nor to laugh whilft the harangue lafted, becaufe they would be affronted at it.

The fpeaker, fome moments after, arofe with two others; one of them filled the pipe of the calumet with tobacco, the other brought fire; the firft then lighted the pipe; the fpeaker fmo-ked a while, and then prefented the pipe to M. *de Bienville,* that he might do the fame; accor-dingly the governor, and all the officers that compofed his retinue, fmoked out of this calu-met, each according to his rank : as foon as this ceremony was over, the old orator took back the calumet, and put it in M. *de Bienville's* hands, in order to be preferved by him. The
                                                    fpeaker

ſpeaker remained ſtanding, and the other ambaſſadors ſat down near the preſent which they
had brought, and which conſiſted of roe-buck
and doe ſkins, and in ſome other furs, all dreſſed white, as a ſign of peace.

The ſpeaker or chancellor was dreſſed in a
robe of ſeveral marten-ſkins ſewed together; it
was faſtened to his right ſhoulder, and paſſed
under his left arm; he wrapped himſelf up in
this robe, and began his ſpeech with a majeſtic
air, addreſſing himſelf to the governor : " My
" heart laughs for joy on ſeeing myſelf before
" thee; we have all of us heard the word of
" peace which thou haſt ſent us : the hearts of
" our whole nation laugh for joy on that occa-
" ſion; the women, forgetting that inſtant all
" that paſſed, have danced; and the children
" have leapt like young roe-bucks.   Thy words
" ſhall never be forgotten, and our deſcendants
" will remember it as long as the ANCIENT
" WORD * ſhall laſt : as the war has made us poor,
" we have been obliged to make a general hunt
" or chace, in order to bring thee ſome furs :
" but we were afraid of going to any great di-
" ſtance, leſt the other nations ſhould not yet
" have heard thy word ; nor are we come hither
" but trembling all the way, till we ſaw thy face.
                                        " How

---

* Thus they call *traditions.*

" How glad are my eyes and my heart to be-
" hold thee this day. Our prefents are fmall,
" but our hearts are great to obey thy word; at
" thy commands thou fhalt fee our legs run and
" leap like thofe of the ftags, to do as thou fhalt
" pleafe."

Here the orator paufed a little; then raifing
his voice, he gravely continued his difcourfe.

" How beautiful is the fun to-day, in com-
" parifon with what it was when thou wert an-
" gry with us! How dangerous is one villain!
" Thou knoweft that a fingle man has killed
" the *chief of the prayer* *, whofe death has caufed
" that of our beft warriors; we have only old
" men, and women with their children remain-
" ing, who all ftretch out their arms towards
" thee as to a good father. The gall that for-
" merly filled thy heart, has given way to ho-
" ney; the great fpirit is no longer irritated
" againft our nation; thou haft required the
" head of a villain from our hands, and in order
" to obtain peace we have fent it thee.

" The fun was red before, all the roads were
" full of thorns and briars; the clouds were
" black, the water troubled and ftained with
" our

* So they call our miffionaries.

" our blood ; our women lamented without inter-
" miſſion the loſs of their relations, and durſt not
" venture to go and fetch wood for preparing
" our victuals ; at the leaſt ſhriek of the birds
" of night all our warriors were on foot ; they
" never ſlept without their arms ; our huts were
" abandoned, and our fields lay fallow ; we had
" all of us empty ſtomachs, and our faces look-
" ed long and meagre ; the game and wild-fowl
" fled far from us ; the ſerpents angrily hiſſed
" at us ; and the birds that perched near our
" habitations ſeemed, by their doleful notes, to
" ſing us ſongs of death.

" To-day the ſun is bright, the ſky is ſerene,
" the clouds are vaniſhed, the roads covered
" with flowers ; our gardens and fields ſhall
" henceforth be cultivated, and we will offer
" their firſt-fruits to the great ſpirit ; the water
" is ſo clear that we ſee ourſelves in it ; the ſer-
" pents fly from us ; the birds amuſe us by the
" ſweetneſs and harmony of their ſongs ; our
" wives and children dance, and forget to eat and
" to drink ; the whole nation laughs for joy, to
" ſee us walk on the ſame road with thyſelf and
" the French ; the ſame ſun ſhall light us, we
" ſhall have but one and the ſame ſpeech, and
" our hearts ſhall make but one ; we will kill
" them that ſhall kill the French ; our warriors
" ſhall

" fhall hunt to make them fubfift, and we will
" eat together: Will not that be good? what
" doft thou fay to it, father?"

To this difcourfe, which was fpoken with a
firm tone of voice, with grace and decency,
and even, if I may be allowed the expreffion,
with the moft majeftic deportment, M. *de Bienville* anfwered in a few words, in the common
language, which he fpoke pretty fluently; that
he was very glad that their nation had recovered
their fenfes; he gave them fomething to eat;
and, as a mark of friendfhip, he put his hand
into that of the fpeaker, and fo fent them home
fatisfied.—Since that time they have always been
inviolably attached to the French, and furnifh
New Orleans with game.

My third letter will prove more interefting;
however, I hope I have hitherto fulfilled my
promifes; and am,

SIR, &c.

New Orleans, the 1ft
of July 1751.

L E T T E R III.

To the fame.

Defcription of the religious Cuftoms and Ceremonies of fome Nations which inhabit the Banks of the great River Miffifippi. *Confpiracy of the Natches againft the French.*

S I R,

I AM now arrived at the place where the great nation of the *Natches* formerly lived, of which the public news have faid fo much. It is afferted, that this formidable nation gave laws to others, on account of the great extent of their country. They inhabited all the fpace of land between the river *Menchak,* which is about fifty leagues from the fea, and the river *Hoyo,* which is near 460 leagues from the fea.

On

On the 20th of Auguſt we ſet out from *New Orleans* on our voyage to the *Illinois*, in ſix boats, on board of which were the four companies about which I wrote to you in my preceding letter, commanded by *M. de Macarty.* We are obliged to row up againſt the current of the river *Miſſiſippi*, on account of the many windings of that river, which runs between two great foreſts, the trees of which appear to be as ancient as the world.

The firſt places you come to on your voyage are two villages peopled with Germans, being the reſt of a grant made, in 1720, by the King to Mr. *Law.* This colony was to conſiſt of Germans and Provençals, to the amount of 1500 perſons; the ground for it was laid out near a wild nation called the *Akanças*; it was four leagues ſquare, and the colony was erected into a dutchy. They had already tranſported thither the ammunition and ſtores for a company of dragoons, and merchandiſes for the value of upwards a million of *livres*; but Mr. *Law* failed, and the India company, which was at that time eſtabliſhed in Louiſiana, took poſſeſſion of all the goods.

The coloniſts ſeparated, and the Germans ſettled ten leagues above *New Orleans:* they are

very laborious, and are looked upon as the pro-
viders and victuallers of the town. The two
villages are under [the direction of a Swediſh
captain *.

Two leagues further you find a nation called
Colla-piſſas, who are diſtinguiſhed by their attachment to the French ; they are now reduced
to a very ſmall number; their true name is *Aque-
lon Piſſas*, that is, the nation who hear and ſee.

Next you meet with the *Oumas*, who adore the
ſun. This nation, with moſt-of the others in
America, believes, that the Supreme Being re-
ſides in the ſun, and that he deſires to be revered in that vivifying orb, as the author of nature : they ſay, there is nothing here that can
be compared to him, and that this wonder by
enlightening the earth, ſpreads joy and abundance on it   Upon theſe principles they wor-
ſhip him, as the viſible image of the greatneſs
and goodneſs of a deity, that condeſcends to
make himſelf known among men, by diſtribut-
ing his benefactions amongſt them.

Fifteen

---

* It is Mr. *Arenſbourg*, who was at the battle of Pultava
in 1709, with Charles XII. This old officer is the head of
a numerous family eſtabliſhed in Louiſiana.

Fifteen leagues above the *Oumas*, in going up the river, you arrive at the *Cut point.* This place is about forty leagues diftant from *New Orleans.* The foil of it is very fertile, and covered with fruit-trees. There are a number of Frenchmen in this part of the country, who apply themfelves to the culture of tobacco, cotton, rice, maize, and other corn; the colonifts likewife trade in building-timber, which they carry down the river to *New Orleans* upon rafts.

Upon the left fhore of the river, a little above the *Cut-point,* you fee the village of the *Tonikas,* an Indian nation who have ever been attached to the French. Their chiefs have always exerted themfelyes to be our allies in war; the laft of them, who was very brave, received a dangerous wound in an expedition againft the *Natches :* the King, on receiving an account of this affair, honoured him with a commiffion, as brigadier of the armies of red men ; and further prefented him with a blue ribbon, from which hung a filver medal, with a reprefentation of *Paris !* he likewife received a gold-headed cane.

After the maffacre of the French by the *Natches,* whereof I intend to give you an account in its place, a part of that nation pretended to be defirous of making peace with the

grand

grand chief of the *Tonikas*: the latter communicated this to the commander-general of the
French, to whom he was very much attached;
the *Natches* prevented the anfwer, and affaffinated
the *Tonikas*, beginning with their grand chief;
his enemies, who feared our advice and our
forces, made hafte to ruin and deftroy a great
number of his fubjects. We fhall always lament,
together with thefe good Indians, the lofs of a
man, whofe great qualities would do honour to
a civilized nation.

After eighty leagues navigation from the capital of *Louifiana*, we arrived at the poft of. the
Natches, which, about twenty years ago, was
very confiderable, but is very infignificant at
prefent.

The fort is fituated on an eminence, which
commands the river *Miffifippi*, from which it is
about the diftance of a cannon-fhot. The
ground, which in this country is always rifing
higher, would be one of the moft fertile, if it
were cultivated; tobacco, cotton, and maize
fucceed very well in it.

I have made fome ftay at this poft, which is
commanded by the Chevalier *d'Orgon*, a natural
fon

fon of the Prince *de Lambefc*, of the houfe of Lorrain.

The *Natches* who lived here formerly were a very confiderable nation. They formed feveral villages, that were under fome peculiar chiefs ; and thefe laft again, obeyed one grand chief of the whole nation. All thefe princes bore the name of *Suns* ; there were five hundred of them, all relations of the great Sun, their common fovereign, who carried on his breaft the image of the fun, from which he pretended to trace his origin, and which was adored under the name of *Wachil,* which fignifies *the great fire* or the *fupreme fire.*

The manner in which the *Natches* rendered divine fervice to the fun, has fomething folemn in it. The high-prieft got up before fun-rifing, and marched at the head of the people with a grave pace, and the calumet of peace in hand ; he fmoked in honour of the fun, and blew the firft mouthful of fmoke towards him. On the appearance of that luminous body, all the by-ftanders began to howl by turns after the high-prieft, and contemplated it with their arms extended to heaven. Then they threw themfelves on the ground ; and their women brought their

D 3

children,

children, and taught them to keep in a devout attitude.

About their harveſt-time, which happened in July, the *Natches* celebrated a great feaſt. They began with blacking their faces; and did not eat till three hours after noon, having previouſly purified themſelves in the baths; the oldeſt man in the nation then offered to their deity the firſt fruits of their crops.

They had a temple in which they kept up an eternal fire; the prieſts took great care to preſerve it, and for this purpoſe they were only allowed to make uſe of the wood of one kind of tree; if unhappily the fire was extinguiſhed, all the people were in the greateſt conſternation, and the neglectful prieſts were puniſhed with death: but ſuch an event happened very ſeldom; for the keepers of this celeſtial fire could eaſily renew it, by fetching common fire under pretext of lighting their calumets; for they were not allowed to employ the holy fire for that uſe.

When their ſovereign died, he was accompanied in the grave by his wives, and by ſeveral of his ſubjects. The leſſer Suns took care to follow the ſame cuſtom; the law likewiſe condemned

demned every *Natchéz* to death, who had married a girl of the blood of the Suns, as foon as fhe was expired. On this occafion, I muft tell you the hiftory of an Indian, who was no ways willing to fubmit to this law : his name was *Etteacteal*; he contracted an alliance with the Suns ; but the confequences which this honour brought along with it, had like to have proved very unfortunate to him. His wife fell fick ; as foon as he faw her at the point of death, he fled, embarked on a piragua on the *Miffifippi*, and came to *New Orleans*. He put himfelf under the protection of M. *de Bienville*, the then governor, and offered to be his huntfman. The Governor accepted his fervices, and interefted himfelf for him with the *Natches*, who declared that he had nothing more to fear, becaufe the ceremony was paft, and he was accordingly no longer a lawful prize.

Etteacteal, being thus affured, véntured to return to his nation; and, without fettling among them, he made feveral voyages thither : he happened to be there when the Sun, called the *Stung Serpent*, brother to the great Sun, died; he was a relation of the late wife of *Etteacteal*, and they refolved to make him pay his debt. M. *de Bienville* had been recalled to France, and the fovereign of the *Natches*

D 4   thought

thought, that the protector's abfence had annul-
led the reprieve granted to the protected perfon; and accordingly he caufed him to be ar-
refted.   As foon as the poor fellow found himfelf in the hut of the grand chief of war, together
with the other victims deftined to be facrificed.
to the *Stung Serpent*, he gave vent to the excefs
of his grief.   The favourite wife of the late Sun,
who was likewife to be facrificed, and who faw
the preparations for her death with firmnefs,
and feemed impatient to rejoin her hufband,
hearing *Etteactcal's* complaints and groans, faid
to him, Art thou no warrior?   He anfwered,
Yes, I am one.   However, faid fhe, thou cry-
eft, life is dear to thee; and as that is the cafe,
it is not good that thou fhouldft go along with
us, go with the women.   *Etteacteal* replied,
True, life is dear to me; it would be well if I
walked yet on earth till to the death of the great
Sun, and I would die with him.   Go thy way,
faid the favourite, it is not fit thou fhouldft go
with us, and that thy heart fhould remain behind on earth; once more get away, and let me
fee thee no more.

Etteacteal did not ftay to have this order repeated to him; he difappeared like lightning:
three old women, two of which were his relations, offered to pay his debt; their age and
their

their infirmities had difgufted them of life ; none of them had been able to ufe their legs for a great while. . The hair of the two that were related to *Etteacteal*, were no more gray than thofe of women of fifty-five years in France. The other old woman was a hundred and twenty years old, and had very white hair, which is a a very uncommon thing among the Indians: none of the three had a quite wrinkled fkin. They were difpatched in the evening, one at the door of the *Stung Serpent*, and the other two upon the place before the temple *.

The generofity of thefe women gave *Etteacteal* life again, acquired him the degree of *confidered*, and cleared his honour, which he had fullied by fearing death. He remained quiet after that time ; and, taking advantage of what he had learnt during his ftay among the French, he became a juggler, and made ufe of his knowledge to impofe upon his countrymen †.

The

* A cord is faftened round their necks with a flip knot, and eight men of their relations ftrangle them, by drawing four one way and four the other ; fo many are not neceffary, but as they acquire nobility by fuch executions, there are always more than are wanting, and the operation is performed in an inftant.

† The jugglers in this country perform the functions of priefts, phyficians, and fortune-tellers, and chiefly pretend to pafs for forcerers.

The morning after this execution, they made every thing ready for the convoy; and the hour being come, the great mafter of the ceremonies appeared at the door of the hut adorned fuitably to his quality; the victims who were to accom- pany the deceafed prince into the manfion of the fpirits, came forth; they confifted of the fa- vourite wife of the deceafed, of his fecond wife, his chancellor, his phyfician, his hired man, that is his firft fervant, and of fome old women.

The favourite went to the great Sun, with whom there were feveral Frenchmen, to take leave of him: fhe gave orders for the Suns of both fexes that were her children to appear, and fpoke to the following effect:

" Children, this is the day on which I am to " tear myfelf from you arms, and to follow " your father's fteps, who waits for me in the " country of the fpirits; if I were to yield to " your tears, I would injure my love, and fail " in my duty. I have done enough for you, by " bearing you next to my heart, and by fuck- " ling you with my breafts. You that are de- " fcended of his blood, and fed by my milk, " ought you to fhed tears? Rejoice rather that " you are *Suns* and warriors; you are bound to " give examples of firmnefs and valour to the " whole

" whole nation : go, my children, I have pro-
" vided for all your wants, by procuring you
" friends ; my friends, and thofe of your father,
" are yours too ; I leave you amidft them ;
" they are the French, they are tender-hearted
" and generous, make yourfelves worthy of
" their efteem, by not degenerating from your
" race ; always act openly with them, and never
" implore them with meannefs.

" And you Frenchmen," added fhe, turning
herfelf towards our officers, " I recommend my
" orphan-children to you ; they will know no
" other fathers than you ; you ought to protect
" them."

After that fhe got up ; and, followed by her
troop, returned to her hufband's hut, with a
furprifing firmnefs.

A noble woman came to join herfelf to the
number of victims of her own accord, being engaged, by the friendfhip fhe bore the *Stung Serpent*, to follow him into the other world. The
Europeans called her the *haughty* lady, on account of her majeftic deportment, and her
proud air, and becaufe fhe only frequented the
company of the moft diftinguifhed Frenchmen ;
they regretted her much, becaufe fhe had the
know-

knowledge of feveral fimples, with which fhe had faved the lives of many of our fick. This moving fight filled our people with grief and horror. The favourite wife of the deceafed rofe up, and fpoke to them with a fmiling countenance: " I die without fear," faid fhe, " grief does not " embitter my laft hours, I recommend my " children to you; whenever you fee them, " noble Frenchmen, remember that you have " loved their father, and that he was till death " a true and fincere friend of your nation, whom " he loved more than himfelf. The difpofer of " life has been pleafed to call him, and I fhall " foon go and join him; I fhall tell him that I " have feen your hearts moved at the fight of " his corps: do not be grieved; we fhall be " longer friends in the *country of the fpirits* than " here, becaufe we do not die there again *."

Thefe words forced tears from the eyes of all the French; they were obliged to do all they could to prevent the *great Sun* from killing him-felf; for he was inconfolable at the death of his

brother,

---

* At the hour intended for the ceremony, they made the victims fwallow little balls or pills of tobacco, in order to make them giddy, and as it were to take the fenfation of pain from them; after that they were all ftrangled, and put upon mats, the favourite on the right, the other wife on the left, and the others according to their rank.

brother, upon whom he was ufed to lay the weight of government, he being great chief of war of the Natches. *i. e.* Generaliffimo of their armies; that prince grew furious by the refiftance he met with; he held his gun by the barrel, and the *Sun*, his prefumptive heir, held it by the lock, and caufed the powder to fall out of the pan; the hut was full of *Suns*, *Nobles*, and *Honourables* *, who were all trembling: but the French raifed their fpirits again, by hiding all the arms belonging to the fovereign, and filling the barrel of his gun with water, that it might be unfit for ufe for fome time.

As foon as the Suns faw their fovereign's life in fafety, they thanked the French, by fqueezing their hands, but without fpeaking; a moft profound filence reigned throughout, for grief and awe kept in bounds the multitude that were prefent.

The wife of the great Sun was feized with fear during this tranfaction. She was afked whether

---

* The eftablifhed diftinctions among thefe Indians were as follows: The *Suns*, relations of the great Sun, held the higheft rank; next came the *Nobles*; after them the *Honorables*; and laft of all, the common people, who were very much defpifed. As the nobility was propagated by the women, this contributed much to multiply it.

whether fhe was ill; and fhe anfwered aloud, "Yes I am;" and added, with a lower voice, " if the Frenchmen go out of this hut, my huf- " band dies, and all the Natches will die with " him; ftay then, brave Frenchmen, becaufe " your words are as powerful as arrows; be- " fides, who could have ventured to do what " you have done? But you are his true friends " and thofe of his brother." Their laws obliged the *great Sun*'s wife to follow her hufband in the grave: this was doubtlefs the caufe of her fears; and likewife the gratitude towards the French, who interefted themfelves in behalf of his life, prompted her to fpeak in the above-mentioned manner.

The *great Sun* gave his hand to the officers, and faid to them: " My friends, my heart is fo " overpowered with grief, that, though my " eyes were open, I have not taken notice that " you have been ftanding all this while, nor " have I afked you to fit down; but pardon the " excefs of my affliction."

The Frenchmen told him, that he had no need of excufes; that they were going to leave him alone, but that they would ceafe to be his friends unlefs he gave orders to light the fires

again

again *, lighting his own before them, and that they fhould not leave him till his brother was buried.

He took all the Frenchmen by the hands, and faid, " Since all the chiefs and noble officers " will have me ftay on earth, I will do it, I will " not kill myfelf; let the fires be lighted again " immediately, and I'll wait till death joins me " to my brother; I am already old, and till I " die I fhall walk with the French; had it not " been for them, I fhould have gone with my " brother, and all the roads would have been " covered with dead bodies."

This prince only furvived the *Stung Serpent* one year, and his nephew fucceeded him. The reign of that young prince proved very unfortunate to the colony. You fhall fee, Sir, by the fequel of this letter, that the colony owes its fafety only to the mother of this fovereign; fhe got from him the fecret of the general confpiracy againft our nation, whom fhe loved very much.

I muft do juftice to the Indians; the project which they formed of deftroying all the French here,

---

* The great Sun had given orders to put out all the fires, which is only done at the death of the fovereigns.

here, was not the result of natural inconstancy
or fickle temper ; it was the bad conduct of an
officer, who insulted a people whom he ought
to have treated gently, that roused their anger.
Free born men, living peaceably in the country
where their anceftors settled, could not bear the
tyranny which the ftrangers exercised over them,
who were come to settle amongft them. The
Sieur de Chepar, commandant of the poft of the
Natches, neglected to gain the efteem of the
French and the Indians under his care ; he abufed thofe who would not enter into his criminal
conduct, and trufted the moft important pofts
to ferjeants and corporals who were entirely devoted to him. You can eafily conceive, Sir,
that the military difcipline was entirely fubvert-
ed by preferences of this kind, which are fo contrary to fubordination.

M. *Dumont*, the fecond officer, made *remonftrances*, which were not attended to, and to
which he gave no other anfwer than by putting
him in irons. As foon as he was fet at liberty,
he went down to the capital to lay his complaints
before M. *Perrier*, then governor of *Louifiana*.
M. *de Chepar* was recalled to give account of his
conduct ; he was to be broken, but his intrigues
and his patrons ferved him, he was acquitted
and fent back to his poft.

Inftead

Inſtead of being correated by this mortification, he conduated himſelf as before, and became the objea of deteſtation and abhorrence of
both the French and Indians; he irritated the
latter, and forced them to come to the moſt
violent extremities. M. *de Chepar*, deſirous of
making his fortune in a ſhort time, ſummoned
the *Sun* of a village called the *Apple*, to retire
with his people, and to leave him the ground
which he occupied, becauſe he wanted to make
himſelf a habitation on it, which ſhould turn
out to good account. The *Cacique* repreſented to
him, that the bones of his anceſtors were repoſed
there: his remonſtrances proved uſeleſs; the
French commandant ordered the *Great Sun* to
cauſe the village to be evacuated, and even
threatened to ſend him loaded with irons to *New
Orleans* in caſe of non-compliance. Perhaps
this officer thought, he could treat the chief as
a ſlave; he did not reflea, that he ſpoke to a
man accuſtomed to command, and whoſe authority was deſpotic over his ſubjeas.

The Great Sun heard him, and retired without ſhewing any paſſion; he aſſembled his
council, where it was reſolved, that M. *de Chepar* ſhould be told, that before they could eva-
cuate the *Apple* village, they muſt make the plan
of another, and that this required two *moons* time.

VoL. I.   E   This

. This refolution was notified to the governor, who fent back the meffengers, and threatened them with the fevereft punifhments, if the village of the Apple was not put in his hands within a very fhort term. This anfwer was brought to the council, where the old men were of opinion that they ought to gain time, during which they fhould confult upon the means of getting rid of thefe troublefome ftrangers, who were going to become tyrants. As they knew M. *de Chepar* to be very felfifh, they agreed to propofe it to him, to grant them a delay of feveral months, during which each hut was to give him a tribute in Indian corn or maize, in game, and in furs. The avarice of the governor made him fall into the fnare; he accepted the propofition, but pretended however that he only did it in order to oblige the nation, whom he loved on account of their conftant friendfhip with the French. The *Great Sun* was not impofed upon by this artful difinterestednefs; he ordered his council to meet again, and informed them, that the term they had defired had been granted, and that it was neceffary they fhould make good ufe of it, confider of the means of getting rid of a heavy tribute, and above all of the tyrannical domination of the French. He obferved, that fuch an enterprize required an inviolable fecret, folid meafures, and, above all, a great deal of cunning;

cunning; he recommended it to them, that they should in the mean while increase the proofs of confidence and friendship to the French; reflect upon what was to be done, and return to the council as soon as they had hit upon some project which might be attended with certain success.

During five or six days the nobles and old men consulted with each other, and met again unanimously resolved to destroy all the French. The oldest man in the council, having saluted his chief, spoke to the following effect:

" We have long experienced, that the neigh-
" bourhood of the French does us more harm
" than good; we old men perceive it, but our
" youths do not see it; the European goods
" please the young people, but of what service
" are they? They seduce our wives, corrupt
" the manners of the nation, debauch our girls,
" and make them proud and idle. The young
" men are in the same case; the husbands must
" over-work themselves, merely to satisfy the
" luxury of their wives. Before the French
" came into these countries, we were men, we
" were contented with what we had; we walk-
" ed boldly on all the roads, because we were
" our own masters; but now we only go by

E 2   " groping,

" groping, for fear of finding thorns in our
" way; we go like flaves, and fuch we fhall
" foon be, fince they ufe us as fuch already.
" As foon as they fhall have power enough,
" they will no longer keep in bounds, they will
" load us with irons; has not their chief threat-
" ened to offer that indignity to ours; and is
" not death preferable to flavery * ?"

Here the orator paufed; and, after taking
breath, continued as follows :

" What fhall we wait for ?   Shall we fuffer
" the French to multiply till we can no longer
" refift them ?   What will the other nations fay
" of us ?   We pafs for the moft fenfible among
" the *red* men †, and they will have reafon to
" fay that we have lefs fenfe than other people.
" Why fhall we wait longer ?   Let us fet our-
" felves at liberty, and let us fhew that we are
" true men.   We muft begin this day to pre-
" pare for it; we muft order our wives to get
" victuals in readinefs, without telling them the
                                    " reafon.

---

* Nature alone has taught thefe favages to refpect their
fovereign, and to cherifh liberty.

† Thus the Indians call themfelves, to diftinguifh themfelves from the Europeans who are white, and from the A-
fricans who are black.

" reafon. Let us bring the *calumet* of peace to
" all the nations of this country, and tell them
" that the French ftrive to fubdue this whole
" continent; and that, as they are ftronger in
" our neighbourhood than any where elfe, we
" fhall be the firft whom they will load with
" their yoke. As foon as they fhall have fuffi-
" cient forces, they will load all the other na-
" tions with it ; let us convince them how much
" it is their intereft to prevent this misfortune,
" which cannot be avoided but by exterminating
" them ; let all the nations join us in this un-
" dertaking ; let us deftroy the French every
" where on the fame day, and at the fame hour;
" let the time of the maffacre be that of the ex-
" piration of the term their chief has granted
" us : thus we can free ourfelves from the tri-
" bute which we have laid on ourfelves ; and
" thus the victuals which we brought them, will
" come into our poffeffion again : On that great
" day of liberty our warriors fhall have their
" fire-arms with them ; the *Natches* fhall fpread
" among the French, there fhall be three or
" four of us in each houfe to one Frenchman ;
" they fhall borrow fire-arms and ammunition
" of them, under pretence of a general chace
" on account of fome great feaft, and they fhall
" promife to bring back fome game. Some
" guns fired near the houfe of the governor of

" the

" the fort, ſhall be the ſignal for them to fall
" upon the French. In order to make all the
" advantage we can of this blow, the other na-
" tions muſt ſecond us; they muſt make the
" ſame maſſacre of the Frenchmen at their ſe-
" veral ſtations; to be ſure of that, we muſt
" make ſome bundles of rods, containing an
" equal number, give each of them a bundle,
" and keep one; let them take notice of the
" number of days they are to wait; every morn-
" ing one rod muſt be cut in pieces and thrown
" into the fire, and when there will be but one
" left, the time of the ſlaughter is come; it
" muſt begin at the firſt quarter of the day (i. e.
" at nine o'clock in the morning); we ſhall fall
" upon our tyrants all at once; they ſhall be
" overwhelmed on all ſides; and when they are
" once deſtroyed, it will be an eaſy matter to
" prevent thoſe from ſettling among us that
" come from the old continent, acroſs the great
" lake. It muſt be recommended before all
" things, to be exact in drawing a rod from the
" bundle every day; the leaſt miſtake can have
" dangerous conſequences; we ſhall charge
" ſome wiſe man with it, and we muſt beg our
" neighbours to imitate us."

Here the orator gave over, and the old men
approved of his propoſal; the *Sun* of the *Apple*
village

village applauded above all; he was the moft
hurt by the injuftice of M. *de Chepar*; his private revenge would accordingly be the moft fatisfied, he feared to fee it fail, and therefore reprefented to the council the confequences of in-
difcretion, and even engaged them to keep the
fecret of this confpiracy from the *female Suns* *.
It now remained to make the grand chief of the
Natches enter into their fcheme; notwithftanding
the great defire he had to be rid of the French,
the projeſt feemed too violent to him; the Sun
of the Apple took upon himfelf to determine
him to it; he was reckoned a man of fenfe and
penetration, and on that account was in great
repute with the nation: he fucceeded; he remarked to the great Sun the neceffity of this
meafure, by telling him what he had to fear for
himfelf; the French governor of the fort had
threatened him, that he would foon drive him
from his village; the great Sun was young, and
confequently a weak man, he that fpoke to him
was a cunning one, the defign was approved of:
the next morning, when the Suns came to falute their fovereign, they received orders to go

E 4   to

---

* The Indians have two words to denote male and female Suns, (after the manner of the Englifh words *prince,*
princefs) which the French author has happily expreffed by
Soleil and *Soleille.*

to the village of the Apple, under some pretence or other, without raising any suspicion that
they went thither in pursuance of some order;
this was executed as required. The seducing
genius of the Sun of the Apple attracted them
all, and they all promised to enter into the con-
spiracy. A council of Suns and old men was
immediately formed; the project was proposed
there again, and carried unanimously; the old
men were appointed ambassadors to the other
nations; they had warriors to accompany them,
and it was forbidden under pain of death to
speak of this to any person. They set out immediately all at once, and unknown to the
French.

Notwithstanding the profound secret that was
kept among the Natches, the common people was
uneasy at the councils of Suns and noble old men
that had been held; it is not uncommon in every
country in the world, to see subjects endeavour
to penetrate the secrets of the court. However,
the curiosity of the people could not be satisfied; none but the female Suns (or princesses)
had a right in this nation to enquire why they
kept their proceedings secret from them. The
young wife of the great Sun was but eighteen
years old, and cared very little about it; only
the female Sun called the *Stung Arm*, mother

of

of the fovereign, and a woman of good fenfe (which fhe was not ignorant of) could take it ill, that they kept the fecret from her. She fhewed her difcontentment to her fon, who anfwered, that the embaffies were fent out for the fake of renewing alliances with other nations, with whom they had long been at peace, and who might think themfelves defpifed if they were longer neglected. This diffimulated anfwer feemed to appeafe the Sun *Stung Arm,* but it did not take off her uneafinefs; on the contrary it redoubled, when fhe faw, upon the return of the ambaffadors, that the Suns affembled in fecret with thofe deputies, to hear how they had been received, whereas fuch councils were generally held in public.

The princefs was vexed at this: What, faid fhe to herfelf, they hide from me what the whole nation ought to know: if her prudence had not checked her anger, fhe would have given vent to it then. It was happy for the French that fhe thought herfelf thus defpifed; fhe juftly feared to augment the impoffibility of coming at the fecret, if fhe laid open her difpleafure. Her genius fuggefted her the means of fatisfying her curiofity; fhe prevailed upon the great Sun, her fon, to go with her to fee a relation who lived in the village of the Apple, and who fhe had
heard

heard was very ill. Under pretence of leading him the fineft road, fhe took him on the longeft, which was indeed the leaft frequented. She had a good deal of penetration ; fhe imagined, that the motive of this fecret arofe from their carrying on fomething to the difadvantage of the French ; what confirmed her conjectures, were the preparations which the Sun of the Apple was making. Finding herfelf in a folitary place with her fon, fhe fpoke to him in the following words :

" Let us fit down here, for I am tired, and " I have likewife fomething to fay to thee ;" as foon as they were feated, fhe added, " Open " thy ears to hear me ; I never taught thee to " lie, and I always told thee, that a liar did not " deferve to be ranked among men, and that a " lying *Sun* deferved to meet with the greateft " contempt, and even from women; therefore " I believe thou wilt tell me truth. Tell me " then, are not all the Suns brothers? How- " ever, they all keep off from me, as if my lips " were cut off, and I could not retain my words ; " or doft thou think that I ever fpoke in my " fleep. I am in defpair to fee myfelf flighted " by my brothers, but above all by thee. " What, art thou not my own offspring? Haft " thou not fuckled at my breaft? And have I " not

" not fed thee with my pureſt blood? Does not
" the ſame blood run in our veins? Couldſt
" thou be a Sun if thou wert not my ſon? Haſt
" thou forgotten, that, without my care, thou
" wouldſt have been dead long ago? Every
" body, and I myſelf have told thee, that thou
" art the ſon of a Frenchman *; but my own
" blood is dearer to me than that of ſtrangers.
" I now walk by thy ſide like a bitch, without
" being looked upon; I wonder that thou doſt
" not kick me away with thy fcot: I am not ſur-
" priſed that the others hide themſelves from
" me; but thou, who art my ſon, canſt thou
" do it? Haſt thou ever ſeen a ſon miſtruſt his
" mother in our nation? Thou art the only
" one of that temper. There is ſuch an uproar
" in the nation, and I am ignorant of the caufe
" of it, I who am the old Sun; art thou
" afraid that I ſhould rebuke thee, or make thee
" the ſlave of the French, againſt whom you
" act? O! I am tired of this contempt, and
" of walking with ſuch ungrateful people."

The

---

* This princeſs had, for a long time, loved an officer of
our nation; there was no doubt of his being the father of
the great Sun, and that took off nothing of the refpect that
his ſubjects owed him; the women gave nobility among
them, and they were contented if they were ſure of a man's
mother, they cared very little to know who was his father.

The fon of this Sun was quite ſtruck with her diſcourſe; he was moved by it to tears, and heard theſe remonſtrances with the uſual tranquility of an American, and with the reſpect due to a princeſs; he afterwards anſwered her to the following purport. " Thy reproaches are
" arrows which pierce my breaſt, and I do not
" think I ever ſcorned or deſpiſed thee; but haſt
" thou ever heard it ſaid, that the reſolves of
" the council of the old men may be revealed?
" Is it not the duty of all men to keep ſecrets,
" and I who am a ſovereign ought not I to ſet
" an example? The great Sun my wife has
" not been informed of the ſecret any more than
" thyſelf. Though it is known that I am a
" Frenchman's ſon, I have not been miſtruſted;
" they have well imagined, that thy great ge-
" nius would find out the ſecret of the council;
" but when it was kept from the great Sun my
" wife, was it fit that thou ſhouldſt be informed
" of it? But ſince thou haſt gueſſed it all,
" what can I tell thee further? Thou knoweſt
" as much of it as myſelf, ſo ſhut thy mouth."

" I was dubious," ſaid ſhe, " about whom
" you were taking ſo many precautions; but
" ſince it is againſt the French, I fear you have
" not taken your meaſures well to ſurpriſe
" them: for I know they have a great deal of
" ſenſe,

" fenfe, though the governor of this ftation has
" loft his; they are brave; they have goods
" in fufficient quantity to make all the other na-
" tions act againft us. If you had a mind to at-
" tack only the red men, I fhould fleep with
" more fecurity; I am no more young*; an
" old woman's life is a trifle, but thine is dear
" to me. If your old men have thought it as
" eafy a matter to furprife the French as the red
" men, they are grofsly miftaken; the French
" have refources which we have not, thou know-
" eft they have the *fpeaking fubftance (i. e.* pa-
" per)."

Her fon told her, that fhe had nothing to fear
with regard to the meafures which had been taken. After telling her all that I have juft now
informed you of, he told her that the bundle of
rods was in the temple, upon the flat piece of
wood (or the table).

When the princefs was fufficiently informed
of every particular, fhe pretended to approve
of the proceedings; and, leaving her fon entirely eafy, fhe only meditated on the means of ren-
dering this barbarous defign abortive; fhe had
but little time left, for the day fixed for the
maffacre was near at hand.

This

* Her lover was already dead fome time.

This woman could not confent to fee all the French deftroyed in one day by the confpiracy of the *Natches*; fhe therefore undertook to bid them keep upon their guard; for that purpofe fhe made ufe of fome Indian girls who had French lovers, but fhe commanded them ex= prefsly not to fay that they acted by her orders.

The *Sieur de Macé*, enfign of the garrifon of the fort at the Natches, received advice by a young Indian girl who loved him; fhe told him crying, that her nation was to maffacre all the French. M. *de Macé*, amazed at this difcourfe, queftioned his miftrefs: her fimple anfwers and her tender fears left him no room to doubt of the plot: he went immediately to give M. *de Chepar* intelligence of it, who put him under arreft for giving a falfe alarm; feven of the inhabitants of the fort, inftructed by the fame means, co-ming to afk his leave to take up arms, in order to prevent a furprife, were put in irons; the go-vernor treated them as cowards, and was vexed that they endeavoured to infpire him with any miftruft againft a nation that fhewed fo much friendfhip: the regularity of their payments kept up his fecurity: he did not fufpect the politics of the Indians; he blindly defpifed them, nor did he think men of their kind capable of fo much cunning.

The

The Sun *Stung Arm* faw with grief, that her cares for the confervation of the French were ufelefs; fhe was determined to ferve them in fpite of themfelves; fhe could not preferve them all, and therefore fhe endeavoured to leffen the number of victims as much as poffible; fhe fe-cretly went to the temple *, fhe drew a couple of rods out of the bundle unnoticed by the priefts; her intention was to forward the day fixed for the execution of the confpiracy; fhe forefaw that the maffacre which would happen at the *Natches* would foon be fpread far about, that the French who were fettled among the other nations would be informed of it, and be upon their guard. That was the only thing that remained for her to do, and fhe fucceeded in it; the Natches found they were come to their laft rod, without perceiving the impofture; they boldly began the intended flaughter, in the per-fuafion that their allies would act at the fame time.

The 28th of December 1729, at eight in the morning, the Indians fpread among the French; fome difcharges of guns, that were to ferve as a fignal, were fired near the door of M. *de Chepar's* houfe;

* Only the Suns among the women could go into the temple.

houſe; and immediately they fell upon the French every where at the ſame time.

Meſſ. *de Rolly*, chief factors of the Weſt India company, were killed firſt. M. *de la Loire des Urſins* houſe made ſome reſiſtance; his ſervants killed eight *Natches* before they were over-powered. M. *des Urſins* himſelf, who juſt was taking a ride, but returned at the firſt firing of the guns, was ſtopped by a troop of Indians: he defended himſelf very bravely, killed four of them, and died pierced with wounds. This is all that the entrepriſe coſt the Indians: they murdered near two thouſand perſons; only twenty-five or twenty-ſix negroes eſcaped, and moſt of them were wounded. One hundred and fifty children, ninety women, and as many negroes, were taken priſoners, in hopes of ſelling them to the Engliſh in *Carolina*.

During this carnage the great Sun was quietly ſitting under one of the India company's ware-houſes; they brought him firſt of all the head of the governor, then thoſe of the chief Frenchmen, which he ordered to be ranged round the firſt. All the others were put in heaps; the corpſes were not buried, and became the prey of vultures; they cut open the bodies of women big with child, and murdered

almoſt

almoſt all thoſe that had children at the breaſt, becauſe their cries and tears importuned them; they made all the reſt ſlaves, and treated them with the greateſt indignity.

Some people pretend, that M. *de Chepar* had the misfortune to periſh laſt of all, and to be the ſpectator of this horrible ſlaughter: he then found, but too late, how wiſe the advices were that had been given him. The Indians told him, that a *dog* as he was did not deſerve to die by the hands of warriors: he was given up to the *ſtinking fellows* *, who killed him with arrows, and afterwards cut off his head.

Such was the death of a man who only followed his own head, his cruelty, his avarice, and his ambition. As no Frenchman eſcaped from this maſſacre, it cannot be exactly aſcertained what kind of death they made the Governor undergo; it is enough to know, that his enemies were a barbarous people, whom he had irritated. A good adminiſtration would have attached them to the French, who drew great advantages from them: thus the fault of one man can draw after it the ruin of a whole colony; one cannot be

VOL. I.   F   ſuf-

---

* The common people among the Natches are called *Mi-chê-Michéquipi*, which ſignifies *ſtinking fellow*.

sufficiently cautious in the choice of those who
are to be sent as governors into those parts. The
Indians, notwithstanding the ideas we have of
them, are not always easily managed; politics and wisdom must necessarily be employed,
in order to obtain their friendship; they will not
be offended with impunity, this history is a
proof of it; nothing could be better conducted
than the plot of the *Natches*; and how unhappy
had it been, without the interposition of Providence! The Sun *Stung Arm* was worthy of the
greatest acknowledgements, but it is not well
known how they have been made to her.

The nations who entered into the plot with
the *Natches*, not knowing the stratagem by
which the stroke had been advanced, believed
they were betrayed: The *Chactaw* nation imagined, that the *Natches* were unwilling to give
them their share of the plunder of the French;
and, to convince the latter that they had no part
in the conjuration, they joined them in order to
chastise the *Natches*. These returned the French
women and the negroes whom they had taken;
some time after they were attacked in their intrenchments, but escaped by the help of a thun-
der-storm, and quitted the country. About a
thousand of them were taken and brought to
New Orleans, and afterwards sold to the isle of
St.

St. Domingo. Among thefe prifoners was the *Great Sun,* his wife, and his mother, who related to the French the above detail of the plot. The *Great Sun* difowned the maffacre; he faid that his nation had abufed his youth, in order to ftrike this blow; that he had always loved the French; that it was their own chief who had compelled the *Natches* to this defperate action, by his extortions upon a free nation. The French were contented with his difavowal; they treated him and his mother and wife with gentlenefs; but as they did not return to their nation, they foon died with grief. Since that time this country is not inhabited: the *Natches,* being purfued by the French, and being too weak to refift them, took refuge among the *Chicachas*,* where they found an afylum.

We ftill have a fort here, but the colony is far from being brilliant; the means of eftablifhing it would be to attract other Indians to it. This is all, Sir, which I can relate to you concerning this part of the country. I fhall now foon leave it, and continue my voyage; and I conclude my letter, by renewing to you the proteftations of thofe fentiments which you know me capable of. And am, S I R, &c.

At the Natches, Sept. 10. 1751. F 2 L E T-

† Chickafaws,

L E T T E R   IV.

To the fame.

The Author arrives at the Akanzas. *Unhappy
Death of the People of* Ferdinando Soto. *Re-
flections on the Folly of Men who feek for a Moun-
tain of Gold. Origin of the famous* Dorado.
Short Account of the tragic Death of M. de la
Salle.

S I R,

AFTER failing about a hundred and
twenty leagues to the north of the
Natches, up the *Miſſiſippi,* without
meeting with any habitation on the road, we
arrived among a nation famous for their friendſhip for the French, and known formerly from
the expedition of *Ferdinando Soto.* I ſpoke to
an old Indian chief of this country, who told
me, he ſaw M. *de la Salle* here in 1682, when
he diſcovered the great river *St. Louis,* known

under

under the name of *Miſſiſippi*, or, as the Indians pronounce it, *Meſhaſſepi*, which ſignifies *all the rivers*, or the *great river*.

M. *de la Salle* paſſed by this nation in coming down the river : he made acquaintance with them, and took poſſeſſion of their country in the name of *Louis le Grand*, of glorious memory *; after fixing the croſs and the arms of France there, he followed the courſe of the *Miſſiſippi*, which enters into the famous gulph of *Mexico*. He took the latitude at its mouth, which he found to be twenty-nine degrees north; he ſailed up again afterwards to the river of *Illinois*, from whence he went to *Canada*, and from thence he returned into *France*.

F 3   On

---

* If tyranny, oppreſſion, and unbridled ambition are ſufficient to immortalize a prince, it is certain *Lewis* XIV. has a juſt claim to be called *great*. It was his happineſs to have great miniſters in the firſt part of his life, in a time when the greater part of Europe had very few manufactures ; but he was weak enough to give ear to the advices ſuggeſted to him by the Jeſuits, and a ſuperannuated and bigotted miſtreſs : this overturned the ſyſtem of grandeur for which the miniſters had laid a good foundation, and Lewis had the misfortune to ſee all the rival nations around him grow powerful and rich, by the emigration of his oppreſſed Proteſtant ſubjects, and thus he outlived his own greatneſs : his death was the moſt fortunate event for France in her weak and exhauſted ſtate.   F.

On his arrival at court, he imparted his difcovery to Meff. *Colbert* and *de Seignelai*, who obtained for him a comnjliion from the King, im-
porting, that all the countries which he fhould
difcover from *New Bifcay* to the *Illinois*, and the
people, both French and Indians, that fhould be
in thofe countries, fhould be under his orders.

It was at the fame nation, called *Akanzas*,
that Mr. *Joutel* arrived, who fet out after the
death of M. *de la Salle*, with guides to find out
the *Miffifippi*. This is the only officer who has
left us an account which may be credited. I
think I ought to give you an abftract of it;
you will find the hiftory of M. *de la Salle* in it,
and of the end of his unlucky expedition.

In regard to *Ferdinand Soto*'s voyage, I fhall
but juft mention, that the general hiftory of the
Weft Indies informs us, that this great officer,
proud and enriched by the conqueft of *Peru*, after imbruing his facrilegious hands in the blood
of the unfortunate family of the *Incas*, intended
to penetrate into this country with the braveft
of his foldiers, to fubdue the nations that inhabit the neighbourhood of this river, of which I
am going to give you a defcription; but he did
not know the interior parts of this vaft continent; perhaps he expected to find effeminate

nations

nations in it, as in South America; he was miftaken in his hopes, part of his people were killed with clubs by the Indians, who flayed the
principal officers of his army, and afterwards
expofed their fkins on the door of their temple,
which fo frightened the Spaniards that they re-
imbarked immediately for Europe.

The hiftorian fays, that *Ferdinand Soto* died
of the fhame which the bad fuccefs of this enter
prize had brought on him, in 1543; and, fince
that time till 1682, this fine country has been
inhabited by no Europeans.

The fate of M. *de la Salle* has been no happier
than that of *Ferdinand Soto.*

There is no virtue in man which is not blend-
ed with fome faults; this is generally the fault
of human nature; and what increafes our humi-
liation, the greateft virtues are often accompanied by the greateft vices. You will eafily perceive this, Sir, by the fhort extract from M.
Joutel's Journal.

M. *Robert Cavelier de la Salle* fet fail from *Rochelle* the 24th of July 1684, with a fquadron of
four fhips, commanded by M. *de Beaujeu*, a
captain of a fhip. Two hundred and eighty-

five

five perfons, together with thirty volunteers *
and fome gentlemen, and a number of workmen
and girls embarked with him. M. *de la Salle*
was on board M. *de Beaujeu*'s fhip, in whom he
repofed no manner of confidence. Whatever
that officer propofed to him, he always anfwered
with an air of haughtinefs, *This is not the King's
intention*; he certainly did not take the proper
fteps to intereft a man in his undertaking, whofe
affiftance he wanted to make it fucceed. Every
one accordingly began to judge difadvantage-
oufly of an expedition, the chiefs of which feemed to act by very different principles; and time
has unhappily confirmed it.

The 28th of December 1684, the fquadron
difcovered the continent of *Florida*; and M. *de
la Salle* having heard much about the current
that fet in to the eaftward in the Mexican gulph,
he made no doubt but that the mouth of the
Miſſiſippi was far to the weft; an error that was
the caufe of all his misfortunes. Accordingly
he bore away weftward; but he advanced very
little, becaufe he went near the fhore from time

to

---

* Among thefe were three priefts of *St. Sulpitius*, one of
them M. *de la Salle*'s brother, *Chedeville* his relation, and
Majulte, befides four recollects, who were to eftablifh the
miffions among the Indians. There were likewife two of
his nephews, *Meranget* and *Cavelier* fourteen years of age.

to time, and failed along the coaft, to try whether he could not difcover what he fought for.

The 2d of January 1685, the fquadron was, according to conjecture, pretty near the mouth of the *Miffifippi*; and on the 10th they paffed by it, without perceiving it. M. *de la Salle*, being perfuaded that the fquadron was but juft oppofite the *Appalachian* mountains, continued his voyage without fending his long-boat on fhore.

It is faid, that people fhewed him the mouth of the river, and that he would not fo much as take the trouble of getting a certainty, becaufe he had taken it into his head, that it could not be the place which was pointed out to him. His obftinacy could not be conquered nor juftified.

He certainly did not know, or did not think of it, that the greateft men in the world have often been, in part, indebted for their greateft fuccefs to people of inferior merit; and that thofe are the wifeft, who profit by the advice and underftanding even of thofe that are lefs endowed than they themfelves.

Some time after, upon fome hints which the Indians on the coaft gave him, he wanted to return;

turn; but M. *de Beaujeu* refufed to do him that favour. They purfued the fame courfe; and the fquadron, in a few days, came to *St. Bernard*'s bay, without knowing it. This bay is one hundred leagues to the weftward of the mouth of the *Miffifippi*; they caft anchor there, and fent the boats upon difcovery, in order to try to get knowledge of the place they were in. They found a very fine river, with a bar at the mouth of it, where there is not above ten or twelve feet water. This difcovery was made after many times failing backwards and forwards, and after feveral meetings of the council, in which nothing was concluded, becaufe whenever one propofed any thing, the other was fure to oppofe it.

M. *de la Salle*, who believed he was near the *Miffifippi*, and whom M. *de Beaujeu*'s prefence conftrained more than it did him any fervice, refolved to land all his people in that place. Having taken this refolution, on the 20th of February he fent orders to the commander of the fhip *La Flute* to land the heavieft goods, and to go up into the river. He intended to be prefent at the execution of his orders; but the Marquis *de la Sablonniere*, and five or fix Frenchmen, having been taken by the Indians as they walked in the woods, he haftened to free them.

He

He was not yet far from the fhore, when, caft-
ing his eye towards the bay, he faw the *Flute*
manœuvring in fuch a manner as to beat againft
the rocks; his bad luck, fays *Joutel* in his relation, prevented his returning to avoid that
misfortune. He continued his journey towards
the Indian village, where his people had been
carried to; and when he came there, he heard a
cannon fired. He took this as a fignal to give
him notice, that the *Flute* was loft; and his
conjecture proved true.

Thofe who were witneffes to this accident
plainly took it to be the effect of a premeditated
defign of M. *de St. Aigron*, who commanded
that veffel. This lofs had many difagreeable
confequences, as it contained the ammunition
utenfils, tools, and in general all that is neceffary to a new fettlement. M. *de la Salle* haftened to the place where the fhip was loft, and
found every body in a total inaction. He begged M. *de Beaujeu* to lend him his boat and canoe, which he obtained very eafily.

He began with faving the crew; next he got
the powder and flower, afterwards the wine and
brandy; he brought on fhore about thirty barrels: had the boat of the *Flute* been able to
                                                        affift

affift that of the fhip *Le Joli*, almoft every thing would have been faved; but that was funk on purpofe, and the night being come, they were obliged to defer the unlading till the next morning. Some hours being paft, the wind, which came from the fea, grew more violent, and the waves increafed; the *Flute* beating againft the rocks burft, and a quantity of goods fell out through the opening, and were carried away by the fea. This was only perceived at break of day; thirty more barrels of wine and brandy were faved, together with fome barrels full of flower, meat, and peafe: all the reft was loft.

To increafe the misfortune, they were furrounded on all fides by Indians; who, notwithftanding the care that was taken to prevent their profiting any thing by the general confufion, took away feveral things which had been preferved from the wreck. The theft was not perceived till they were retired with the booty. They had left feveral of their canoes on the fhore, which were feized upon: very weak reprifals indeed, which coft much more than they were worth. The Indians came at night to take their canoes; they furprifed thofe who were left to take care of them, and, finding them afleep, they killed two volunteers, whom M. *de la Salle*

regretted

regretted very much, and wounded his nephew and another perſon.

So many misfortunes, one after another, diſguſted ſeveral perſons who were upon the expedition; and, among others, Meſſ. *Doinmaville* and *Mignet*, two engineers, who were willing to return to France, to which the diſcourſes of M. *de la Salle*'s enemies contributed greatly; for they never ceaſed to cry down his conduct, and tax his project as a ſilly and raſh undertaking. He, on the contrary, never ſhewed more reſolution and firmneſs; he conſtructed a warehouſe ſurrounded with good intrenchments; and taking it into his head, that the river, in which he was, might poſſibly be one of the branches of the *Miſſiſippi*, he prepared to go up in it.

They immediately began erecting a fort; as ſoon as the work was ſomewhat advanced, M. *de la Salle* gave *Joutel* orders to finiſh it, left him the command of it, and about one hundred men: he took the reſt of his people, about ſixty in all, with himſelf, and embarked on the river, with the reſolution of going up as high as he could. *Joutel* ſtayed but a ſhort time after him in the fort which had been begun; every night the ſavages were roving in the neighbourhood; the French defended themſelves againſt
them,

them, but with loffes that weakened them. On the 14th of July, *Joutel* received an order from M. *de la Salle* to join him with all his people.

Many good ftout men had been killed or taken by the Indians; others were dead with fatigue, and the number of fick increafed every day; in a word, nothing could be more unhappy than M. *de la Salle*'s fituation. He was devoured with grief; but he diffimulated it pretty well, by which means his diffimulation degenerated into a morofe obftinacy. As foon as he faw all his people together, he began in good earneft to think of making a fettlement, and fortifying it. He was the engineer of his own fort, and being always the firft to put his hand to work, every body worked as well as he could to follow his example.

Nothing was wanting but to encourage this good-will of the people, but M. *de la Salle* had not fufficient command of his temper. At the very time when his people fpent their forces with working, and had but juft as much as was abfolutely neceffary to live upon, he could not prevail on himfelf to relax his feverity a little, or alter his inflexible temper, which is never feafonable, and lefs fo in a new fettlement. It

is

is not fufficient to have courage, health, and watchfulnefs, to make any undertaking fucceed; many other talents are requifite. Moderation, patience, and difintereftednefs, are equally neceffary. It is ufeful to diffimulate now and then, to prevent making evil worfe. Gentlenefs is the beft method which every commander can follow.

M. *de la Salle* punifhed the leaft faults with an unheard-of cruelty; and feldom any word of comfort came from his mouth to thofe who fuffered with the greateft conftancy. He had of courfe the misfortune to fee all his people fall into a ftate of languor and defpondency, which was more the effect of defpair, than of excefs of labour or fcantinefs of good nourifhment.

Having given his laft orders at his fort, he refolved to advance into the country, and began to march on the 12th of January 1687, with M. *de Cavelier* his brother, *Moranget* and the young *Cavelier* his nephews, Father *Anaftatius* a Francifcan friar, *Joutel, Duhaut, L'Archeveque de Marne*, a German whofe name was *Hiens*, a furgeon named *Liétot*, the pilot *Teffier, Saget*, and an Indian who was a good huntfman. I mention them all, becaufe they fhall be fpoke of in the fequel.

As

As they advanced further into the country, they found it inhabited; and when they were but forty leagues from the nation of the *Cenis*, they heard that there was a Frenchman among those Indians. It was a sailor from Lower *Bretany*, who had lost himself when M. *de la Salle* first came down the *Missisippi:* this poor wretch lived among the *Cenis* since 1682, having been adopted by them. He did not hope to see Europe again, nothing but chance could procure him the means of returning thither : *Joutel* went to fetch him from amongst those Indians. He only quitted them to be witness of a crime.

The 17th of May, *Moranget* being on a hunting party, and having, as it is said, abused with words *Duhaut*, *Hiens*, and the surgeon *Liétot*, those three men resolved to get rid of him as soon as possible, and to begin with the servant of M. *de la Salle*, and his Indian huntsman who was called *Nika*, who both accompanied *Moranget*, and could have defended him. They communicated their design to *L'Archeveque* and the pilot *Tessier*, who approved of it, and desired to take part in the execution. They did not speak of it to the Sieur *de Marne*, who was with them, and whom they wished to have been able to get away. The next night, whilst the three unhappy victims whom they would sacrifice to their revenge

revenge flept very quietly, *Liétot* gave each of them feveral blows with the hatchet on the head. The Indian and the fervant died immediately. *Moranget* raifed himfelf fo as to fit upright, without fpeaking a word; and the murderers obliged the Sieur *de Marne* to difpatch him, threatening to kill him too if he refufed; thus, by making him an accomplice of their crime, they wanted to fecure themfelves againft his accufing them.

The firft crime is always followed by uneafinefs; the greateft villains find it difficult to conquer it: the murderers conceived, that it would not be eafy to efcape the juft vengeance of M. *de la Salle,* unlefs by preventing him; and this they refolved upon, after deliberating on the means of effecting it. They thought the fafeft way was to meet him, and furprife all that accompanied him, and fo open themfelves a way for the murder which they intended to perpetrate.

So ftrange a refolution could only be infpired by that blind defpair, which hurries villains into the abyfs which they dig for themfelves: an unexpected incident became favourable to them, and delivered into their hands the prey which

Vol. I.   G   they

they fought for. A river that feparated them
from the camp, and which was confiderably increafed fince they paffed it, kept them two days:
this retardment, which at firft feemed an obftacle to their projeƈt, facilitated the execution
of it. M. *de la Salle*, wondering that his nephew
did not return, nor either of the two men that
were with him, determined to go and feek them
himfelf. It was remarked, that he was uneafy
when he was going to fet out, and inquired with
a kind of uncommon concern whether *Moranget*
had quarrelled with any one.

He then called *Joutel*, and intrufted him with
the command of his camp, ordering him to go
his rounds in it from time to time, and to light
fires, that the fmoke might bring him on his
road again, in cafe he fhould lofe his way; he
likewife bid him give no body leave to abfent
himfelf. He fet out on the 20th, attended by
Father *Anaftafius* and an Indian. As he ap-
proached to the place where the affaffins had
ftopt, he faw fome eagles foaring pretty near the
place, and concluded that there was fome carrion: he fired his gun; and the confpirators,
who had not yet feen him, gueffing that it was
he who was coming, got their arms in readinefs.
The river was between them and him: *Duhaut*
and

and *L'Archeveque* croffed it; and feeing M. *de la Salle* advancing flowly, they ftopped. *Duhaut* hid himfelf in the long grafs, with his gun cocked, *L'Archeveque* advanced a little more: and a moment after, M. *de la Salle* knowing him, afked him where his nephew was? He anfwered, that he was lower down. At the fame inftant *Duhaut* fired; M. *de la Salle* received the fhot in his head, and fell down dead.

It was the 20th of May 1687 that this murder was committed near the *Cenis*. Father *Anaftafius*, feeing M. *de la Salle* drop down at his feet, expected that the murderers would not fpare him, though they fhould have no other view in it than to get rid of a witnefs of their crime. *Duhaut* came near him to quiet him, and told him, that what they had done was an act of defpair, and that they had long thought of revenging themfelves on *Moranget*, who had endeavoured to ruin them. Father *Anaftafius* informed M. *Cavelier* of his brother's death; that gentlemen told them, that if it was their intention to kill him likewife, he would forgive them his death before hand, and he only demanded, as a favour, a quarter of an hour to prepare himfelf for death. They replied, that he had nothing to fear, and that nobody complained of him.

Joutel

Joutel was not then in the camp; *L'Arche-* *veque*, who was his friend, ran to inform him, that his death was certain if he shewed any re- sentment of what had happened, or if he pre- tended to take advantage of the authority with which M. *de la Salle* had invested him. *Joutel*, who was of a very gentle temper, answered, that they should be content with his conduct, and that he believed that they ought to be plea- sed with the manner in which he had hitherto behaved; and then he returned to the camp.

As soon as *Duhaut* saw *Joutel*, he called out to him, that every one should command by turns. He had already taken all the authority into his hands; and the first use he made of it, was to make himself master of the magazine. He divided it afterwards with *L'Archeveque*, say- ing, that every thing belonged to him. There were about thirty thousand livres worth of goods, and near twenty-five thousand livres both in coin and in plate.

The assassins had force and boldness on their side; they had shewn themselves capable of the greatest crimes, accordingly they met with no resistance at first. They soon divided, and quar- relled among themselves; they found difficul- ties

ties in dividing the treafure ; they came to blows, and *Hiens* fired his piftol at *Duhaut*'s head, who reeled, and fell four yards from the place where he ftood. At the fame time *Rutel* the failor, whom *Joutel* fetched from the *Cenis*, fired a gun at *Liétot*. That wretch lived yet feveral hours, though he had three balls in his body ; fo the two affaffins, one of M. *de la Salle*, and the other of his nephew *Moranget*, were themfelves the victims of that fpirit of fury, which they had infpired to this unhappy colony.

The Indians knew not what to think of thefe murderers ; they were quite fcandalized by them. They were in the right, and could with more reafon treat thofe Frenchmen as barbarians, than we had to confider them as fuch. Be that as it will, fuch was the tragic death of *Robert Cavelier, Sieur de la Salle*, a man of abilities, of a great extent of genius, and of a courage and firmnefs of mind which might have carried him to fomething very great, if, with thefe good qualities, he had known how to get the better of his fullen, morofe mind, to foften his feverity, or rather the roughnefs of his temper, and check the haughtinefs with which he treated not only thofe who depended entirely upon himfelf, but even his affociates. The moft unhappy thing

G 3   for

for the memory of this famous man is, that he
has not been pitied by any body, and that the
bad fuccefs that has attended his undertakings
has given him the appearance of an adventurer
among thofe who only judge from appearances.
Unhappily they are commonly the greateft number, and their voice is, in a manner, the voice of
the people. He has further been reproached with
never taking advice from any body, and with having ruined his private affairs by his obftinacy *.

Thus ended this unlucky undertaking; many
things confpired to make it abortive: it would
at leaft have had part of the wifhed-for fuccefs,
if a fettlement on the mouth of the Miffifippi
had been the only thing in view, as many people
thought it was. It is certain, that when M. *de
Beaujeu* abandoned M. *de la Salle* in St. *Bernard's
Bay*, the latter foon found out, that he was to
the

---

* In order to diminifh the villainy of the deed of *Duhaut*,
it has been fpread, that M. *de la Salle* had killed young
Duhaut with his own hands, and that he had treated feveral
others in the fame manner; that it was defpair and revenge
that animated the confpirators, who feared to perifh themfelves by his injuftice and feverity. One ought to be fo
much the more upon one's guard againft fuch calumniating
difcourfes, as it is but too common to increafe the faults of
the unhappy, and to attribute to them even thofe which they
really have not.

the weftward of the river he fought for; if it had been his intention to find it, he might on his firft journey to the *Cenis* have obtained guides from thofe Indians, becaufe they granted fome in the fequel to *Joutel* *; but he wifhed to come near the Spaniards, in order to take cognizance of the mines of *St. Barbara*, and to feek likewife a *Dorado*. By endeavouring to do too much, he not only did nothing at all, but made all his people perifh, and perifhed himfelf, and was pitied by nobody.

Before I conclude this letter, let me add fome reflections on the folly of men.

The avidity of the Spanifh captains muft have been very great, as it engaged them to feek for an imaginary *Dorado* or mountain of gold, whilft the whole country they were in abounded in all

G 4 parts

---

* The Sieur *Joutel* found the *Miffifippi* by means of the Indians, who brought him to the *Akanzas*, and from thence into *Canada*, ; where he arrived, accompanied by one prieft, a Recollet friar, a foldier, a failor, a colonift, and an Indian, who compofed a ftrange fort of caravan. They were all that returned from this expedition. The remains of this unhappy colony perifhed either through the Indians or through the Spaniards, who took them prifoners, and fet them at work in their mines.

parts with that metal. This is a proof, that all the treasures in the world are incapable of satisfying man, as soon as avidity has once gained the empire in his heart.

The Spaniards were not contented with the riches of *Peru*; they muft ftill go to difcover a *Dorado*, that is, a country where the rocks and ftones are all of gold. The Indians, in order to flatter the avidity of their enemies, and at the fame time to get them out of their country, never ceafed amufing them with accounts of the gold, filver, diamonds, and pearls with which that country abounded. Their defire of getting rid of their unwelcome guefts, induced them to fpare nothing towards perfuading them of the exiftence of this pretended country. The Spaniards believed thefe accounts, in which they were interefted; and this is faid to be the origin of the famous *Dorado*, which has made fo much noife in the world.

The report was current, that, after paffing a long chain of mountains covered with fnow, one entered upon a vaft plain exceedingly well peopled, in which was the *Dorado* that every one wifhed to difcover.

Quefada,

Quefada, with two hundred and fifty brave foldiers, fet out immediately in fearch of it. On *St. James's* day they perceived, from the top of a mountain, fome vaft plains which refembled a fea; and when they were defcended to the foot of the mountain, they built there a town, and called it *San-Yago*, in remembrance of the day on which they difcovered the plain; they likewife furnamed it *Las Atalayas* *, in order to point out the defign of their journey, which was to difcover the *Dorado*. This town exifts ftill in the place, which is marked in the maps as a monument which feems to engage pofterity to go out upon the difcovery of this unknown treafure. *Quefada* paffed through the woods of *Ayrico* with exceffive trouble, and arrived at *Timana* in 1543, having loft almoft all his people.

Orellana undertook the fame voyage in that year; he fet out from *Peru*, defcended the river *Maragnon* or of the Amazons, came to the coaft, and neglected nothing towards arriving at the mountain of gold; but all his pains were ufelefs, and he gained no more honour by the

under-

---

* *Atalayar* fignifies to difcover, or to fpy, in Spanifh: *Atalaya*, a tower or fort from whence one difcovers: *Las Atalayas* is the plural.

undertaking than that of having completed one of the moſt horrible voyages that ever were heard of. About the ſame time *Philip de Ure,* fearing that *Queſada* would profit alone by this diſcovery, ſet out from *Coro* in the province of *Venézuela,* together with *Aquito,* the Lieutenant *Velalcazar,* and one hundred and twenty men; but a *Cacique* having told him, that moſt of the people of *Queſada* had periſhed in the undertaking, he went to the ſouthward along the river *Guabari,* and ſtopped, as Father *Simon* and Father *Piedrahata* aſſure us, at the firſt ſettlement of *Omaguas,* in a very bad plight. But what will not men undertake for the ſake of gold! *Auri ſacra fames, quid non mortalia pectora cogis* * ?

But to what purpoſe is all this philoſophy.— The ſtay which I intend to make here, will enable me to ſend you a new letter on the ſubject of the moſt intereſting particulars of the politics and form of government of the nations who inhabit this country. I am,

S I R, &c.

At the Akanzas,
Oct. 29. 1751.

---

* Here follows a dull quotation from a Spaniſh author upon this ſubject, which we thought proper to omit. F.

LETTER V.

To the same.

Description of the Manners of the Nation of Akan-
*zas, their Religion and Manner of carrying on
War ; the Goodness and Fertility of their Country.*

SIR,

I Hope the description I shall give of this Indian nation, by drawing your attention upon their particular character, will convey a general idea of all the nations of North America. There is indeed very little difference among them, in regard to their cu-
stoms and their way of thinking, and especially in regard to a Supreme Being, which in their language they call *Coyocopchill,* which signifies *the great Spirit,* or the *Master of life.*

The

The *Akanzas* live on the banks of a river that bears their name; it arifes in *New Mexico*, and falls into the *Miffifippi*. Thefe Indians are tall, well made, brave, good fwimmers, very expert in hunting and fifhing, and entirely devoted to the French, of which they have given marks on feveral occafions.

I fpoke, in my preceding letter, of an old man of this nation, who faid he had feen M. *de la Salle*. This good Indian added, that from that time he conceived a very great efteem for the French; that they were the firft nation of white men he had feen, and fince that time he had always recommended it to his nation, whofe chief he was, never to receive any other European allies than the French, who were immediately received at his requeft: in reality thefe people never would have any thing to do with the conjuration of the general maffacre of the French colony at the *Natches*. I muft do thefe good Indians that juftice; they are always at war with the *Tchicachas* (Chickfaws) who gave the *Natches* a retreat.

The country of the *Akanzas* is one of the fineft in the world; the foil of it is fo fertile, that it produces, without any culture, European

wheat,

wheat, all kinds of food, and good fruit, unknown in *France*; game of all kinds is plentiful there; wild oxen *, ſtags, roebucks, bears, tygers,

---

* The here enumerated animals, we intend to make better known, by adding the names in Dr. Linnæus Syſt. Nat. and Mr. Pennant's Syn. of Quadr. or his Britiſh Zoology.

1. WILD OXEN. Bos Biſon, *Linn.* American ox, *Penn. Syn. Quad.* 8.

2. STAGS. Cervus Elaphus, *Linn.* Stag deer, *Penn. Syn. Quad.* 49.

3. ROEBUCKS. As it is dubious whether this ſpecies is in *North America,* this is probably the Dama Virginiana, *Ray. Syn. Quad.* 86,; or Virginian deer, *Penn. Syn. Quadrup.* 51.

4. BEARS. Urſus Arctos, *Linn.* Black bear, *Penn. Syn. Quad.* 190.

5. TYGERS. There are no true tygers in all the new continent, and what is called thus muſt be the Cugacurana of *Marcgrave,* and *Ray. Syn. Quad.* 169. or Brown cat, *Penn. Syn. Quad.* 179.

6. LEOPARDS. Felis Pardus, *Linn.* Panther, *Penn. Syn. Quad,* p. 171. note. Mr. Pennant has proved, from very good authorities, that this ſpecies is found in America, contrary to what M. *de Buffon* ſays; who, though a very great naturaliſt, by far ſuperior to many who make free

with

tygers, leopards, foxes, wild cats, rabbets, turkies,   grous,   pheafants,   partridges,   quails,
turtles, wood-pigeons, fwans, geefe, buftards,
ducks

---

with him, is however a man who never departs from an opinion which he once has embraced, and which he will carry
by his eloquence in fpite of the moft creditable authorities to
the contrary.

. 7. FOXES.   Canis Vulpes, *Linn.*   Fox, *Penn. Syn.
Quad.* 152. with all its varieties, the crofs fox, the black
fox, and the brand fox.

8. WILD CATS.   Felis filveftris tigrina, *Briffon. Quad.*
193. Cayenne Cat, *Penn. Syn. Quad.* 182.

9. RABBETS.   There were originally. no rabbets in America, but they were imported by the Spaniards, and are now
greatly increafed ; whether thefe, here called rabbets, on
the river *Miffifippi,* are the true rabbets, or whether they
are that kind of hare which is peculiar to North America, cannot be decided.   The North American hare feems to
be the Alpine hare, *Penn. Syn. Quad.* 249 ; it is lefs in
fize than the European common hare, and a medium between
hare and rabbet, according to Kalm's *North Amer.* I. p. 105.

10. TURKIES.   Meleagris Gallopavo, *Linn.* Le dindon,
Planches enluminées, 97.

11. GROUS.   There are about feven different kinds of
grous in *North America.*

(*a*) Tetrao

ducks of all kinds, teals, divers, fnipes, water-hens, golden plovers, ftares, thrufhes, and
other birds which are not known in Europe.

On

(*a*) Tetrao Phafianellus, *Linn.* The long-tailed grous, *Edward,* 117.

(*b*) —— Canadenfis, *Linn.* The fpotted grous, *Edw.* 71.

(*c*) —— Lagopus, *Linn.* The white grous, *Edw.* 72.
Pl. enl. 129.

(*d*) —— Cupido, *Linn.* The pinnated grous, *Cat.* III. 1.

(*e*) —— Umbellus, *Linn.* The ruffed grous, *Edw.* 248.

(*f*) —— Canace, *Linn.* The ftriated grous, *Pl. enl.* 131.
& 132. *Briff.* I. 203. t. 20. f. 1. 2.

(*g*) —— Togatus, *Linn.* The fhoulder-knot grous, *Pl.
enl.* 104. *Briff.* I. 207. t. 221. f. 1.

Which of thefe are found fo far fouth as *Louifiana* cannot be
determined.

12. PHEASANTS. This is fo vague a denomination, that
it is next to impoffible to find out which kind of pheafant
the author means; for there is but one pheafant in *America*,
in *Cayenne*, and *Guiana*, and therefore it is dubious whether
this bird is found fo far north as *Louifiana*: I am therefore
inclined to believe, the author meant the *long-tailed grous*,
which bears a great fimilarity to a pheafant, and is found as
far as *Virginia*, which is not above three or four degrees
more north than the *Akanzas*.

13. PARTRIDGES. This feems to be the American par-
tridge, *Cat.* III. 12. Tetrao Virginianus, *Linn.*

14. QUAILS.

On my arrival at the *Akanzas*, the young warriors received me with the dance of the calumet. It is neceſſary that I ſhould inform you, that

---

14. QUAILS. Tetrao Mexicanus, *Linn.* Louſiana quail, *Pl. enl.* 149.

15. TURTLES. Columba Canadenſis, *Linn.* Canada turtle, *Pl. enl.* 176.

16. WOOD-PIGEONS. Columba migratoria, *Linn.* Migratory pigeon. *Kalm,* II. p. 82. t. 2. Columba Carolinenſis, *Linn.* Caroline pigeon, *Cat.* I. 24.

17. SWANS. Anas Cygnus, *Linn. Br. Zool.* p. 440. *Edward* 150.

18. GEESE. Anas Anſer, *Linn.* Wild gooſe, *Br. Zool.* 447. Anas crythropus, *Linn.* White fronted gooſe, *Br. Zool.* 450. *Edw.* 153. Anas Canadenſis, *Linn.* Canada gooſe, *Edw.* 151. *Pl. enl.* 346.

19. BUSTARDS, ~~Otis Tarda~~, *a ſpecies of ye above by miſtake called Ji.* *Linn.* This is the firſt time that I find a buſtard mentioned among the American birds. As they are not uncommon in France, I am inclined to think the author's account to be true; and as he has already mentioned the turkies before, it is not likely that he ſhould confound the buſtard and turkey.

20. DUCKS of all kinds. There are at leaſt twenty kinds of ducks known to be in America. Vid. *Forſter's Catalogue of North American animals,* p. 16. 17.

that dancing enters into all forts of tranfactions with thefe nations; they have religious, phyfical, merry, ceremonious, warlike, pacific; nuptial, funeral, playful, hunting, and lewd dances: the laft is abolifhed fince our arrival in America.

The dance of impudicity was performed privately and in night-time, by the light of a great fire. All that entered into the lafcivious affembly,

---

21. TEALS. I fuppofe the author means by teals the leffer kinds of ducks, as the harlequin, pied, brown, whitefaced, blue-wing, &c. and common teal.

22. DIVERS are of four kinds in North America. Vid. Forfter's Cat. N. Amer. 16.

23. SNIPES. There are likewife feveral birds of th's kind in North America; fo that without a more detailed denomination, it is impoffible to determine the fpecies.

24. WATER-HENS. Of this kind is the Rallus Carolinenfis, Linn. the Carolina rail, and the common water-hen, or Fulica chloropus, Linn. in N. Amer.

25. GOLDEN PLOVERS. Charadrius apricarius, Linn. Edw. 140.

26. STARES. Sturnus Ludovicianus, Linn. Pl. enl. 256. Briff. II. 449. t. 42. f. 1. Cat. I. 13. This bird has miftakenly appeared in the books of the modern ornithologifts

bly were obliged to *ftrike againft the poft* *, that
is, to fwear that they never would reveal what
they had feen or done in this diffolute ball : the
dancers of both fexes appeared quite naked
there, in attitudes and geftures of proftitution,
accompanied with fongs of the fame kind, which
you muft excufe my tranfcribing, though, in the
language of the Indians, they are purely pieces
of genteel wit.

The *Akanzas* have expert fellows among
them, who would perhaps amaze our jugglers.
I faw

---

under two names : *Briffon* calls it, in II. 242. an American
ouzel; and II. 449. he reprefents it as a Louifiana ftare.
Linnæus makes likewife two birds of it; he calls it a lark,
p. 289. Alauda magna, and p. 290. a ftare, Sturnus Ludovicianus ; but, upon comparifon, it may be eafily determined, that both are but a ftare, and that it ought to be
erafed from among the *Larks* and *Ouzels*.

27. THRUSHES. There are at leaft feven *North American*
thrufhes, which of them are upon the river *Miffifippi* cannot
be determined for want of information, F.

* Whenever the Indians fwear or take oaths, they take a
club with which they ftrike againft a poft, calling to mind
their fine actions in war, and promifing to keep their word
religioufly : an oath of this nature is irrevocable among them :
every Cacique fwears to lead his nation well, and ftrikes the
poft; without taking that oath, he cannot be inftalled in the
dignity.

I faw one of them, who, in my prefence, performed a trick which will appear incredible to
you; after fome wry mouths, he fwallowed a
rib of a ftag feventeen inches long, held it with
his fingers, and drew it out of his ftomach again.
He went to *New Orleans* to fhew his agility to
the governor and the officers of the garrifon;
this the Indians call acting the phyfician.

The *Akanzas* declare war with the following
ceremonies. They make a feaft in the hut of
the chief, where dog's flefh is ferved up, which
is the principal food of warriors; becaufe they
fay, that a creature which is fo brave as to be
killed in the defence of his mafter, muft give them
valour. He that kills one of the enemy's dogs
is likewife received as a warrior; but he muft
bring the fcalp of the dog, that is, the fkin from
the head, as if it were the fcalp of a man, without which the others would not believe him.
The Indians have dogs in great numbers, both
for hunting, and to fecure them from being furprifed by the enemies.

After the feaft of which I have fpoken, the
great chief calls together an affembly of warriors.

The

The affembly is held in the middle of the village, in a great hut made on purpofe, which
they call the hut of the council. The chief
and moft confiderable men place themfelves, according to their refpective ranks, on mats or on
tyger-fkins.   When they are all feated, the
chief or orator puts himfelf into the midft of the
affembly, and holds his fpeech with a loud
voice: he reprefents to his nation, that it would
be a fhame for them not to revenge the affront
they received from fuch or fuch a nation; that
if they did take them to account for it, they
would for the future be looked upon as women *.   At that inftant all the affembly ap-
plauds, by faying, *Heu! heu!* The chief then
takes a bundle of rods, and prefents it to the
affembly; all that are defirous of going to war
take one of the rods, and by this means they are
enlifted.

The next morning the women run through
the village, crying, " Young men and warriors,
" who received the rods, fet out, go to war, re-
" venge the deaths of our relations, allies, and
" friends;

---

* When an Indian is called a *woman* or an *old woman*, it
is an affront, which fignifies a man without courage, a
coward.

" friends; and do not return till you are ftained
" with the blood of our enemies, and bring with
" you their fcalps *."

Then a young Indian takes the trouble to
paint red a club, which they call a *head-breaker*;
this club is brought upon the limits of the enemies country; there they cut a piece out of a
tree, and with vermilion they draw on it two arrows acrofs each other, which is their fymbol of
war: the red colour fignifies, that the nation
defires revenge, and will not be fatisfied till it
has fhed the blood of their enemies.

Before they fet out, the chief of the nation
calls another affembly, which is generally followed by a feaft, to which he invites his allies.
The chief prefents the confederates with rods,
to engage them to march with them as auxiliary
troops. At the end of the repaft they fing and

H 3   dance

---

* The Indians are ufed to pluck the fkins from their enemies heads whom they kill in battle; they count the number of the flain by thefe fcalps, which they bring home like
trophies on poles. We generally give them, in goods, for
the King's account, the value of ten crowns (écus) for each
fcalp of our enemies.

dance the dance of war *. All the young men
are painted red ; it is really curious to fee them
dance. He that expreffes by dance the difcovery or the furprife, watches his enemy, keeping in a ftooping pofture ; all at once he falls
upon him, his club in hand, making horrible
cries, as is done in a real action. His comrade
drops as if he were thunderftruck, ftiffening all
his mufcles as an epileptic ; after which the
other reprefents, dancing, the method of fcalping
the dead enemy ; this is done with a knife which
he has in his hand, he makes an incifion on the
forehead, and round the neck of his enemy; he
places his long nails therein, he puts both his
knees againft the fhoulders of the captive, and
with a fudden pufh with his knees and pull with
his hands, he takes up the fkin with the hair on
it, from the head. All this is reprefented in
finging and dancing to the tune of a drum and
                                                  a *chi-*

---

* The fong of war is conceived in the following terms :
" I go to war to avenge the death of my brothers ; I fhall
" kill, I fhall exterminate, I fhall plunder, I fhall burn my
" enemies : I fhall bring away flaves, I fhall devour their
" heart, dry their flefh, drink their blood ; I fhall bring
" their fcalps, and make cups of their fculls ;" and more
fuch expreffions, which are full of cruelty, and fhew a thirft
after revenge and flaughter.

a *chichikois* *, which marks the time and the cadence.

The Indians never go to war without consulting their *Manitou* †, to whom they attribute all their good or bad luck. If the *Manitou* has not been favourable to them, they quit him without any ceremony, and take another. The chief, before he goes to war, undergoes a very rigid fasting, and paints his body black during that time. After the fast, he washes himself, and paints his body and his face red. He harangues his warriors before the false deity, after which every one prepares his baggage. Sometimes they go to war four or five hundred leagues from their own country.

Their baggage, in time of war, consists of a bear's skin, which serves as a bed; a wild ox's skin, with which they cover themselves; a tyger-cat's skin, which serves as a sack to put the calumet or tobacco-pipe in; a *head-breaker* or club;

H 4

---

* This is a gourd in which they put a kind of little beads, they likewise fasten such beads to their feet.

† False Indian deity; sometimes a dried raven or a snake; they likewise employ for that purpose amphibious creatures and quadrupeds.

club; and a little hatchet, which they make use of in order to make huts in the woods.

Their arms confist of a gun or musket, the horn of an ox to put the gun-powder in, which they hang round the body with a string, together with a little bag in which they put their balls, the flint, and a screw; besides this, a bow and a quiver full of arrows; the latter are very useful for hunting. They never employ their fire-arms at any animals, when they are upon any expedition against their enemies, lest the noise might serve to discover them. They agree amongst themselves upon the method of surprising their enemies; for the Indians place all their glory in the knowledge of this kind of war, which is generally fatal to those who are the object of it.

They take very little care with regard to victuals; every one has a little bag of flour of Indian corn or maize, roasted as we do coffee, and when he is hungry he takes a spoonful of water in which some of this flour or meal is diluted, which he keeps till they are very near the enemy.

Though

Though the Indians are sometimes three or four days without eating, they are not ill at all from it, but continue their road as before : they contract their girdle round their belly, in proportion as it grows more empty, and diminishes in size ; in a word, they are indefatigable.

When the Indians have made a stroke at the enemy, as they term it, some young warriors immediately set out, to bring the news of the victory to the village. They make their arrival known, by some cries, which mark the number of prisoners, that of the dead, and that of the scalps which they bring with them. The women prepare to receive the prisoners, and to give them a hearty drubbing with sticks. They have likewise a right to decide who of the captives shall die, for they are brought before them with their hands tied, and painted black *. Those women who have lost their husbands, or sons, are at liberty to take captives to replace them. They can adopt them as husbands or as sons, and they are then immediately set free.

Those who are not adopted must be burnt at a slow fire ; to that purpose their head is scalp-
ed,

---

* Those who are thus painted are to be burnt in the midst of the village, unless the women adopt them.

ed, and they are faſtened to two poſts which
are driven into the ground, with a piece of wood
lying acroſs them *; then all the young people
exerciſe their fury upon them, and they endure
the greateſt torments without complaining ; on
the contrary, they ſing till they expire, ſaying
that they are true men, and that they fear neither fire nor death; they laugh at their tormentors, and tell them that they do not make
them ſuffer enough ; that if they were in their
hands they would plague them much worſe;
that the fire muſt be applied to ſuch and ſuch
parts, and that they are there the moſt ſenſible
to pain. It is to be remarked, that when they
diſpoſe themſelves to march againſt their enemies, they take care to paint their bodies red ;
ſo that, when they attack the enemy, with ſuch
howls as if they were bewitched, they really
look like a troop of devils let looſe from hell †.
They are good towards their friends, but very
cruel towards their enemies.

As

---

* The captives are obliged to ſing and dance round theſe
poſts.

† The Indians in general, both men and women, have
no hair on their bodies, beſides thoſe on the head; they
ſay, that in this particular we reſemble the beaſts, and they
ſay the ſame when they ſee us eat herbs and ſallad.

As to religion, they believe the exiftence of a great Spirit, whom they adore under the form of a ferpent or a crocodile; they give him a kind of divine fervice. They fear the devil, whom they call a bad fpirit. They likewife adore the fun and moon. When it thunders, they imagine that the Lord of life fpeaks to them in an angry tone.

I muft not clofe my letter without informing you of a fingular event, which, though of very little importance, may however be very ufeful to me, during my ftay in America. The Akanzas have adopted me; they have acknowledged me as a warrior and a chief, and have given me the mark of it, which is the figure of a roe-buck imprinted on my thigh. I have willingly undergone this painful operation, which was performed in the following manner: I was feated on a tyger's fkin; an Indian burnt fome ftraw, the afhes of which he diluted with water: he made ufe of this fimple mixture to draw the roe-buck; he then followed the drawing with great needles, pricking them deep into the flefh, till the blood comes out; this blood mixing with the afhes of the ftraw, forms a figure which can never be effaced. I fmoked the calumet after that; they fpread white fkins under my feet,

on

on which I walked; they danced before me crying out for joy; they told me afterwards, that I
could go to all the people who were their allies,
prefent the calumet, and fhew my mark, and I
would be well received; that I was their brother, and that if any one killed me, they would
kill him; now I am a noble *Akanza*. Thefe
people think they have done me all the honour
due to a defender of their country, by thus
adopting me: and I regard this honour almoft
like that which the *Marfhal de Richelieu* received,
when his name was infcribed in the golden book
at *Genoa* among the noble Genoefe. It is true,
there is fome difference between an infcription
and the operation I have undergone; I cannot
exprefs it to you how much I have fuffered by
it; I did all I could to prevent fhewing how
much I was affected; on the contrary, I joked
with the Indian women that were prefent; and
all the fpectators, amazed at my infenfibility,
cried out for joy, and danced round about me,
faying, I was a true man. The pain has been
very violent, and I have had the fever from it
for a week together. You cannot believe how
fond the *Akanzas* are of me fince that time.
This is all I had to fay upon this fubject: fome
time this month we intend to continue our journey to the *Illinois*. As the feafon is much advanced,

vanced, and we have yet three hundred leagues to go, we run the rifk of being ftopped by the ice, and of wintering on the road. We have been obliged to ftop here for preparing the bifcuit neceffary for fo long a voyage; for in this feafon we muft combat both the current and the north wind. According to all appearances, I fhall not be able to write before next year. This letter fets out by a boat, which will arrive in time before the departure of a man of war for *France*, where I hope my letter will find you in good health. I beg you would let me hear from you; for I affure you, you can do me no greater pleafure.

I am, &c.

At the Akanzas, the 6th
of November 1751.

P. S. I found a Meftizo Indian among the *Akanzas*; and, upon queftioning him concerning his origin, I heard that he was the fon of *Rutel*, that failor from *Bretany* who loft himfelf, when M. *de la Salle* came down the *Miffifippi* in 1682, and of whom I have had the honour of fpeaking before.

This

This demi-Indian added, that *Rutel* his father was found by the *Cenis*, an Indian nation, who adopted him; he received one of their girls as his wife, in the quality of a warrior; becaufe, having made ufe of his mufket in a battle againft fome enemies of the *Cenis*, the explofion of that weapon, which was as yet unknown to them, frightened them, and put them to flight.

This *Rutel* having afterwards taught the Indians the method of going with oars and fails in their canoes and piraguas, he enabled them to defeat a little fleet of their enemies; this manner of navigating being till then unknown to the nation, and drew their gratitude and veneration upon him; they revered him as the greateft man in the world; and the famous *Ruiter*, who, from a common failor, became Lieutenant and Admiral of the United Provinces, was perhaps lefs revered than *Rutel* was among the *Cenis*.

LETTER VI.

To the same.

An Account of the Author's Navigation from the A-kanzas to the Illinois. The King's Boat St. Louis, on which the Author was, is overset; he falls into the Miffifippi, and an Akanza faves his life.

SIR,

I AM now, thank God, arrived at Fort *Chartres,* after running many rifks on this long and troublefome voyage. We fet out from the *Akanzas* the 7th of November, on our voyage hither. We have gone three hundred leagues without meeting with any village or habitation. As this extent of country is abfolutely uninhabited, there are happily great flocks of wild oxen, ftags, and roe-bucks, to be met with, efpecially in this feafon when the wa-

ters

ters are low. Thefe animals are obliged to come in flocks to the river to drink, we often killed them as they croffed it, and likewife fome bears were thus got. The *Akanza* Indians generally come to hire themfelves to the French, in order to make them fubfift by hunting upon the road. Thefe hunters fet out in the morning in pira-guas; they kill the oxen which they meet on the banks of the river, and the boats that fol-low after them take on board the meat, which lies ready for them on the fhore.

The Indians take care to keep the tongue, and the flefh from the back of the animals which they have killed, and to prefent thefe bits to the commander and officers of the convoy; af-ter which a ferjeant or a corporal diftributes the flefh to the foldiers in each boat: the pleafure of hunting amply repays for the fatigues of the voyage. The game is fo common in the neigh-bourhood of the river *St. François* *, that, when we went on fhore in thofe parts, it was impoffible to fleep, on account of the multitudes of fwans, cranes, geefe, buftards, and ducks, that were continually going up and down in thefe watery places. On approaching the country of the
Illinois,

---

* This river comes from the country of the *Hautaux.*

Illinois, you fee, in the day-time, whole clouds of turtle-doves or wood-pigeons. A circumftance that will perhaps be incredible, is, that they often eclipfe the fun ; thefe birds, living merely upon acorns and the feeds of beech-trees, in the woods, are excellent in autumn ; fometimes eighty of them are killed at one fhot. What a pity that fo fine a country is not inhabited, or is only inhabited by brutes !

M. *de Macarty*, an Irifhman, and commander of the convoy, having had fome fits of the gout, and fearing to be obliged to winter on the road, refolved to go before the reft, when we were at the juncture of the *Ohio* with the *Miffippi*, thirty leagues from the *Illinois*. He took the beft rowers out of all the boats, and put them on board his boat, and, without troubling himfelf about the others, he left them behind, contrary to M. *de Vaudreuil*'s injunctions ; however, the law of nature dictates to every body the order of affifting others mutually, in cafe of an attack from an enemy, or fome other accident, fuch as happened to the boat *St. Louis*, on board of which I was. It got upon a fand-bank, and they were obliged to unload it almoft entirely before they could fet it a-float again, which made me lofe two days, and prevented my joining the convoy again.

To increafe my misfortunes, when I was but fourteen leagues from the *Illinois*, my boat, three days after it was ftranded, ran againft a tree, of which the *Miſſiſippi* is full, and efpecially in time of low water; the fhock burft the boat, and fuch a quantity of water got in, that it funk in lefs than an hour's time. By this accident I loft all I had: I ran the rifk of perifhing too; for I had thrown myfelf into a piragua, but it was fo full of goods faved from the wreck, that it overfet; feveral foldiers were drowned, and I fhould have fhared the fame fate, had it not been for a generous *Akanza*, who, not fearing the feverity of the feafon, leapt into the water, and feized me by my riding-coat.

After thefe adventures I am at laft arrived at Fort *Chartres*: I had not been long here, when I was witnefs to an event which might have had very unhappy confequences. The *Pehen-guichias* and the *Ouyatanons* had agreed upon the total ruin of five French villages among the *Illinois*. M. *de Mccarty* had fent me before-hand to prepare quarters for fome troops that came in

a cona convoy. The Indians had meditated their en-: terprife, and intended to come before the con-: voy. I was then at the *Kafkakias*, where M. *de Montcharvaux* commanded, who could not juftly know the whole extent of the plot of thofe barbarians. Thefe were fpread in the houfes of the inhabitants; by their careffes, their affecta- tion, and calling to mind the maffacre of the Natches, we fufpected their defign.

On fuch occafions as thefe, an officer feels all the weight of the command. M. *de Montchar- vaux* was not difcouraged; he was feconded by M. *de Gruife*, an intelligent, brave officer. He held a council with the oldeft and moft confider- able people of the place; and did me the ho- nour to confult me in this circumftance : it was more through his goodnefs than through necef- fity, becaufe I was newly arrived, and confe- quently little acquainted with the fituation of af- fairs in that neighbourhood. I will however venture to fay, that he was pleafed with the ad- vice I gave, though it was a very fimple one. My opinion was, that, in order to penetrate the defign of thefe Indians, we fhould keep on the defenfive, without fhewing the leaft fufpicion : that we fhould fend out fome armed inhabitants on horfeback, as if they went a-hunting; recom-

mending

mending it to them, that, after they had gone
the rounds, they fhould return into the village
full gallop, as if fomething had happened to them:
this was to give a falfe alarm. There remained nothing further to be done in that cafe, but
to examine the countenances of the Indians,
who would certainly betray themfelves. This
advice was followed; the Indians believed the
French had difcovered their plot; they intended to execute it on Chriftmas-day, when the
people came from the great mafs; they had exactly inquired after that day, afking, in their
way, when that day came on which the Son of
the great Spirit came into the world.

As foon as they believed they were difcovered, they thought only of making their efcape;
we fired upon them, and killed twenty-two on
the fpot. A ferjeant, called *La Jeuneffe*, a
Creole, and a good hunter, killed four in my
prefence. M. *de Gruife*, on his fide, attacked
thofe who were in the Jefuits houfe, he wounded
feveral of them, and took five alive, among whom
there was one *Illinois*; they were put in irons.

M. *de Macarty* haftened to difpatch meffengers
to *New Orleans* to the Marquis *de Vaudreuil*, to
give him an account of this expedition; the governor

vernor fent back orders to deliver the prifoners
to their countrymen, who came crying, the calumet in hand, and difavowed the plot, faying
their people had loft their fenfes, and that the
Englifh had taken their fenfes from them. They
received peace very thankfully, and all is quiet
at prefent; however, for precaution's fake, the
inhabitants have received orders to carry their
mufkets when they go to mafs; and the officer
of the guard to place two fentinels at the church-
door during divine fervice.

I muft not forget to mention to you, Sir,
that all this paffed without our having a fingle
man killed or wounded. The Indians threw
away their cloaths and their clubs to run the
better; the vigilance of M. *de Montcharvaux*
the commandant, and of M. *de Gruife* the major, has prevented the confpiracy, at the moment when the plot was to be executed. I am
now returned to Fort *Chartres*, where we lead a
pretty peaceable life; I cannot fend any great
news, but I will communicate fome little anec-
dotes which may amufe you, and will at leaft
give you an idea of our Indians.

I had hired an Indian for my hunter during
winter; he belonged to the village of the *Mit-*

chigamias;

chigamias ; one day having got a very great quantity of game, inſtead of bringing it to me, he went to treat * with ſome Frenchmen, who gave him brandy in exchange, of which he drank ſo much as to loſe the uſe of his reaſon.   As he entered my lodgings in this condition, I received him very ill; I took away the muſket which I had given him, and turned him off by puſhing him out of doors: he came, however, into my kitchen againſt my will, lay down in it, and would not go out of it.   As ſoon as he was in his ſenſes again, he well conceived what a great fault he had committed ; and, being willing to atone for it, he took a gun, powder, and ſhot, and went out. The next day he returns, and comes in, very haughtily, loaded with game : he had round his naked body a girdle, between which all the heads of the wild fowls were put ; he looſened it, and threw them into the middle of my room ; he then ſat down near my fire, without ſpeaking ; he lighted his calumet, and giving it me to ſmoke out of it, he ſaid, " I own I had loſt my " ſenſes yeſterday, but I have found them again:
" I ac-

---

* They call *treating*, the exchange or barter of European merchandize againſt the furs which the Indians take in hunting.

" I acknowledge my fault ; and I beg thee to
" excufe it. I agree that I had deferved the
" treatment I received, being turned out of thy
" hut ; thou haft done well to let me come in
" again, becaufe, if the other Indians had heard
" of it, they would at the leaft difpute reproach
" me with having been turned out of the hut of
" the chief *Great Nofe* *."

Many Europeans make no difference between
the Indians and brutes, imagining that they
have neither reafon nor common fenfe. However, the circumftance which I have now related, and a great many more, fufficiently fhew,
that thefe people are fufceptible of fentiments
of honour ; they know how to do themfelves juftice when they are wronged, and know very
well when they do ill. There are nations among
the Europeans, of whom one may remark as
ridiculous and barbarous cuftoms as among
the American Indians.

To return to my hunter : you know very
well, that drunkennefs debafes men to the rank

I 4   of

* An epithet the Indians gave me to diftinguifh me from
the other officers, to each of whom they gave fuch denominations, relative to the good or bad qualities they obferved
in them.

of brutes, and that this vice is corrected with difficulty even amongst the French. The Indians imitate them eafily in it, and fay the white people have taught them to drink the *fiery water* *.

One day my Indian found the door of the King's magazine open; he fneaked in like a ferpent, got to a barrel of brandy, and fhed half of it, by endeavouring to fill a bottle with it. This accident obliged me to difmifs him; however, as he was a good hunter, and had only one fault, his wife begged me to give him phyfic, to prevent his drinking: I willingly undertook the cure, with the affiftance of his wife and relations. Once this hunter was drunk, but defired ftill more brandy; I got the people to tell him I had fome, but that I was very tenacious of it. He came immediately, and afked me for fome: I faid, I had brandy, but I would not give it for nothing. He faid he was poor; however, if I would take his wife, he would hire her to me for a month. I anfwered, that the chiefs of the white warriors did not come to the red men to enjoy their wives; that if he would fell me his fon, I would willingly take him as a flave,

and

---

* Thus they call *brandy*.

and give him in return a barrel of brandy ; we made the bargain in prefence of feveral witneffes, and he delivered his fon to me.

I was ready to laugh at this farce, from the very beginning of it. I made him drink upon the bargain fome brandy, into which I had put long pepper. When he had drunk it, he was bound, and brought to fleep. When he was recovered of his drunkennefs, the Cacique of the village and his relations, who were in the fecret, came to him into his hut, where he lay upon a mat ; they difplayed to him all the horror of the unnatural action he had committed by felling his own offspring. The poor Indian came crying to me, and faid, *Indagé wai panis,* i. e. I am unworthy of living ; I do no longer deferve to bear the tender name of father. He was very angry at the brandy I had given him to drink, and which had fired all his ftomach ; he called it *urine of the chief of hell,* that is, of the evil fpirit that caufed it.

His wife, who is naturally humorous, and who was diverting herfelf at his expence, afked him very coolly where his fon was ? He ftill ex-cufed himfelf, faying, that, knowing me to be very kind, he expected I would return him his

fon ;

fon; that he knew the grand chief of the
French *, and the father of the red men, had no
flaves in his empire. I told him he was in the
right, but that I had adopted his fon, and
would take him in that quality with me to
France, in order to make him a Chriftian, and
that all the furs of his nation would not be fufficient to redeem him.

As the relations feemed to be grieved, they
advifed the drunkard Indian to go to the *chief
of the prayer*, or the man that fpeaks with the
great Spirit; for thus they call the priefts : I
told him, that if the chief of the prayer † required it, I fhould not be contrary to him; I
would return him his fon, on condition that he
fhould be baptifed, and that I fhould be his
godfather; that as to himfelf, I required from
him an abjuration of drunkennefs, which had
proved fo fatal to him. He faid my words were
ftrong, and he fhould remember them while he
lived; he begged I would adopt him as a brother, and faid he was going to ftrike at the poft ‡.

Since

---

* The French King.

† The Abbé *Gagnon*, of the order of St. Sulpitius, and
chaplain of Fort *Chartres*.

‡ The Indian method of taking an oath.   See Letter V.

Since that time he has never drank wine, or any
fpirituous liquors; I have fent people to offer
them to him, but he always refufed them, faying, that he had ftruck at the poft, and that
the Lord of life would be angry with him; that
I had told him that this Spirit could not be deceived: he rocollected that once I had named
the number of glaffes of brandy which he had
drunk, without my having feen him; to which
he had anfwered, that it was very true, and that
he believed that the great Spirit that fees every
thing muft have told me of it. I took the following method when I wanted to know how many
drams my Indian had taken. I left a clean
glafs near a barrel of brandy; the Indian, being
alone, was tempted to drink a glafs; after
which I ordered the glafs to be wafhed in hot
water, and put in its place again; and every
time he drank, my people always did the fame
thing. Accordingly it was very eafy for me to
tell him, thou haft taken fo many drams; he
was always amazed at it, and thought I was a
forcerer.

I have often remarked, that the Indians are
highly pleafed when the French carefs their little children; likewife, in order to make myfelf
beloved and feared by them at the fame time,
when-

whenever I had reason to be displeased with their behaviour, I made use of this method: the more I seemed vexed and angry at the fathers, the more I affected friendship for their children; I caressed them, and gave them European toys. The Indians readily guessed, that as I had no reason to complain of their wives and children, I did not love them less than before, and was only vexed at those who had offended me, without extending my anger upon their families. This moved their heart, and consequently they went out, killed some wild fowls, brought them to me, and, throwing them on the floor, said, " This is to appease thee, be no longer angry " with us." I immediately answered, I willingly forget the past, when I see you come back with your wits, meaning when you do not come empty handed. A father's heart is the same all over the world; every father is pleased with the friendship which is shewn to his children, who make returns by their caresses.

You can well conceive, that a mere trifle can gain me the friendship of these people; and that it depends only upon the method of acting with them, to attach them to one's self at all events. But let this suffice for this time; I think I must recall to your mind the plan I purpo-

fed

fed to follow; I only examine the fituation of the places where I ftop, and, during my ftay, I fhall apply particularly to know the genius of the people with whom I am to live for a time; and I think this ftudy not beneath a traveller. You are a foldier and a philofopher; I am perfuaded, that what I fhall give you an account of will pleafe you; for I flatter myfelf, that you depend upon the fidelity of your hiftorian: indeed, I mean to affert nothing but what I am an eye-witnefs of; for I can neither invent nor exaggerate. I am, S I R, &c.

At Fort Chartres, among the Illinois,
   the 28th of March 1752.

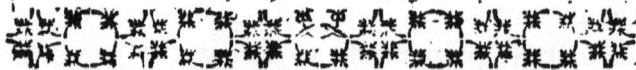

L E T T E R VII.

To the fame.

Defcription of the War of the Nations of Foxes' againft the Illinois, of which the Author has been an Eye-witnefs. Account how the French fettled among thefe People.

S I R,

I HAVE enquired after the manner in which the French fettlement has been made here. The country of the *Illinois* was difcovered by our Canadian hunters; they found its climate very good, being in forty degrees north latitude, fettled on it, and made an alliance with the natives. Many people among them married Indian girls, of which the greateft part became Chriftians : and after the difcovery of *Louifiana*, the India Company fent many fami-

lies

lies over hither, who lived and multiplied here. There are now five great villages of French inhabitants in thefe parts *. The moft confiderable place is called *Kafkakias*, a name of the tribe of an *Illinois* fettlement, which is about half a league from it. The Sieur *Sauffier*, an engineer, has made a plan for conftructing a new fort here, according to the intention of the court. It fhall bear the, fame name with the old one, which is called Fort *de Chartres*.

The *Illinois* country is one of the fineft in the world; it fupplies all the lower parts of *Louifiana* with flower. Its commerce confifts in furs, lead and falt. There are many falt fprings †, that attract the wild oxen, and the roe-bucks, which like the paftures around them very much. Their flefh and tongues are falted, and furnifh another branch of commerce to *New Orleans*; and they cure hams, which equal thofe of *Bayonne*. The fruits are as fine as in *France*.

* The India Company were poffeffed of Louifiana; but they gave it back to the King in 1731. The five villages of the French are that of the *Kafkakias*, the Fort *Chartres*, St. *Philip*, the *Kaokias*, and the *Prairie du Rocher* (meadow on the rock); there is now a fixth, called St. *Genevieve*.

† Called *Salt-licks*, by the Englifh Planters. F.

The

The *Illinois* have very near the same manners and customs as the Nations I have already spoken of; they only differ in their language. They marry, and often, when they return from hunting, leave each other again, each party going a different way.

The marriage of the Indians is quite in the state of nature, and has no other form than the mutual consent of the parties. As they are not tied by any civil contract, whenever they are dissatisfied with each other, they separate, without ceremony, saying that marriage is a tie of the heart, and that they only marry in order to love each other, and help each other mutually in their wants. I have seen very happy marriages among these people; divorces and polygamy are uncommon amongst them, though the latter is allowed by the laws. An Indian may have two wives if he hunts well; sometimes one Indian marries two sisters, giving it as a reason that they will agree better among themselves, than two that are strangers to each other. The Indian women in general are very laborious; they are commonly told, when they are young, that if they be idle or heavy, they will get a wretched husband. Here avarice, ambition, and many other passions, so common among the

Europeans,

Europeans, never ſtifle the feelings of nature, in a father's breaſt, or incline him to force his children, and much leſs to controul them in their Inclinations. By an admirable ſympathy, deſerving of admiration, thoſe only are married, who love each other.

The *Illinois* Indians were formerly the moſt formidable in *Louſiana*, but the continual wars, which they have been engaged in, againſt the northren nations, have reduced them to a very ſmall number. The hatred of the *Canada Indians* againſt them, ariſes from the incurſions which the *Illinois* were uſed to make into their country, and becauſe they took and killed in theſe inroads, both the male and female beavers, which among theſe nations is reckoned a crime and cowardice, becauſe they make a great commerce with the ſkins of theſe *amphibia* *, which they exchange for European goods.

In 1752, the Indians of the tribe of *Koakias* met ſix Indians of the nation of *Foxes*, hunting †;

VOL. I.   K   they

Beavers are quadrupeds and probably called, by our author, *amphibia* for no other reaſon, but becauſe they may be eaten as fiſh on the *jours maigres* F.

† Their true name is *Outagamis*; they inhabit the coun try to the weſt of the Lake *Michigan*.

they took them prifoners, though they were not
at war, and refolved to burn them, that they
might not give any account of them. One of
the *Foxes*, or *Outagamis* was happy enough to
efcape from the ftake he was faftened to, and being purfued by his tormentors, he leaped into a
lake, and eluded their refearches, by fwimming
under water. He remained hidden in the rufhes,
only putting out his head from time to time to
take breath. He had the firmnefs to remain in
that pofture while his comrades were broiling.
In the night time he efcaped the watchfulnefs of
the *Illinois*, who thought he was either drowned
or eaten by the *armed fifh* *. As he was naked
and without arms, he was obliged, in order to
fubfift upon the road, to eat grafs like a beaft.
Being returned to his nation, he told them what
had happened to him with the *Illinois*, and the
unhappy fate which they had made his fellow-
travellers undergo. Their relations immediately
began to grieve for them after their manner. The
chief of the nation called an affembly together,
for they undertake nothing without a council ; the
                                              refult

---

* The armed fifh in *Louifiana* is exceedingly voracious.
His teeth cut the iron of the fifh hooks in pieces.

refult was to fend bundles of rods * to the chiefs of the tribes, who were their allies, among whom were the *Sioux*, the *Sakis* and the *Kikápous* who marched as auxiliary troops under the ftandard of the *Foxes*. The army confifted of a thoufand warriors ; every thing being in rea- dinefs, the general of the *Foxes* marched towards the *Illinois*, and chiefly towards the *Mitchigamias* who had given fhelter to the *Koakias*.

The warriors being come together to the num- ber of one thoufand, they embarked in one hundred and eighty canoes made of birch tree bark, on the river *Ouifconfing* which falls into the *Miffifippi*. By the current of the river, and the help of their oars, they were foon brought to their enemies, the *Illinois*.

They paffed in good order by the fort of *Koa- kias* where the Chevalier *de Volfei*, an officer of my detachment, commanded. The van of this fleet of the *Foxes*, confifted of the beft runners, who were to go on fhore to reconnoitre. They

landed

* As the Indians have not got the art of writing, the rods mark the number of warriors, and the day of affembling for the departure of the army.

landed about a quarter of a league from the *Mitchigamias* village, which was furrounded within a mufket fhot by a wood; their enemies being far from expecting fuch a vifit.

The *Foxes* had fixed upon *Corpus Chrifti* day for fighting the *Illinois*. They knew that the latter would come to Fort *Chartres* to fee the ceremony which is performed by the French on that folemn day; the fort was only a league from the Indian village.

Every thing being in readinefs for the attack, the general of the *Foxes* ordered ten or twelve of the beft runnners to throw away their bodies †. Thefe young men immediately fell upon the enemy's village and killed all they met as they came in, crying the cry of death, and having difcharged their arms, they fled with as much quicknefs as they came.

The *Illinois* took up their arms and purfued them; but the army of the *Foxes*, lying on the ground,

---

* This is a great holiday with the French.

† To *throw away* their bodies, is among the Indians to *expofe* their bodies *to danger*, as thofe do that are obliged to mount firft of all the breach to ftorm a place.

ground, in the high grafs, difcharged all their arms and killed twenty-eight *Illinois* : at the fame time they fell upon the village, and killed men, women and children ; fet fire to the village, and bound and led away the reft as captives.

The *Foxes* loft but four men in this glorious expedition, one of them being a chief with a medal *, of the nation of *Sioux*, who went with them as an ally.

I was a fpectator of this flaughter, which happened on the fixth of June 1752. I was at that time on a hill which overlooks the plain and the village of the *Mitchigamias*. I had the opportunity of faving the life of a girl of fifteen years of age, who came to bring me fome ftraw-berberries. At the time of the attack, fhe ran away, and as the enemies purfued her, fhe ran into my arms, where the barbarians did not venture to fhoot at her, for fear of hitting me.

K 3

This

---

* This diftinction, of which I have already fpoken, is granted by order of the King, through his general, to the moft valiant Indians, and who are moft attached to the French nation.

This account will inform you, that nothing can be more dangerous, than being taken unawares by thefe nations. None but thofe, who were gone out of curiofity to fee the proceffion at the French fort of *Chartres*, efcaped the revenge of the *Foxes*, who contented with their victory, re-embarked in their boats, and put the prifoners well bound in the van; and paffing by the French fort of *Koakias*, they gave a general falute with their guns.

The chief, or admiral of the *Foxes*, had hoifted the French colours on his canoe, and was as proud of his victory, as if he had fubdued a great empire.

M. *de Macarty*, our governor, has written to thofe in the pofts of Canada, to treat with the *Foxes* concerning the ranfom of the *Illinois*, whom they have taken prifoners.

Thefe cunning Indians had conducted their undertaking fo well, that we knew nothing of it till it was executed; they hid the knowledge of it from us, juftly fearing that we fhould interpofe our mediation between them and the *Illinois*, as being the friends and allies of both; but the
offended

offended nation was defirous of vengeance only.

The village of the *Mitchigamias* has loft about eighty perfons, both killed and prifoners, in this fatal affair.

On the fixteenth of *June*, I was ordered by the commandant of Fort *Chartres*, to affemble the remains of the conquered tribes of *Koakias* and *Mitchigamias*, and I held this fhort fpeech to them, by means of the King's interpreter.

I fpeak to you, my children *, on the part of your father, M. *de Macarty*, who takes a great fhare in your misfortune, at the fame time he exhorts you to take care in fowing your maize, that you may efcape the want in which you are at prefent. Here is fome maize, which he gives you, becaufe his heart fuffers to fee you weakened by hunger. He has likewife told me to give this little quantity of powder, fhot and flints; we cannot do better at prefent, becaufe we have our enemies as well as you, and we do not know when the boats will come from the great village (i. e. *New Orleans*) Your father

K 4   recom-

---

* The Indians are ufed to call every officer, *my father*.

recommends it to you to go a hunting, and to take your families with you, that they may have somewhat to live upon, leaving only a certain number of men, to take care of the fields, and to prevent the wild beasts from ruining them; you must likewise take care to send one of your people from time to time, to inquire how matters stand here.

The Answer of the Chiefs of the Tribes.

" It is very well, my Father, that the great chief *
" pities us. It was a very brave action to be sur-
" prized in the manner we have been; thou hast been
" an eye-witness of it, for thou hast saved the life
" of one of our girls; our tribe have been killed
" by the *Foxes*, who have burnt our huts with our
" victuals, and taken our booty, during our re-
" treat at the *Kaskakias*. Thou must think, that
" we cannot leave any here, or they must starve,
" and would ever lament the death of our rela-
" tions, who perished in this sad action. But to
" convince our father of our fidelity, tell him,
" by means of the speaking substance (paper),
" that from time to time we shall send some one
" of

---

* Thus these nations call the superior officers of a province or district.

" of our people to him with game to know what
" happens here,

" We hope the grand chief of the French
" will protect and help us to shelter ourselves a-
" gainst the enemy. We beg thee likewise to make
" interest with him that he may be so good as to
" send word to several families of our people,
" who stayed among the *Kaskakias*, to join us,
" in order to assist us in the common defence of
" the intended fort, of which we have drawn
" the plan on the shore of the *Missisippi*."

Speech of Chikagou, a Chief with a Medal.

" I beg, my father, that thou wouldst get our
" arms mended, and we shall decamp after that
" immediately : and that thou wilt tell the grand
" chief not to hear the bad words, which our
" enemies will not fail to throw out against our
" nation, let him remember the promise I made
" him, it shall be a true one ; and I preserve his
" words in my heart."

Answer.

If what thou sayest be true, thy father will
receive thee well, and all the other chiefs will
endeavour

endeavour to please thee, if thy heart agree with thy tongue. It is necessary thou shouldst set out soon : consider the damage which the dogs of thy village have done among the cattle belonging to the French inhabitants *, and with what tranquility they suffer it ; that they have hitherto said nothing about it, is in consideration of your misfortunes, which grieve them, and they cannot see you reduced to this sad condition without being moved at it : but they begin to be tired, therefore you must remedy it. Your father will be satisfied when he knows that you are gone to the hunting country, because his heart is afflicted to see you suffer hunger, and he pities his children.

As to myself, I heartily wish you good success in hunting, and a plentiful crop at your return. I hope the *Great Spirit* will have pity upon you ; do not slight him : recommend it to your young people not to play the fool, that is, not to destroy the female beavers in the lakes

and

---

* The Indians have many dogs for hunting ; and they themselves having lost their provisions, their dogs were hungry, and devoured the cattle of the French. The Indian dogs are of a breed which partakes of the wolf and the dog.

and hunting places of your enemies, who will not fail to be revenged for it, as you have unhappily experienced.

Your father has written to Mr. *Adamville*, who commands at the *Peorias*, to make your peace with the *Foxes*, and to treat with them about the ranfom of your wives and children, whom they have taken prifoners; the merchandizes fhall be furnifhed for that purpofe for the account of the king, your father, grand chief of the white men and of the red men.

Among the Indians, thofe who run away or defert in an action, where their honour, and the defence of their country is at ftake, are not punifhed; but they are confidered as the difgrace of human nature. The others are continually reproaching them, that they are not men, but old women; they are defpifed by the very women, and the uglieft girls will not accept of them for hufbands, and if ever it happened that a girl fhould be willing to marry a coward, her relations would not allow of it, for fear of having men without courage, and ufelefs to their country in their family. Thefe men are obliged to let their hair grow, and to wear an *alkonan*,

like

like the women *. I faw one of them, who being afhamed of his figure, went by himfelf to fight the *Tchikachas*, who are our enemies and theirs. He came near them, creeping like a fnake, and hiding himfelf in the great grafs during three or four days, without eating or drinking. As the Englifh bring goods to the *Tchikachas* (Chickfaws) in caravans, our *Illinois* killed one of them who had ftrayed from the caravan, cut off his head, mounted his horfe, and got off. He was out three months upon this fine expedition. On his return the nation received him with due honour, and gave him a wife, that he might beget warriors. Before his departure he eat of dog's flefh, conformably to the opinion current among his people, and of which I have already had the honour of fpeaking to you.

The grand chief of the *Illinois* is defcended from the family of the *Tamaroas*, who were formerly fovereigns of this country. This Cacique or Indian king, is the fon of him that went to France with his attendants in 1720. He was prefented to the King, who gave him a medal with his portrait, which the fon now wears on

his

---

* A fhort petticoat, which the Indian women make ufe of, to cover their nakednefs.

his breaft. There was likewife a woman of the nation of the *Miffouris*, who was called the princefs of the *Miffouris* *. The Sieur *Dubois*, a ferjeant, and interpreter of thofe American ambaffadors, having been created an officer by the King, married this *Miffourian* lady at his return. She became a widow; and afterwards married the Sieur *Marin*, a captain of the militia, by whom fhe had a daughter, who is ftill alive.

The Indian princefs defcribed to her countrymen the magnificence fhe had feen at the court of France, where fhe had been well received, and loaded with prefents; fhe had, amongft other things, got a fine repeating watch fet with diamonds, which the favages called a fpirit, on account of its motion, which feemed fupernatural to them.

I have here fpoken with an old Indian, who was in the retinue of the Prince *Tamaroas*; I afked him feveral queftions concerning France, and

* She was the daughter of the grand chief of this nation. It is faid fhe was M. *de Bourmont*'s miftrefs, who, during his command among the *Miffouris*, never ceafed to praife and extol the wonders of France, and by that means engaged feveral to follow him: this girl went over to the Chriftian religion, and was baptifed at the church of *Notre Dame*.

and efpecially what fine fights he had feen at *Pa-ris:* he anfwered, that it was the *Rue de Bouche-ries,* (the fhambles) becaufe there was a great abundance of flefh ; and after that the *Rue St. Honoré.* When he told his countrymen that he had feen the opera, and that all the people there are jugglers or forcerers ; and that he likewife faw, upon the *Pont-Neuf,* fome little men who danced and fung *, they would not believe him. When he faid, that, in the great village of the French *(Paris),* he had feen as many people as there are leaves on the trees in their forefts, (an hyperbole which the Indians make ufe of to ex-prefs a great number, having no words to ex-prefs a number above a hundred), they anfwer-ed, that the Europeans probably had fafcinated his eyes, that it was impoffible, and that they had always offered the fame objects to his eyes. He faid that he had feen the huts of the grand chief of the French, *i. e. Verfailles* and *Louvre,* and that they contained more people than there are in their country: he likewife added, that he had feen the hut of the old warriors, (the royal hofpital of invalids). As this old Indian began already to doat, he agreed with the other Indians, that the French had bewitched him. Another
Illinois,

---

* A puppet-fhow.

Illinois, who had made the fame voyage, told his countrymen, that, in the *Thuilleries*, and other public walks, he had feen men who were half women, having their hair dreffed like women, wearing the fame ear-rings, and great nofe-gays on their breaft; that he fufpected they put *rouge* on their faces, and that he found they fmelled like crocodiles *.

This Indian fpoke with the greateft contempt of that race of mortals, whom we know under the name of *petits-maitres*, or beaus, who are born with the weaknefs and the delicacy peculiar to women; nature feeming to have begun making them fuch, and afterwards to make a miftake in the formation of their fex.

The Indian had likewife remarked the enormous height of the head-dreffes of our women in that time †, and of the heels of their fhoes. But what would he have faid, if he had feen the extravagant width of their hoops, and their fine

fhape

---

* The crocodile in the *Miffifippi* has follicles with mufk, which fmells ftronger than the Eaft Indian mufk; its effluvia are fo ftrong, that you can often fmell the animal before you fee it.

† During the regency.

ſhape forced, from their, infancy, into that elegant cuiraſs called ſtays.   Theſe coquets are
not leſs ridiculous by their artifices, than their
ſilly adorers.   You have made. the obſervation,
as I have done, in the courſe of your travels
through Europe, that the foreigners and country gentlemen, who come to *Paris* to copy our
beaus and our belles, have rendered themſelves
inſupportable to their countrymen by this unnatural method of acting : indeed, ſaid our American, ſuch effeminate manners diſhonour are-
ſpectable nation.

I have received a letter from the Marquis *de
Vaudreuil*, in which he expreſſes great concern
for the unhappy accident which has befallen me,
by the wreck of my boat.   This governor, from
a pure effect of his generoſity, which is natural
to him, has been willing to alleviate, as much
as is in his power, the fate of an unhappy officer, who loſt all he had in the King's ſervice.

He has given me leave to come to *New Orleans*, and offered me his purſe and his table ; I
am afraid he will be gone for France by the time
I arrive at *New Orleans*. It may be ſaid with
truth, that he has deſerved the eſteem and friendſhip of every body.   The Indians inceſſantly
                                                        com-

compare him now to M. *de Bienville*, his predeceffor. When thefe people do not fpeak in
praife of a governor, but, on the contrary, agree
with all the inhabitants in detefting him, it is the
ftrongeft accufation againft him.

Before I conclude, I fhall add a word about
the *Miffouris*. Baron *Porneuf*, who has been governor of Fort *Orleans* eftablifhed in that nation, and who knows their genius perfectly well,
has informed me, that they were formerly very
warlike and good, but that the French hunters
had corrupted them, by their bad conduct, and
by fome difunions among them ; they had
made themfelves contemptible by frauds in
trade ; they feduced and carried off the Indian
women, which, among thefe people, is a very
great crime ; for they never pardon fuch forts of
robberies. All the irregularities of thefe bad
Frenchmen irritated the *Miffouris* againft them ;
and therefore, during M. *de Bienville*'s government, they maffacred the Sieur *Dubois*, and the
little garrifon under his command ; and as no
foldier efcaped, we have never been able to know
who was right and who was wrong.

The ftory I fhall tell you will convince you,
that thefe people are only nominally favages, and

that the French, who endeavoured to impofe
upon them, have deceived themfelves.   About
forty years ago, when thefe Americans did not
yet know the Europeans, a traveller or hunter
penetrated into their country, made them acquainted with fire-arms, and fold them mufkets
and gunpowder: they went out a-hunting, and
got great plenty of game, and of courfe many
furs.   Another traveller went thither fome time
after, with ammunitions ; but the Indians being
ftill provided, they did not care to barter with
the Frenchman, who invented a very odd trick,
in order to fell his powder, without much troubling his head with the confequences that might
refult from his impofture to his countrymen. He
thought he had done a great action in deceiving
thefe poor people.

As the Indians are naturally curious, they
were defirous of knowing how powder, which
they called *grain*, was made in France. The
traveller made them believe, that it was fown in
favannahs, and that they had crops of it as of
indigo or millet in *America*.

The *Miffouris* were pleafed with this difcovery,
and fowed all the gun-powder they had left,
which obliged them to buy that of the Frenchman,

man, who got a confiderable quantity of bea-
ver-fkins, otter-fkins, &c. for it, and afterwards went down the river to the *Illinois*, where
M. *de Tonti* commanded.

The *Miſſouris* went from time to time to the
ſavannah, to ſee if the powder was growing:
they had placed a guard there, to hinder the
wild beaſts from ſpoiling the field; but they
ſoon found out the Frenchman's trick: It muſt
be obſerved, that the Indians can be deceived
but once, and that they always remember it;
accordingly theſe were reſolved to be revenged
upon the firſt Frenchman that ſhould come to
them. Soon after, the hopes of profit excited
the traveller to ſend his partner to the *Miſſouris*,
with goods proper for their commerce; they
ſoon found out, that this Frenchman was aſſo-
ciated with the man who had impoſed upon
them; however, they diſſembled the trick which
his predeceſſor had played. They gave him the
public hut, which was in the middle of the village, to depoſit his bales in; and when they
were all laid out to view, the *Miſſouris* came in
confuſedly, and all thoſe who had been fooliſh
enough to ſow gun-powder, took away ſome
goods; ſo the poor Frenchman was rid of all
his bales at once, but without any equivalent

from

from the Indians. He complained much of thefe proceedings, and laid his grievances before the great chief, who anfwered him very gravely : That he fhould have juftice done him, but that for that purpofe he muft wait for the gun-powder harveft, his fubjects having fown that commodity by the advice of his countryman ; that he might believe upon the word of a fovereign, that, after that harveft was over, he would order a general hunt, and that all the fkins of the wild beafts which fhould be taken, fhould be given in return for the important fecret, which the other Frenchman had taught them.

Our traveller alledged, that the ground of the *Miffouris* was not fit for producing gun-powder, and that his fubjects had not taken notice, that France was the only country where it fucceeded in. All his reafoning was ufelefs; he returned much lighter than he came, and afhamed of having been corrected by favage men.

This leffon did not prevent others from going to the *Miffouris*; one of them intended to play a good trick there; he got ready a piragua, which he loaded with trifles; and, being informed of the preceding adventure, he filled a little cafk

with

with aſhes and pounded charcoal, at the top of which he put ſome gun-powder. When he arrived, he put all his goods in the great hut, in order to tempt the *Miſſouris* to rob him; it happened as he expected. The Frenchman made a great noiſe, gave the Indians abuſive language, and, running to the caſk of gun-powder, he opened it, took a burning match, and cried out, I have loſt my wits, I will blow up the hut, and you ſhall come with me to the country of the ſpirits. The Indians were frightened, and knew not what to do; the other Frenchmen who came with him were out of doors, and cried out, our brother has loſt his ſenſes, and he *will* not recover them again, till he gets his goods back, or till he gets paid for for them. The chiefs went through the village, to exhort the people to pay; thoſe who had any relations in the hut joined them; the people were moved, and every one brought all the furs he had into the hut; the Frenchman then ſaid he had found his ſenſes again. The chief preſented him with the calumet, he ſmoked, and poured water upon the gun-powder to make it uſeleſs, or rather to hide his fraud from the Indians. He brought home fine furs to the value of a thouſand crowns. The Indians have ever

ſince

fince held him in great efteem, giving him the
name of a *true man*, or *man of courage.*

I fhall finifh my letter with the defcription of
a very odd and extraordinary ceremony, performed by the *Miffouris*, who came hither as ambaffadors, at the time when the Chevalier *de
Boifbriant* commanded here. This tragic ftory
will at the fame time ferve to teach officers,
who, through a noble ambition, afpire to military commands, that both the theoretical and
the practical part of geography ought abfolutely
to be underftood by them ; and that it is neceffary they fhould carefully ftudy the interior fituation of a country where they are at war, in order to avoid all furprifes of the enemy, and to
preferve the lives of the men who are under
their care. What I fhall now tell, will fufficiently convince them of this neceffity.

Spain faw, with great difpleafure, during the
regency, our fettlements on the *Miffifippi :* The
Englifh too, on their fide, fpared no intrigues to
ruin this growing colony, as they do ftill in regard to thofe upon the banks of the river *Ohio,*
which they fay belongs to them ; and they have
likewife laid claim to the *Miffifippi.*

In

In 1720, the Spaniards formed the defign of fettling at the *Miſſouris*, who are near the *Illinois*, in order to confine us more to the weſtward ; the *Miſſouris* are far diſtant from *New Mexico*, which is the moſt northerly province the Spaniards have.

They believed, that in order to put their colony in fafety, it was neceſſary they ſhould entirely deſtroy the *Miſſouris* ; but concluding that it would be impoſſible to fubdue them with their own forces alone, they reſolved to make an alliance with the *Oſages*, a people who were the neighbours of the *Miſſouris*, and at the fame time their mortal enemies, hoping . with their aſſiſt-ance, to furprife and deſtroy their enemies. With that view they formed a caravan at *Santa-Fé*, confiſting of men, women, and foldiers, having a *Jacobine* prieſt for their chaplain, and an engineer-captain for their chief and conduct-or, with the horfes and cattle neceſſary for a per-manent fettlement.

The caravan being fet out, miſtook its road, and arrived at the *Miſſouris*, taking them to be the *Oſages*. Immediately the conductor of the caravan orders his interpreter to fpeak to the chief of the *Miſſouris*, as if he had been that of

the

the *Ofages*, and tell him that they were come to make an alliance with him, in order to deſtroy together the *Miſſouris* their enemies.

The great chief of the *Miſſouris* concealed his thoughts upon this expedition, ſhewed the Spaniards ſigns of great joy, and promiſed to execute a deſign with them which gave him much pleaſure. To that purpoſe he invited them to reſt for a few days after their tireſome journey, till he had aſſembled his warriors, and held council with the old men : but the reſult of this council of war was, that they ſhould entertain their gueſts very well, and affect the ſincereſt friendſhip for them.

They agreed together to ſet out in three days. The Spaniſh captain immediately diſtributed fifteen hundred muſkets amongſt them, with an equal number of piſtols, ſabres, and hatchets ; but the very morning after this agreement, the *Miſſouris* came, by break of day, into the Spaniſh camp, and killed them all except the *Jacobine* prieſt, whoſe ſingular dreſs did not ſeem to belong to a warrior : they called him a *mag-pie*, and diverted themſelves with making him ride on one of the Spaniſh horſes, on their days of aſſembly.

The

The prieft, though he was careffed and well fed, was not without uneafinefs, fearing that thefe jokes would end in facrificing him to the *Manitou*, or deity of the Indians ; therefore, one day, taking advantage of their confidence in him, he took his meafures to get away before their faces. All thofe tranfactions the *Miffouris* themfelves have related, when they brought the ornaments of the chapel hither. They were dreffed out in thefe ornaments : the chief had on the naked fkin the chafuble, with the paten fufpended from his neck, having driven a nail through it, and making ufe of it as a breaft-plate ; he marched gravely at the head of all the others, being crowned with feathers and a pair of horns. Thofe that followed him had more chafubles on ; after them came thofe who carried the ftole, followed by thofe who had the fcarfs about their necks ; after them came three or four young Indians, fome with albs, and others with furplices on. The Acolothifts, contrary to order, were at the end of this proceffion, not being adorned enough, and held in their hands a crofs or chandelier, whilft they danced in cadence. Thefe people, not knowing the refpect due to the facred utenfils, hung the chalice to a horfe's neck, as if it had been a bell.

Reprefent

Reprefent to yourfelf the ridiculous fight which the fingular order of this proceffion muft offer to the eye, as they arrived before the houfe of M. *de Boifbriant* the King's lieutenant, marching in cadence, and with the great calumet of peace difplayed according to cuftom.

The firft Frenchman who faw this mafquerade arrive, ran laughing to give M. *de Boifbriant* intelligence of it; this officer, who is as pious as he is brave, was overcome with grief at the fight of the Indians, and knew not what to think of the event; he feared they had deftroyed fome French fettlement; but when he faw them near by, his fadnefs vanifhed, and he had much to do to keep himfelf from laughing with the reft.

The *Miffouris* told him, that the Spaniards intended to have deftroyed them; that they brought him all thefe things, as being of no ufe to them, and that, if he would, he might give them fuch goods in return as were more to their liking. Accordingly he gave them fome goods, and fent the ornaments to M. *de Bienville*, who was then governor-general of the province of *Louifiana.*

As

As the Indians had got a great number of Spanish horses from this caravan, the chief of the *Miſſouris* gave the fineſt to M. *de Boiſbriant.*

They had likewiſe brought with them the map which had conducted the Spaniards ſo ill, who came to ſurrender themſelves, by confeſſing their intention to their enemies.

I ſhall profit of the permiſſion which I have obtained to go down to *New Orleans.* If I find our general, and a letter from you there, it will be a double pleaſure to me.

I am, S I R, &c.

At the Illinois, the 15th
of May 1753.

L E T T E R VIII.

To the same.

The Author leaves the Country of the Illinois, and goes to New Orleans. Arrival of Monsieur de Kerlerec. Departure of the Marquis de Vaudreuil. The Author's second Voyage to the Illinois. Heroic Action of a Father, who sacrificed himself for his Son.

S I R,

IN June I arrived at the Capital of *Louisiana*, where I found a letter from you, which gave me real pleasure, by informing me that you continue to enjoy your health, and it made up for the loss I had of our dear governor's presence; when I came hither I heard he was already gone to France; and to compleat my misfortunes, Mr. *Michel de la Ruevilliero* was dead of an apoplexy; he had

wrote

wrote to me that he had with sorrow heard of
the loss of my boat, and that notwithstanding
it was not the king's custom to re-imburse such
expences, yet he would repair this loss with pleasure for my relief: that I should make an exact
account of all I had lost, and join to it a certificate from M. *de Macarty*, the commander of the
convoy : this was, he said, an indispensable ne-
cessity, that this article may at least have some
appearance, and thus be entered in the accounts ;
he promised that as soon as he should have this
paper, he would settle what I was to receive.
The Marquis de *Vaudreuil* had recommended me
at his departure to his successor M. *de Kerlerec*,
who has not paid any attention to his recommendation ; his qualities are quite the reverse of
those of his predecessor ; but this new governor
alledges, that he is not come so far, merely for
the sake of changing the air. He kept me at
New Orleans, and only allowed me to rejoin my
garrison in 1754, with the convoy which M. de
Faverot commanded. I could not find any
room to embark my provisions for the voyage,
on account of the number of goods every one
was allowed to take as a venture, and which
filled the king's boats : I made my just repre-
sentations on this subject to M. *de Kerlerec*, who
made me suffer all kinds of disagreeable circum-

stances

ftances on this occafion. After which, having
afked me what venture I took with me, I anfwered, that I underftood nothing of commerce;
that being a foldier, his majefty had fent me to
Louifiana to ferve him, and that I placed all my
glory in that fervice, at laft M: *de Kerlerec* gave
me leave to join my garrifon.

I left *New Orleans* the feventeenth of Auguft,
but the boats, as I have already faid, were fo
much laden with ventures, that being overtaken
by the froft, we could not get to the *Illinois*, but
were obliged to winter on the road; and the
convoy only arrived in January, 1755, which
occafioned extortions and immenfe cofts for the
king's account. The fatigue of fo long a
voyage ruined my health fo much, that I was
reduced to the utmoft extremity. I was conducted on foot by Indians, and when I was tired,
they carried me in a dreffed ox hide, made in
the form of a hamock, hung upon a great
pole, as a litter. They changed fucceffively,
and in this manner I came once more to the
old fort *Chartres*, where I lay in a hut, till I
could get a lodging in the new fort, which
is almoft finifhed. It is built of free ftone,
flanked with four baftions, and capable of containing a garrifon of three hundred men. I
afked

afked M. *de Macarty's* leave to go to change the air at the *Kaokias*, who are a day's journey from Fort *Chartres*, and the road to it is either by water or by land. In this poft there is a little fort on the' left fide of the *Miſſiſippi*, it is the great road of the *Illinois* to *Canada*, and the center of commerce of *New France*, or *Louiſiana*, which is confiderable in furs.

The priefts of the order of St. *Sulpicius*, to whom the ifle and town of *Montreal* belong, have eftablifhed a miffion here under the name of the *Holy Family of Jeſus*. There are but three priefts. I have been particularly acquainted with the Abbé *Mercier*, a Canadian by birth, and vicar of the whole country of *Illinois*. He was a man of probity, whofe friendfhip could not fail of being of ufe to me, by the knowledge he had acquired of the manners of the Indians, who were edified by his virtue and difintereftednefs. He fpoke the language of the country, and on account of the fluency with which he expreffed himfelf in it, he was highly efteemed among the Indians, who confult him in all their affairs. He has fpent forty five years in cultivating the Lord's vineyard in thefe diftant countries, and the Indian nations of thefe parts
have

have always refpected him.   A man of his character could never have lived long enough for
the happinefs of thefe people. This worthy
apoftle of *Louifiana*, fell into a confumption in
Lent, and he died of it one Friday at half an
hour after eleven at night, expiring as a Chriftian
hero. He had an admirable prefence of mind,
and I have regretted him very much. The
French and the Indians were inconfolable; the
latter fent their deputies according to their cuftom to lament him on his tomb. They came
in fwarms, and as foon as they arrived near the
houfe of the late Abbé, they cried out aloud and
made doleful lamentations. Thefe poor people
were in a great confternation, and grief was
painted on their faces. Thefe people, whom
we call favages, know the true virtue in man;
this man had worked almoft during his whole
life for their welfare; they called him their father and the chief of the prayer.

What a difference is there between this miffionary and another anterior to him, who falfely
attributed to himfelf the difcovery of *Louifiana*;
I mean the father *Hennepin*, a Recollet friar, of
whom I fhall fpeak to you. In 1683, he publifhed a relation, the title of which is not right:
for

for the country which the Recollet, and the Sieur
Decan difcóvered in going up the *Miſſiſippi* from
the river of *Illinois* to the fall St. *Anthony*, does
not belong to *Louiſiana*, but to *Canada*.   The relation of a fecond voyage of father *Hennepin*, in
the *Recueil des Voyages du Nord*, bears a title which
is equally falfe : voyage to a country greater
than Europe, between the frozen ocean, and
new *Mexico* ; for though they have gone very
far up the *Miſſiſippi*, they have ſtill been at a
great diſtance from the frozen ocean.   When
the author publifhed this fecond relation he had
quarrelled with M. *de la Salle* ; it feems that he
was actually forbid returning to *America*, and
that the difpleafure this reſtriction gave him,
prompted him to retire to Holland, where he
publifhed a third work, intitled a new defcription of a very great country, fituated in *America*
between new *Mexico* and the frozen ocean, with
reflections on M. *de la Salle's* undertakings and
other things concerning the defcription and hiftory of *North America.*

The author there not only vents all his ill-na-
ture on M. *de la Salle,* but likewife throws it
upon *France,* pretending to have been ill-treated
by the nation.   He means to fave his honour by
declaring that he was born a fubject of the Ca-

tholic king * ; but he ought to reflect that it
was at the expence of France that he travelled
in *America*, and that it was in the name of his
moft Chriftian majefty, that he and the Sieur
Decan took poffeffion of the countries which
they had difcovered. He did not fear
to advance, that it was with the confent of
his Catholic majefty, his firft fovereign, that
he dedicated his relation, to William the
Third, king of Great Britain, in which he
folicits that monarch to conquer thefe vaft regi-
ons, and to fend Miffionaries thither, to teach
the Indians the Chriftian religion ; a proceeding
which excited the ridicule of the Catholics, and
fcandalized the Proteftants, who were furprized
to fee a prieft who called himfelf a miffionary,
exhort a Proteftant fovereign to found a Roman
church in *America*. All his works are befides
written in a pompous ftile, which fhocks the
reader, and offends him by the liberties which
the author takes, and by his indecent invectives.
Father *Hennepin* thought he might make ufe of
the privilege of a traveller ; but he has likewife
been much cried down by his fellow-travellers,
who have often declared, that he was very un-
faithful

---

* Father Henneppin was a native of *Douay*.

faithful in all his accounts. It appears that there was more vanity in his undertaking, than true zeal in making profelytes in America.

Whilft I was at the *Koakias*, fome Indians of the nation of *Ofages* arrived there; their *Manitou*, or falfe deity, was a dried ferpent, of a monftrous fize. Thefe people faid that this prodigious animal had committed great devaftations in their country; that it fwallowed a tyger-cat all at once; that confequently they had declared war againft it, and were gone to attack it. They followed it by the track, but neither balls nor arrows could penetrate its body, which was covered with very hard fcales, like thofe of a crocodile. They fucceeded at laft in putting it to death by fhooting balls and arrows at it, which blinded it. He that had killed it carried the mark or impreffion of it on his body, in the fame manner as the *Akanzas* imprinted the roe-buck on my thigh. They make this lafting mark in the following manner. They firft draw with black, or with gun-powder the figure of the animal or object they mean to reprefent, on the flefh; after which they fting the fkin in the out-line, with one or more needles to the blood; the figure is then flightly wafhed

over

over with a fine fpunge dipt in a folution of rock
falt, which mixes the blood with the black, con-
tracting the fkin which has been ftung, and ren-
ders the figure indelible.   This is not done without fome pain ; but as it is a kind of knighthood
to which they are only intitled by great actions,
they fuffer. with pleafure, in order to pafs for
men of courage. Thefe marks of diftinction
multiply in proportion to the fine actions they
do in war.

If one of them fhould get himfelf marked,
without having previoufly diftinguifhed himfelf
in battle, he would be degraded, and looked
upon as a coward, unworthy of an honour,
which only belongs to thofe who generoufly expofe their lives in defence of their country. The
Indians only value the fons of Caciques, in as
much as they are brave and virtuous after the
example of their fathers and anceftors.

I faw an Indian, who, though he had never
fignalized himfelf in defence of the nation,
however chofe to get a mark on his body, in
order to deceive thofe who only judged from appearances.   He would pafs for a man of courage
with a view to obtain one of the prettieft girls
of the nation in marriage, who, favage as fhe was,
                                             was

was however not without ambition. As he was
on the point of concluding the match with her
relations, the warriors, full of indignation on
feeing a coward boaft with a mark due only to
military merit, held an affembly of chiefs of
war, in order to punifh fuch audacioufnefs.
The council agreed, that, to obviate fuch an
abufe, which would confound brave men with
cowards, he who had wrongfully adorned himfelf with the figure of a club on his fkin, without ever having ftruck a blow at war, fhould
have the mark torn off, that is, the place fhould
be flayed, and that the fame fhould be done to
all who would offend in the fame cafe.

As there was no pardon to hope for, his con-
demnation being pronounced by an act of this
Indian fenate, who is jealous of maintaining the
honour of the nation, I offered, in commifera-
tion of the poor wretch, to cure him in the
French manner; I faid I would take off the fkin
and the mark without hurting him, and that my,
remedy would change the blood into water. The
Indians, ignorant of my fecret, believed I jeft-
ed with them: therefore, counterfeiting their
jugglers, I gave the pretended bravo a calabafh
full of fyrup of the maple-tree, into which I had
put a dofe of opium; and, whilft he was afleep,

M 3   I ap-

I applied Spa..ifh flies to the figure of the club which he bore on his breaft, and over them fome plantain leaves, which caufed tumours; the fkin and the mark went off, and a watery matter came out. This method of proceeding furprifed the Indian jugglers, who were ignorant of the Spanifh flies, or Cantharides, which are very common in *North America*. They give a light in night-time ; and even the fmalleft types can be read, by holding the infect near to the letters, and following the lines.

There is often a fimilarity in the manners of the Indians and of the Europeans, though they may appear ever fo different amongft themfelves. The following example is a proof of it. An officer belonging to the regiment of the *Ifle de France*, having fallen in love with a young lady at *Paris* in 1749, the mother of the lady told him, that fhe would willingly give him her daughter, provided he was adorned with the crofs of *St. Louis*. In order to accelerate his marriage, love infpired him with the thought of taking that diftinction from himfelf, which the King alone can give away. The lady already looked upon him as her fon-in-law ; but a few days after, the falfe chevalier is met by an officer of his regiment, who, being before him in the fervice, is

furprifed

surprifed to fee him obtain the crofs before himfelf. The new chevalier told him, that, with
protections, one could get at every thing. The
officer, who knew nothing of the other's
views, goes immediately to M. *d'Argenfon*, and
reprefents to him the injuftice done to him, by
giving the order of St. Louis to his junior officer. The minifter denies it, and fends for the
lift of promotions, in which the officer is not
comprifed: accordingly he is taken up, and
brought before the tribunal of the Marfhals of
France. A court was held at the hofpital of
invalids, wherein Marfhal *Belle-ifle* prefided.
The falfe chevalier was fentenced to have the
crofs taken from him, to be degraded, and to
be confined in a fortrefs during twenty years.

The Indian women are allowed to make marks
all over their body, without any bad confequences; I have feen fome of them who had
marks even on their breafts, though that part
be extremely delicate; but they endure it firmly,
like the men, in order to pleafe them, and to
appear handfomer to them.

To return to the *Manitou* of the *Ofages*, I
wifhed to have this pretended relic in my poffeffion, in order to adorn your collection of na-

tural

tural curiofities with it; I was willing to treat about it with the Indian prieft who ferved it, offering him European goods in return, and reprefenting to him that the adoration of this animal was an abufe; that he ought, as we do, to worfhip the *Great Spirit*, or *Author of Nature*; but this cunning prieft of the devil, in owning that his fuperftitious countrymen adored every thing uncommon, told me, that he expected to make a great profit of his *Manitou*; that, being a phyfician, and a juggler befides, he could eafily make them believe that his deity eat with the evil fpirit at night, and that they muft bring him victuals into his hut, and fine furs to drefs him out.

Thus this impoftor, by his artful difcourfes, gives weight to the errors and prejudices of thefe ignorant people. Thefe fellows make them believe, that they converfe with the devil at night, whom the Indians are much afraid of, becaufe he can only do harm; whereas they fay the *Great Spirit*, being good, can do them no hurt.

I fhall finifh my letter by an account of the tragic death of an Indian of the nation of *Collapiffas*, who facrificed himfelf for his fon; I have

admired

admired this heroic deed, which raifes human generofity to the higheft pitch.

A *Chaɛɛaw*, fpeaking very ill of the French, faid, that the *Collapiſſas* were their *dogs*, i. e. their flaves; one of thefe, vexed at fuch abufive language, killed the *Chaɛɛaw* with his gun. The nation of *Chaɛɛaws*, which is the greateft and moft numerous on this continent, armed immediately, and fent deputies to *New Orleans* to afk from the governor the head of the murderer, who had put himfelf under the protection of the French. They offered prefents to make up the quarrel, but the cruel nation of *Chaɛɛaws* would not accept any; they even threatened to deftroy the village of *Collapiſſas*. To prevent the effufion of blood, the poor unhappy Indian was delivered up to them. The Sieur *Ferrand*, commander of the German fettlement on the right fhore of the *Miſſiſippi*, was charged with this commiſſion. The rendez-vous for this purpofe was given between the village *Collapiſſa* and the fettlement of the Germans; and the facrifice was performed there as follows:

The Indian was called *Tichou Mingo*, i. e. Cacique's fervant. He ftood upright, and held a fpeech, according to the cuftom of the people, faying,

saying, " I am a true man, that is, I do not
" fear death ; but I pity the fate of a wife and
" four children, whom I leave behind me very
" young, and of my father and mother, who
" are old, and for whom I got fubfiftence by
" hunting *.   I recommend them to the French,
" becaufe I die for having taken their part."

He had hardly fpoken the laft word of this
fhort and pathetic fpeech, when his good and
tender father, penetrated with his fon's filial
love, got up, and fpoke to the following effect:
" It is through courage † that my fon dies ; but
" being young, and full of vigour, he is more
" fit than myfelf to provide for his mother, wife,
" and four little children ; it is therefore necef-
" fary he fhould ftay on earth to take care of
" them. As to myfelf, I am near the end of my
" career, I have lived long enough, and I wifh my
" fon may come to the fame age, in order to
" educate my little children. I am no longer fit
" for any thing, fome years of life more or
" lefs are indifferent to me. I have lived as a
                                      " man,

---

* He was the beft hunter in the nation.

† Courage is a word which, in their language, fignifies —
fomething great or extraordinary.

" man, and will die as fuch; therefore I go to
" take his place *."

At thefe words, which expreffed paternal affection in a very ftrong and moving manner,
his wife, his fon, his daughter-in-law, and their
little children, fhed tears round the brave old
man ; he embraced them for the laft time, and
exhorted them to be faithful to the French, and
to die rather than to betray them by any meannefs unworthy of his blood : at laft he told them,
that his death was a neceffary facrifice to the nation, which he was contented and proud to
make.   With thefe words he prefented his head
to the relations of the dead *Chattaw*, and they
accepted it : after that he laid himfelf on the
trunk of a tree, and they cut off his head immediately with one ftroke of a hatchet.

Every thing was made up by this death ; but
the young man was obliged to give them his father's head † ; in taking it up, he faid to it,
" Pardon

---

* Thefe nations follow the *lex talionis*, death is avenged
by death ; and it is fufficient to fubftitute any one of the nation, if even he were not a relation of the criminal ; flaves
only are excepted.

† They put it on a pole, and carried it as a trophy into
their tribe.

" Pardon me thy death, and remember me in
" the country of fpirits." All the French who
affifted at this tragic event were moved to tears,
and admired the heroic conftancy of this vene-
rable old man, whofe virtue is equal to that
celebrated Roman orator, who, in the time of
of the triumvirate, was hidden by his fon. The
latter was cruelly tormented, in order to extort
from him the place where his father was concealed, who, being no longer able to bear that
fo tender and fo virtuous a fon fhould fuffer fo
much, came to prefent himfelf to the murderers,
and begged the foldiers to kill him, and to fave
his fon's life; the fon conjured them to kill
him, but to fpare his father ; the foldiers, more
barbarous than the favage Indians, killed them
both together, at the fame time, and in the
fame place.

M. *Ferrand*, my fellow-traveller in my laft
voyage to the *Illinois*, fell into the *Miffifippi* in
the fevereft feafon, whilft his foldiers were exer-
cifing ; and, at the very moment that the rapidity of this river carried him into an abyfs, an
Akanza hunter, who was happily on board his
boat, faved him from the precipice. The officer told him, that he hoped to recompenfe him
generoufly for this piece of fervice ; but the Indian

dian' immediately anfwered, that he had only done the duty of a brother, who ought to fuc-cour the unhappy in time of danger; that, as the *Great Spirit* had taught him to fwim like a fifh, he could not employ his fkill better than to fave the life of his fellow-creature.

All the Indians, both men and women, learn to fwim from their infancy. I have often feen the mothers put their little children into pools of frefh water, and I took great delight in feeing the little creatures fwim naturally. Would not fuch an education be better than thofe methods which people are fo fond of in Europe? The queftion I fpeak of here is of the utmoft confe-quence, efpecially in a country where almoft eve-ry body goes by water, and on fea-voyages. I fhall not enter into thefe details, which might prove tirefome: I fhall only fay, that, accord-ing to found reafon, the firft thing which it is neceffary to know in nature, is how to preferve one's exiftence; and that it is to be wifhed, that the European mothers would imitate the Ame-ricans in that particular, and likewife in fuck-ling their own children. This action, which is dictated by nature, would prevent many acci-dents with regard to children fuppofed to be legitimate; and, without quoting many facts

to

to this purpofe from the *Caufes Celebres*, I have
a recent example before my eyes of the confufion often caufed in families by thofe mercenary
nurfes. A gentleman, who was an officer of
the fame detachment which I was in, had long
been fuppofed to be loft by his nurfe. As foon
as he was born, he was fent down into the midft
of *Normandy*; and his relations have only found
him out, when he was twenty-two years old,
through mere chance, after he had gone through
a feries of miferies and dangers during that
time.

I remember, that, in 1749, upon the road
between *Paris* and *Arpajon*, I was witnefs of an
accident which happened to one of the little victims which parents put from them, in order not
to be importuned by their cries. The nurfe
who was trufted with this child, had put it in
her apron; as fhe was ftepping into one of thofe
carriages deftined for thefe journies, her apron,
which was tied behind, got untied, and the
child fell upon the pavement, and expired.

Give me leave to fay, that there is an entire
difference between the way of thinking of the
European and the Indian women. The latter
would think themfelves abufed, if they were to
leave

leave their children to the care of a woman far from their own infpection : they are not afraid, as fome European women, that their hufband's tendernefs will diminifh, becaufe they have borne the tokens of their mutual affection; on the contrary, the flame increafes on both parts, and the pleafure of feeing their race perpetuated, and to fee another felf grow up in a little creature which they brought into the world, amply re-pays the trouble they have of fupporting them.

The white women, whom we call *Creoles*, fol-low in *America* the European cuftom, difdaining to fuckle their own children ; they give them, as foon as they are born, to a tawny or red flave, without reflecting, that her blood may be cor-rupted. Many able phyficians have demonftra-ted, that the milk has an influence on the incli-nations of the children. I have often feen many an innocent fall a victim to the irregular life of their nurfes in *America* ; which is a circumftance fatal to the propagation of the human fpecies. I leave this fubject to the gentlemen of the fa-culty, who will certainly handle it better than myfelf.

I conclude, by affuring you that I am, *&c.*

P. S. An

P. S. An Indian courier has juft brought us the agreeable news of the taking of *Choaguen*, and the places dependent on it, upon the famous lake *Ontario*.

The garrifon of that place, to the number of fifteen hundred regular troops, have furrendered prifoners of war ; and have accepted the articles of capitulation which M. *de Montcalm* has granted them ; that general immediately fent the five pair of regimental colours which he found in the place to *Quebec*.

M. *Rigaud* *, the governor of *Trois Rivieres*, commanded the Canadians and Indians ; he had taken poffeffion of an advantageous poft, in order to oppofe all fuccours, and cut off the retreat of the enemy.

The land troops, thofe of the colonies, the Canadians, and the Indians, have all equally diftinguifhed themfelves : we know not yet the number of men which the enemies have loft ; all we have heard is, that their general was killed

at

---

* Brother of the Marquis of *Vaudreuil*, who returned into *America* with the title of Governor-General of *Canada* and *New France*.

at the beginning of the attack : we, on our side, have loft but three foldiers. M. *de Bour-lamaque*, a colonel of foot, has been flightly wounded, together with feven or eight Canadians; but unhappily M. *Decomble*, the engineer, was fhot by one of our own Indians, who took him for an Englifhman, on account of his uniform, which was different from that of the other French officers.

The Marquis *de Montcalm* is now employed in deftroying the forts of *Choaguen*, and in fending the provifions and ammunition, and a hundred pieces of cannon which have been found there, to *Frontenac*.

At the Illinois, the 21ft
  of July 1756.

L E T T E R   IX.

To the same.

The Author sets outs from the Koakias for Fort Char-
tres. His Observations on the Population. Ac-
count of a Caravan of Elephants arrived in the
Neighbourhood of the Ohio.

S I R,

Ccording to all appearances, this is the
A last letter I shall write to you from the
Illinois; I prepare to set out by order
of the physicians, who have judged it necessary
that I should return to France, to use the baths
of *Bourbon*, in order to prevent the bad conse-
quences of a shot I received, many years ago, at
the assault of *Chateau Dauphin* *.

Yester-

---

* This is a fort in Piedmont, at the top of a mountain of
the

Yefterday an exprefs arrived here from Fort *du Quêne* to our commander, who informs us, that the Englifh make great preparations to come to attack that poft again. M. *de Macarty* has fent provifions to victual the fort. The Chevalier *de Villiers* commands it in my ftead, my bad ftate of health not allowing me to undertake that voyage ; it would have enabled me to examine the place on the road, where an Indian found fome elephant's teeth, of which he gave me a grinder, weighing about fix pounds and a half.

In 1735, the Canadians who came to make war upon the *Tchicachas* (Chickfaws) found, near the *fine river* or *Ohio*, the fkeletons of feven elephants ; which makes me believe, that *Louifiana* * joins to Afia, and that thefe elephants came from the latter continent by the weftern part, which we are not acquainted

N 2   with :

---

the Alps. It was taken the 19th of July 1744, under the command of the Prince of Conti.

The brigade of Poitou, commanded by the brave M. *de Chevert*, diftinguifhed itfelf in this action by an uncommon valour, which has been admired by all Europe.

* The French fet no bounds to the weftward to Louifiana. F.

with: a herd of thefe animals having loft their way, probably entered the new continent, and having always gone on main land and in forefts, the Indians of that time not having the ufe of fire arms, have not been able to deftroy them entirely; it is poffible that feven arrived at the place near the *Ohio*, which, in our maps of *Loui-fiana*, is marked with a crofs. The elephants, according to all appearance, were in a fwampy ground, where they funk in by the enormous weight of their bodies, and could not get out again, but were forced to ftay there *.

In 1752, the Baron *Porneuf*, who command-ed Fort *François* in the country of the *Miffouris*, received the fkin of an animal from the Indians, which was hitherto unknown in *America*. That officer fent it to the Marchionefs *de Vaudreuil*, who made a muff of it: this creature was about twice as big as an European fox, and its hair as fine

* It appears from modern geographical obfervations, that our author's fuppofition of a migration of elephants is im-probable and it is further confirmed by the examination of the teeth of thefe animals, which are very different from thofe of the common elephant, and confequently they cannot be of the fame fpecies. See Kalm's Travels, vol. I. p. 135. Philofoph. Tranf. vol. LVIII. and Pennant's Synopfis of Quadrupeds, p. 91. F,

fine and foft as velvet, mottled with black and pearly white.

Many authors pretend, that it is poffible that people went through *Nova Zembla*, (fituated northward of the ancient continent) over the ice to *Greenland*; they think, that this is the track on which thofe went who firft peopled *America*, and that the ftreights which feparate it from the continent, has high mountains of ice on its eaftern fhore: but all thofe who have tried to go to India through this northern part, have been eaten by white bears, or have perifhed amidft the ice.

This is my obfervation on the fubjeÐ: if men did go through thofe parts to inhabit *North America*, they probably would have preferred *Canada*, *New England*, and *Louifiana*, the northern parts of which are analogous to their country; whereas it is known, that when the French and Englifh difcovered *North America*, there were but few inhabitants in it; but, on the contrary, the Spaniards who conquered *Peru* and *Mexico*, found kings and emperors, who fet on foot great armies, and who annually facrificed twenty thoufand captives to their falfe deities. Therefore there is reafon to believe, that men went from

the

the weft to *Mexico* and *Loufiana* *. The elephants who came thither are a proof which confirms my obfervations †. Further, when I afked the Indians called *Sioux des prairies*, who are
a nomadic nation, they told me, that they had
heard other Indians fay, that, to the weftward
of their country, there lived a nation of clothed
people, who navigated on great falt-water lakes
with great piraguas ‡; that they inhabited great
villages built with white ftones; that the inhabitants obeyed one defpotic grand chief, who
fent great armies into the field.

The *Mexicans* adore idols as the Indians do;
the *Natches* Indians had a temple, and a kind of
fervice; in their language intelligent people
have found Chinefe words. Some Indians cut
off their hair, leaving only a tuft as the crown

· of

---

* *Louifiana* formerly touched *Canada* on the north-eaft, *Florida* and the *Englifh colonies* on the eaft, and *New Mexico* on
the weft fide. Its north-weft boundaries were not determined.
See more on this fubject in a note to Kalm's Travels, vol. III.
p. 125. F.

† But this proof does not hold good. See the note on
p. 180.

‡ The Indians call the fea a great lake, and the fhips
great piraguas,

of a friar, to which they faften feathers of various colours. They never cut their nails; and among the Chinefe it is a mark of nobility to let the nails grow very long.

If we fuppofe that men went over from our continent to *America*, they would have kept their white colour, fince we fee, that, during two centuries and a half after *Columbus* difcovered this new world, the Europeans who fettled in it preferve their white complexion from generation to generation. The animals which have been found there are entirely different from ours, and neither *Pliny* nor any other old naturalift fpeak of them. We muft be contented with admiring the works of the Creator, without defiring to dive into his myfteries *.

N 4

I fhall

---

* This way of arguing is very ftrange, and greatly promotes barbarifm. Man has got reafon for the purpofe, that truth fhould be the object of his enquiries; and if he fhould carry them no further, out of fear to dive too deep into the myfteries of the Creator, this would patronize ignorance and barbarifm. Many a thing, which feemed too abftrufe, has been difcovered by an indefatigable application. The way in which America was peopled, and the manner in which the fkeletons of great bulky animals approaching to the kind of elephants came to the river *Ohio*, are now a myftery, but may one day or other be difcovered by a lucky accident, or a great and original genius. F.

I fhall add here, by the way, that when the Spaniards difcovered the ifles of *St. Domingo* and *Cuba*, they found them well peopled with Indians, whom they murdered under pretence of a religious principle, but really in order to get their gold. Therefore a Cacique or petty king of the ifland, efcaping from the Spaniards, gave his people to underftand, that gold was the deity of their enemies, fince they came fo far, and expofed themfelves to fo many dangers, in order to get poffeffion of it; and that it was neceffary they fhould abandon every thing, in order to be left in quiet. Another Cacique being condemned to be burnt by the inquifition, was folicited by a Jefuit to become a Chriftian, in order to go to Paradife; but he openly declared he would not go there, if there were any Spaniards in it. Thefe unhappy Indians abhorred the Spaniards fo much, that they did not even converfe with their wives for fear of begetting flaves to fuch mafters: and whenever they eat of their flefh, it was more through revenge than any appetite; for they plainly faid, that the flefh of a Spaniard was good for nothing.

I forgot to tell you in my laft, that I have been invited to the feaft of war, given by the grand chief of the *Illinois*, in order to raife warriors,

riors, and march with the Chevalier *Villiers*. This gentleman obtained leave from the governor to raife a party of French and Indians, and to go with them to avenge the death of his brother, M. *de Jumonville*, who was killed by the Englifh before the war broke out. /

The grand chief of the *Illinois* is called *Papapé-chángouhias*; he is related to feveral Frenchmen of diftinétion, fettled among thefe people. This Cacique fucceeded Prince *Tamaroas* furnamed *Chikagou*, who died in 1754. He wears the medal of the late Cacique: this *Illinois* prince has convinced the French, that he is worthy of wearing it, by his friendfhip for our nation. The detachment of the Chevalier *de Villiers* * being ready to fet out, *Papapé-changou-hias*

---

* The Chevalier *de Villiers*, who commanded this detachment, muft not be confounded with M. *de Villiers*, called the *Great Villiers*, who went to avenge the death of *Jumonville* immediately after his murder in 1753. See the poem which the famous M. *Thomas* wrote on this fubjeét.

Of the feven brothers who compofed this family of *Villiers*, fix were killed in Canada in defence of their country. The Chevalier *de Villiers* is the laft; he was taken prifoner in the aétion at *Niagara* in 1759, being in the party of M. *Aubry*: this officer had defeated a body of Englifh troops at Fort *du Quefne*.

hias defired to ferve him as a guide with his warriors. They left Fort *Chartres* on the firft of
April 1756, and arrived, towards the end of
May, on the boundaries of *Virginia*, where the
Englifh had a little fort furrounded with great
pales. The Indians came near it in the night-
time, each having a fafcine of refinous combuf-
tible wood, which they fet on fire clofe to the
pales of the fort. The Englifh commanding
officer, appearing to give orders for putting out
the fire, was aimed at by an Indian, who killed
him on the fpot. The fame Indian called
out in their language : " Surrender, you Eng-
" lifh dogs, or elfe you fhall be burnt or eaten."
The foldiers, intimated by his threats, and being without a commander, furrendered at difcretion the next morning; the Indians then
bound them two by two, like captives, except
the ferjeant, whom one of the Indians found out
to be the perfon who had beaten him with a
ftick in time of peace. The poor ferjeant became the victim of the refentment of thefe barbarians, who burnt him without any mercy. I
have already faid, that the Indians never forgive,
and that they think themfelves free and independent: therefore one muft take care not to
ftrike them, for they revenge themfelves fooner
or later.

The

The Englifh prifoners, to the number of forty, taken in the fort, were divided among the French and Indians, who ftripped them according to their cuftom, plucked out their beards and hair, and, at the requeft of the French, they only made them flaves. But the French officers, and the humaneft among the French inhabitants of the *Illinois*, joined together, and releafed them, by making a prefent to that nation who treated their prifoners like dogs, only becaufe they were our enemies, and becaufe they thought of making themfelves great with us *.

From the village of the *Koakias* we arrived at the *Peorias*, allies of the *Illinois*, through a fine large meadow, which is twenty-five leagues long. The favages who were with me, killed fome little birds with fticks, and called them ftrawberry-bills. Thefe birds, whofe plumage is varied with many colours, are as good to eat as the *beccafigos* in Provence. The Indians told me, that they are birds of flight or of paffage, and that they affemble in flocks every year like fparrows,

---

* From a natural kind of antipathy between the two nations, the French take every opportunity to deprefs the Englifh, and to raife themfelves above them, fometimes at the expence of truth. F.

fparrows, to feed on the ftrawberries in this meadow, which is red all over with them in the feafon. The village of the *Peorias* is fituated on the banks of a little river, and fortified after the American manner, that is furrounded with great pales and pofts.

When we were arrrived there, I enquired for the hut of the grand chief; they brought me to a great hut, where the whole nation was affembled, on account of a party of their warriors, who had been beaten by the *Foxes*, their mortal enemies.

I was well received by the Cacique and his firft warriors, who came one after another to fqueeze me by the hand in fign of friendfhip, faying, *hau, hau!* which fignifies, *you are welcome*, or I am glad to fee you. A young Indian or a flave, lighted the calumet of peace, and the chief gave it to me to fmoke out of, according to the common cuftom.

After the firft ceremonies were over, they brought me a calebafh full of the vegetable juice of the maple tree. The Indians extract it in January, making a hole at the bottom of it, and apply a little tube to that. At the firft thaw, they

they get a little barrel full of this juice, which they boil to a fyrup : and being boiled over again, it changes into a reddifh fugar, looking like *Calabrian manna*; the apothecaries juftly prefer it to the fugar which is made of fugar canes. The French who are fettled at the *Illinois* have learnt from the Indians to make this fyrup, which is an exceeding good remedy for colds, and rheumatifms.

At the end of the feffion of this affembly, they brought a kind of bread which they call *Pliakmine,* bears paws, and beavers tails; I likewife eat of the dog's flefh through complaifance, for I have made it a rule to conform occafionally to the genius of the people, with whom I am obliged to live, and to affect their manners, in order to gain their friendfhip: they likewife brought in a difh of boiled gruel, of maize flour, called *Sagamité,* fweetened with fyrup of the maple tree; it is an Indian difh which is tolerably good and refrefhing. At the end of the repaft, they ferved a defert of a kind of dry fruits which our Frenchmen call *bluets,* and which are as good as Corinth raifins; they are very common in the *Illinois* country.

The

The next day I faw a great croud in the plain : this affembly was for making a dance in favour of their new *Manitou*; the priefts were dreffed in a remarkable manner : their bodies were covered with a clay in which they had made burlefque drawings, and their faces were painted red, blue, white, yellow, green and black. The high prieft had a bonnet of feathers, like a crown on his head, and a pair of horns of a wild goat, * to fet the feathers off. I own the appearance of this prelate tempted me to laugh ; but as thefe ceremonies are ferious, one muft take care, not to burft out, becaufe it would be reckoned a want of religion, and an indecent action amongft them : nor do the Indians ever interrupt the Roman Catholics, in the exercife of religion. But what a fight prefented itfelf to my eyes ; I faw a living monfter confidered as a divinity : I was at the door of the temple of this falfe deity ; the mafter of the ceremonies begged me to go in ; I was not yet fufficiently acquainted with their cuftoms, and fhewed fome reluctance, but one of the Indians who accompanied me, perceiving it, told me, that if I did not go in, the people would take it as an offence,

---

* Thefe animals are found at the *Mifouris*, their horns are of a fine black, and bent backwards.

fence, or at leaft as a contempt. This difcourfe determined me and I went in * : this is the picture of their *Manitou* ; his head hung upon his ftomach, and looked like a goat's, his ears were like a lynx's ears, with the fame kind of hair, his feet, hands, thighs and legs were in form like thofe of a man: this falfe divinity feemed to be about fix months old, the Indians found it in the woods at the foot of a ridge of mountains, called the mountains of *Sainte Barbe*, which communicate to the rich mines of *Santa Fé* in *Mexico*. The general affembly was called together on purpofe to invoke the protection of this monfter againft their enemies.

I let thefe poor people know, that their *Manitou* was an evil genius, as a proof of it, I added, that he had permitted the nation of *Foxes*, who were their moft cruel enemies, to gain a victory over fome of their countrymen ; that they ought to quit him as foon as poffible,

and

---

* The mafter of the ceremonies, or prieft, that is appointed to guard the temple, before he made his offerings, anointed his body with rofin ; he then ftrewed the foft feathers of a fwan, or the hair of a beaver all over this melted gum, and in that ridiculous plight he danced in honour of the falfe deity.

and be revenged on him. They anſwered, *tika-labé, houé nigué*, i. e. we believe thee, thou art in the right. They then voted that he ſhould be burnt, and the great prieſt pronounced his ſentence, which, according to the interpreter's explanation, was conceived in theſe terms : " Mon-
" ſter, ariſen from the excrements of the evil
" ſpirit, to be fatal to our nation, who has
" wrongfully taken thee for her *Manitou* ; thou
" haſt paid no regard to the offerings which we
" have made thee, and haſt allowed our enemies,
" whom thou doſt plainly protect; to overcome
" a party of our countrymen, and to make
" them ſlaves : therefore our old men aſſembled
" in council have unanimouſly decreed and with
" the advice of the chief of the white warriors,
" that to expiate thy ingratitude towards us,
" thou ſhalt be burnt alive." At the end of this ſentence all the aſſembly ſaid, *hou, hou, hou, hou.*

As I wiſhed to get this monſter, becauſe I could not get that ſnake I ſpoke to you of before, I took the following method : I went to the prieſt, made him a ſmall preſent, and bid my interpreter tell him, that he ſhould perſuade his countrymen, that if they burnt this evil genius, there might ariſe one from his aſhes which
would

could prove fatal to them ; and that I would go on purpofe a-crofs the great lake in order to deliver them of it. He found my reafons good, and by means of the little prefent I gave him, he got the fentence changed, and he was ordered to be killed with clubs : As I defired to have the monfter, without being mutilated, I informed them that they muft deliver it to my people, who would ftrangle it ; for if any of their .nation killed it, fome misfortune or other might happen to him from it. They ftill approved my reafons, and delivered the animal to me, on condition that I fhould carry it far from their country. It was accordingly ftrangled ; but having neither fpirits of wine nor brandy to preferve it in, I was obliged to get it diffected, in order to be able to bring it to France, to fatisfy your curiofity in regard to fubjects of natural hiftory *.

I fhall finifh this letter by another account of the fuperftition of thefe people, and of the divine fervice they give to horrid animals. In

Vol. I.   O   1756

---

* The fkeleton of this monfter, or falfe divinity, is now in the natural hiftory cabinet of M. *de Fayelles*, clerk of the office of the American colonies belonging to the French.

1756 there arrived a deputation of Indians at
Fort *Chartres,* of the nation of *Miſſouris* * ;
there was an old woman among them, who
paſſed for a magician ; ſhe wore round her naked
body, a living rattle ſnake, whoſe bite is mortal, if the remedy is not applied the moment
after.

This prieſteſs of the devil, ſpoke to the ſer-
pent, which ſeemed to underſtand what ſhe ſaid :
I ſee, ſaid ſhe, thou art weary of ſtaying here ;
go, then, return home, I ſhall find thee at my
return : the reptile immediately ran into the
woods, and took the road of the *Miſſouris.* If
I had been inclined to be ſuperſtitious, I ſhould
have told you that I had ſeen the devil appear
to theſe nations under the figure of a ſnake.
Many Miſſionaries have been willing to perſuade
us in their relations and edifying letters, that the
devil appears to theſe people, in order to be
adored by them, but it is eaſy to ſee, that there
is nothing preternatural in it, and that it is a
mere juggle.

You

* A nation living to the weſtward of *Louiſiana,* on a river which bears their name, and falls into the *Miſſiſippi.*

You know befides, that all animals, even the moft ferocious, are tamed by man, I do not pretend to fay that the fnake of the pretended witch went into her country. All I can tell you is, that I always had a very great antipathy againft thefe animals, and that when I meet with them, I take a pleafure in crufhing their heads.

I remember, that in the village of the *Péan-guichias*, a nation allied to the *Illinois*, one of our foldiers was very near getting into a very bad fcrape. He went into an Indian hut and found a live fnake, which he killed with a hatchet, not knowing that the mafter of the hut had made his *Manitou* of it. The Indian arrived at the fame time in a terrible paffion to find his deity dead; he afferted that it was the foul of his father, who died about a year before; he having fhot two ferpents which were pairing upon the point of a rock, fell fick and died foon after.

The imagination of the old man being troubled by the height of the fever, he thought he faw the two fnakes coming to reproach him with their death; he therefore recommended it to his fon in dying, never to kill any of thefe ani-

O 2   mals,

mals, fearing that they would likewife be
the caufe of his death *. Knowing the
genius of thefe people, I advifed the foldier, whom the Indian looked upon as one
who had flain a deity, to pretend to be
drunk; and to do as if he would kill me
and his comrades. The Indians, not knowing that it was only a farce, were the
firft to cry out, that the white warrior † had
loft his wits. I afked for cords to tie him;
and as I feemed very angry with him, the
chiefs and the warriors came to intercede for
him, faying that it was a man who had loft
his fenfes by drinking; that the fame often
happened to the red men: in order to give
more colour to the impofture, I waited yet for
the Cacique's wife to beg me, and appeared
pacified in deference to her fex, which I refpected very much.

I prefented the mafter of the fnake with
a bottle of brandy, to drown his grief. The
Indians

---

* I have feen a peafant in France, who had killed an owl
on his neighbour's roof; and his father dying fome time after, he believed that his death was caufed by that bird of ill
prefage.

† So they call our foldiers.

Indians are exceſſively fond of this liquor, and grow furious when they have drank too much of it. After their drunkenneſs is over, they ſay that they have neither ſpoken nor done any thing, and attribute all their follies to the brandy believing to juſtify their conduct by acknow-ledging that they had loſt their wits. When a drunken Indian kills another, the death is not revenged. But theſe people take care ſeldom or never to drink all at once, thoſe who are ſober keep in bounds the reſt, and the women hide both offenſive and defenſive weapons. Brandy may be reckoned among the pernicious things which have contributed towards the depopula-tion of North America : this liquor makes men brutes, and often kills them. I have ſometimes ſeen drunken Indians kill each other with hatchets and clubs,

I am now ready to leave the *Illinois*, and ex-pect to be in *New Orleans* in January 1757. This letter ſets out in a piragua, which M. *de Macarty* ſends with diſpatches to the governor.
I am, &c.

At the Illinois, the 10*th*
November 1756.

L E T T E R   X.

To the same.

The Author leaves the Illinois: His Navigation down the Miſſiſippi: he encamps in an Iſland formed by that River.   His Soldiers make him Governer of it.

S I R,

YOU inquire, whether the Indians have captains amongſt them, and whether they are governed by a king? The time I have ſpent among them procures me the pleaſure of ſatisfying your curioſity on that head. You muſt know, then, that they are divided into tribes or nations, each of which is governed by a petty king or Cacique, who only depends on the *Great Spirit*, or Supreme Being ; theſe Caciques reign deſpotically, without making their authority odious, and know how to make them-

ſelves

felves refpected and beloved. They likewife
have the fatisfaction of being regarded by their
fubjects almoft as demi-gods, born for the happinefs of this world ; for they have the tendernefs of fathers for the people of their tribe ; and
that name flatters them much more than all the
pompous titles of the *Grand Signior* or the *Great
Mogul.* Thofe Afiatic emperors are often expofed in their extenfive dominions to revolutions,
by which their life is endangered ; for often tri-
butary kings rebel againft them, and kill them
with their whole family.

The crime of high treafon is unknown among
the *Americans* ; the chiefs and Caciques go every
where without fear. If any one fhould be bold
enough to attempt any thing againft their lives,
he would be punifhed as a horrible monfter, and
the whole family of the murderer would be ex-
terminated without mercy.

As to the captains or chiefs of war, who command their armies againft their enemies, this
poft is occupied only by fuch as have given fignal proofs of courage in defence of their country in feveral combats ; and as the generals go
naked, as well as the other Indians, the marks
of wounds they bear upon their body are fuffi-

O 4

cient

cient to diftinguifh them from the reft, and ferve inftead of teftimonials to them.

The old men, who cannot go to war any more, are not ufelefs to the nation. They hold fpeeches, and the people hear them as oracles. Every thing is done as they advife it; and the young men fay, that they having lived longer than themfelves, muft of courfe have more experience and knowledge. When I admired the countenance which thefe old men enjoyed, they told me, that fince they could no longer fight for their country, they taught others to defend it. The warriors, when they return from an expedition, never fail to throw part of the booty into the huts of thofe old men, who have exhorted them, and excited their courage. The prifoners of war are always given to the oldeft people in the nation, who make them their flaves. The old warriors who cannot go to war any more, harangue the foldiers. The orator begins with ftriking againft the poft with a club, and mentions all the fine actions he has done in war, that is, how many fcalps he has taken from different nations. The hearers anfwer, *hau, hau*, *i. e.* that is true. The Indians abhor lying, and fay that a liar is not a true man.

The

The old fpeaker begins his difcourfe, and fays : " If I were younger and more vigorous, " to conduct you againft our enemies, as I have " formerly done, you fhould fee me go on the " tips of my toes. Go my comrades, as men " of courage, and with the heart of a lion *; " never fhut your ears, fleep like hares, go " like the roe-buck, do not fear the cold, nor " hefitate to go into the water like ducks; " when you are purfued, hide well your retreat. " Above all, do not fear the arrows of your ene- " mies, fhew them that you are true warriors " and men. Laftly, when you find an oppor- " tunity, ufe all your arrows on the enemy, and " after that break in upon them with your clubs " in hand; ftrike, flay, and extirpate; it is " better to die fighting than to be taken and " burnt."

At the end of this harangue, the old warrior prefents the calumet to the *Tacha-Mingo*, that is, the general or chief of war, and to all his offi- cers, who fmoke it, each after their rank; and all thofe who have not yet been to war come to

fmoke

---

* An hyperbole no Indian in America would make ufe of, not knowing that creature, which is not to be met with in that country. F.

smoke it, by way of enlisting themselves; they dance the dance of war, and, after that ceremony, they distribute dog's flesh, which, as I have already observed, is a dish principally appropriated to warriors *.

M. *du Tissenet* told me of an accident that happened to his father, who was one of the first officers that came to *Louisiana* with M. *de Bienville.* M. *du Tissenet* being at an Indian nation, together with some Frenchmen who came to barter goods; the Indians wanted to scalp them; M. *du Tissenet* had learnt their language, and heard their discourse, and as he wore a wig, he took it from his head, and threw it on the ground, saying from time to time, You will have my scalp, take it up, if you dare to do it. The astonishment of these people was inexpressible, for M. *du Tissenet* had got his head shaved a little before this happened; he told them afterwards, that they were very much in the wrong to attempt to hurt him, for he only came to make

an

---

* It is very remarkable, that, when the ancient kings of *Macedonia* performed the lustration of their armies, a dog was killed, and divided into two parts, and the whole army, with the king at their head, went through the two halves of the dog. F.

an alliance with them; that, if they compelled him, he would burn the water in their lakes and rivers, to hinder them from failing, and fet fire to their forefts; he got a little pot, and put fome brandy in it, and fet it on fire with a match; the Indians, who were not yet acquainted with brandy, were amazed; at the fame time he took out of his pocket a convex glafs, and fet fire to a rotten tree by means of the fun. Thefe people really believed, that the officer had the power of burning their rivers and their woods; they careffed him, loaded him with prefents, and fent him home well efcorted, that no one might do him any harm. Since that time M. *de Bienville* has made ufe of M. *du Tiffenet* in feveral negociations towards making alliances with the Indians,

M. *du Tiffenet*'s adventure puts me in mind of that of an Italian, who was in the fuite of M. *Tonty*, the then governor of Fort *Louis* among the *Illinois*. This Italian fet out from thence by land, to join M. *de la Salle*, to whom he could have been very ufeful, by teaching him the road which he was to take in order to come to the *Miffifippi*, if he could have been with him in time; he likewife faved his life by a fingular ftratagem. Some Indians being willing to kill him,

him, he told them they were much in the wrong
in attempting to deftroy a man that bore them
all in his heart. This difcourfe amazed the Barbarians; he affured them, that, if they would
give him time till the next morning, he would
convince them of the truth of what he had afferted; adding, that if he deceived them, they
fhould do what they pleafed with him. Then,
fixing a little mirror on his breaft, the Indians,
who were much fuprifed to fee themfelves, as
they imagined, in the heart of this man, granted him his life.

I have commanded the convoy in defcending
the river, which M. *Aubri* brought up : M. *de
Macarty* trufted the Englifh prifoners to my care
to bring them to *New Orleans*; they are the
fame which the Chevalier *de Villiers* and the Indian chief *Papéchangouhia* took. I have made
hafte to come to the capital before the thawing
of the ice, which breaks loofe in the northern
rivers, and follows the current; I ran the rifk
of being ftopt by it, if I had not given orders
for rowing as hard as poffible; I even made ufe
of the Englifh prifoners to relieve my foldiers :
as every one has an equal right to his life on fuch
occafions, the officers likewife lent a helping
hand, to encourage the crew.

After

After paffing the rocks at *Prudhomme* ⃰, there
are no others in the *Miffifippi*; and when there
are feveral boats, they are faftened together,
and go down with the current day and night.
There is only one man at the helm, and one at
the head of every boat, to take care of the
floating trees. It is a pleafure to go down this
fine river: the fame diftance which, in going
up, takes three months and a half, in defcending
is performed in ten or twelve days, when the
water is high in the river.

I muft not forget to mention, that on the
firft of January the foldiers come in the morning
to wifh their officers a happy new year, who generally return the civility by a prefent of brandy. I was juft encamped on a little ifland about
two leagues in circuit, fituated on one of the
branches of the *Miffifippi*, which I was defcending. This ifle was furrounded with very tall
trees. A facetious gafcoon foldier, as thofe of
this nation generally are, gave his comrades to
under-

⃰ Thefe rocks form the fhores of the *Miffifippi*, which are
on both fides like walls of five hundred feet high. Formerly
there was the Fort *Prudhomme* in this place, fo named from
a fellow-traveller of M. *de la Salle*, who died there, and
occafioned the fort to be called after him.

underftand that they might get an extraordinary
new year's gift if they would perform the ceremony of receiving me governor of the ifland.
The ferjeant approved this droll thought, and
immediately gave his orders for it. He began
with graving my name on the bark of a tree, ordered the fwivels to be charged with powder,
and made the troops appear in arms. The
drummer beat a whirl, and the ferjeant as mafter of the ceremonies, taking off his hat, faid
" *in the king's name* *, ye tygers, wolves, bears,
" oxen, ftags, roe-bucks, and other animals of
" this ifland, fhall acknowledge our commander
" as your governor, and obey him in all that he
" he fhall command you for his fervice ;" one
of the foldiers then fired the fwivels of the
boats, which were accompanied with a general
falute from the fmall arms. The fudden explofion of thefe fire arms, frightened the wild
oxen, who went into the river in order to fwim
through it and to gain the continent : the foldiers went after them in a piragua and killed
four of them, together with two roe-bucks that
juft reached the fhore, and prefented them to
me as my property, which obliged me to ftay
here in order to dry the flefh for confumption,
during

* *De par le Roi.*

during the remaining part of our voyage. In order to take advantage of the fun of my soldiers, which I took good care to reward immediately, I had a mind to vifit the interior parts of my government : but I was hardly gone half a league, when I faw a bear, who was quietly eating acorns under a great oak : I fired my piece at him, but the ball only went into the lard of the animal, which was monftroufly fat ; as foon as he felt the wound, he wanted to come up to me, but he was too heavy to run ; then feigning to run from him, I drew him towards my foldiers, who foon furrounded and killed him as guilty of felony and rebellion. They held a court martial, where the ferjeant prefided. The corporal, who acted as the king's attorney-general, gave it as his opinion, that in order not to ruin the fine coat of the bear, who had revolted againft his mafter, he fhould only be fhot in the head, which was punctually executed.

He was then flayed, and I have taken his fkin, which is a very black one, and which I fhall not relinquifh, any more than Hercules did that of the *Nemean* lion which he conquered.

The

The foldiers melted the fat, and got above one hundred and twenty pots of oil from it*, you muſt know that the bears come out of their holes as foon as the fruits begin to ripen, and they do not go in again till they are all eaten up. They then ſtay in their retreats till the next feaſon, and neither eat nor drink during that interval; their greafe is the only thing they feed upon, by fucking their paws. It is dangerous to meet a lean one without company. The Indians make a great trade with bears' ſkins, and treat their friends with their paws and tongues; they have often regaled me with them on my voyages, and I found them extremely good.

I direct this letter to *Campeach*, to M. *de Arragory*, the agent of the French marine, who will fend it to *Cadiz*, from whence it will come fafer to you than by our veſſels, as Spain is not at war with England: I do not write duplicates of this letter, befides, I hope to fet out for Europe next April.

I am, S I R, &c. &c.

At New Orleans, the 25th of February 1757.

L. E T-

---

* *Bears oil* is very good to eat, in *Louiſiana* they make ufe of it for fallad, for frying, and for fauces, and prefer it to hog's lard. The pot holds about two quarts Engliſh.

L E T T E R   XI.

To the Same.

The Author sets out for Europe. He fights an English Privateer. He embarks at Cape Fran-çois on a Vessel belonging to a Fleet of twenty-six Merchantmen, which were almost all taken in his Sight by Privateers. Taking of a little Vessel from the Enemy. Arrival at Brest.

SIR,

HAVING found no vessel here to return to *France*, I was obliged to go on board the brigantine *Union* fitted out as a sloop of war, and commanded by captain *Gau-Jean* who is well know for having taken five English ships during the war, on his voyage from France to *Louisiana*.

We fet fail from the *Balife* on the firft of April 1757, for Cape *François*. On the 20th of April being in fight of *Turk*'s ifland *, we perceived a fhip, which we fuppofed to belong to the enemy; fhe chafed us at night, and being a prime failer, came up with us in three hours' time: the Englifh privateer faluted us with a bullet from his cannon, and called out to us to furrender to the king of England; to which we returned a broadfide, and a volley of the fmall arms; after which I haled him to ftrike his colours for the king of France, or elfe he fhould be funk; the privateer finding that he had to meddle with a dealer in bullets, made off, and got among the rocks near Turk's ifland, hoping to draw us nearer to the fhore, where we might have been loft. But our captain, who was very prudent, and a good mariner at the fame time, faw the fnare which was laid for him; therefore, inftead of following the privateer, he continued his voyage, and we happily arrived in the harbour of Cape *François* on the firft of May. There we found the fquadron of M. *de Beaufremont*, deftined for the fuccours of *Canada*, having on board M. *de Bart*, whom the king had appointed governor and lieutenant-general

* L'ifle *Turque*.

neral on the ifle of *St. Domingo.* My firft care
on going on fhore was to pay my refpects to
him. That general, who is always ready to
ferve unfortunate officers, prevented my cares,
by difpatching me four days after my arrival,
and fparing me the expence I fhould have been
at if I had ftayed on this ifland, he procured me
a free paffage at the king's expence, as a fleet of
twenty-fix merchantmen were. ready to fail for
France, under the convoy of M. *de Beaufremont,*
who brought them as far as the *Cayques* iflands,
where he left them, in order to proceed on
his deftination according to the orders of the
court.

I muft tell you that I preferably chofe a *Bor-
deaux* veffel, called the *Sun,* captain *Odouoir;*
(imitating the Indians, who indeed make a divinity of the fun). But the event has fhewn that
I was very happy in my choice; for almoft all
the veffels which compofed the fleet have been
taken in my fight. Only four arrived in France,
the *Sun* was the firft: fhe came to *Breft* in forty-
five days, after taking an Englifh fhip in the latitude of the *Newfoundland* bank. I landed at
Breft the fifteenth of June 1757, and immediately waited on the Count *du Guai,* commander
of the marines in this port; I then paid a vifit to

P 2　　　　　　　M.

M. *Hocquart*, the counsellor of state and intendant of the marine in this department, whom I informed of the death of M. *Auberville*, who had succeeded for a time to M. *Michael de la Rouvilliere*, as commissary general of the marine, and regulator of the provisions of * *Louisiana.* M. *Hocquart* was known for his probity when he was intendant of *New France*; it is certain that he came back from thence indebted forty-thousand livres, which the king, contented with his services, has made him a present of; a fine example for M. *Bigot*, his successor; but if he has not brought back treasures from his administration, he has at least the satisfaction of passing for one of the gallantest men of his rank : he has been regretted by all the Canadians, and even by the Indians, who, as I have already said, know how to distinguish merit.

On owning to this gentleman, that I had no money to go to court with, he was so kind as to order M. *Gaucher*, clerk of the treasurer of the colonies to give me some. He likewise offered me his table during my stay in this town, which I intend to leave the twenty-second of this month.

You

---

* *Ordonnateur.*

You will, perhaps, be amazed to hear, that in the fpace of eight months, I have feen two winters, two fummers, and two fprings ; I fhall now explain it to you. I wrote to you, that I left the *Illinois* at the end of December, 1756, when the *Miffifippi* began to freeze, and defcending that great river, I came to *New Orleans* in January 1757, the climate of which is comparable to that of the *Hierian* iflands, where our regiment was in 1744. That is, it was the feafon of gardening or fpring. I left *Louifiana* the firft of April 1757, and came to Cape *François* the firft of May, and found fummer there : I embarked for Europe on the fourth, and after coming out of the *Bahama Channel* we met with fpring ; continuing our voyage to the great fands of *Newfoundland*, we faw on the twenty-fecond, at fun-rifing, a floating mountain of ice, which at firft we took to be a fail ; but the keen air coming from it convinced us at laft that it was a piece of ice from the frozen ocean. On the fifteenth of June 1757, we came to *Breft*, where we found fummer. This therefore is a pretty extraordinary cafe.

I am, S I R, &c.

At Breft, the 18*th*
   of June 1757.

P 3

L E T-

L E T T E R XII.

To the Same,

The Author arrives at Court, receives a Gra-
tification from the King, and an Order
to go to Rochefort. *He embarks there for*
Louisiana.

S I R,

I AM now once more at *Rochefort*
from whence I failed for *Louisiana,*
eight years ago. I come from the
court, where I prefented to the comptroller
general and minifter of the marine, M. *de*
Moras, the governor's letter, which explains
the motives of my voyage. He was fo
kind as to fpeak with me in his cabinet,
in prefence of M. *de la Porte,* chief of
the

the board of plantations. He questioned me on the present state of *Louisiana*. I assured the minister that I had left in our interest all the nations of that vast continent, which I had visited, and that the *Cherokees* were come to treat of peace with the French. He likewise asked me, whether I thought the colony could be attacked. I answered that there was little probability of the English attempting to attack it, on account of the difficulty of coming in through the mouth of the *Missisippi* at the fort of *Balise*; and that the colony wanted no other fortifications, than those which nature had provided it with.

M. *de Moras* obtained for me from the king a gratification of a thousand livres in order to enable me to go to the waters which my health required I should take; after which I received an order from his majesty to go back to *Louisiana*, and continue my services there; therefore I came hither without loss of time in order to embark; we intend to set sail as soon as the convoy will be fitted out for *Cape Breton*.

M. *Druis Imbuto* succeeds M. *Normant de Mesi*, as *Intendant* of the marine. The king

could

could not choofe a better perfon both on account of his abilities, and of his integrity, and likewife on account of his zeal for the king's intereſt in this important place. This intendant made me the fame offer as his predeceſſor,

I am, S I R, &c.

At Rochefort, the 12th
of September 1757.

L E T T E R XIII.

To the same.

The Author leaves Rochefort; *he meets with three Englifh Merchant-Ships, taken by M.* de Place, *of which one was burnt and another funk. He ftops at the Ifle of* Grenada. *Navigation along* Jamaica.

S I R,

Wrote to you from *Rochefort,* that we intended to fet out in December 1757; but the convoy deftined to fuccour *Cape Breton* having in part been taken by the Englifh fleet, we were obliged to fit out another. During that time a fquadron of ten great Englifh men of war having alarmed the coaft of *Aunis,* that has retarded us till the month of *May.* This fquadron difappearing, we fet fail on the tenth of the fame month.

I was

I was on board the King's frigate *La Fortune*, together with M. *de Rochemore*, commiſſary-general of the marine, and *ordonnateur* of the province of *Louiſiana*. M. *de Place*, a captain of a man of war, commanded the *Eopalme* frigate of thirty guns, deſtined for our convoy: we met with three Engliſh veſſels on our voyage, which only coſt us three cannon-ſhot. M. *de Place* ſunk one of them, and burnt the other, after taking the crew and the goods out of them. As to the third, it came from the coaſt of *Guinea*, was richly laden, and had on board four hundred and forty negroes, who were in part ſold to the iſle of *Grenada*. The Baron *de Bonvouſt*, who has juſt been appointed governor of this iſland, entertained us very generouſly and politely during our ſtay there. We remained there till the twenty-ſecond of July, when we ſailed for *Louiſiana*, keeping alongſide of *Jamaica*, to avoid the great ſhips of the enemy, which never come to thoſe ſhores: we took that courſe in order to deceive the ſpy, and we arrived happily at the mouth of the *Miſſiſippi* on the twelfth of Auguſt.

M. *de Rochemore* *, an honeſt *ordonnateur*, who is very zealous for the intereſt of the King, will have

---

* The brother of a M. *Rochmore* who is now commodore.

have a great deal of trouble in reforming the abuſes that have crept into the management of the colony's affairs, ſince the war; and during our voyage, I foretold him, that he would be much diſturbed in his adminiſtration : what I foreſaw really happened ; and by the ſame ſhips which brought us hither, the court has been prejudiced againſt him, with a view to deprive him of his place. I was but juſt arrived at *New Orleans*, when the governor gave me orders to prepare to go with a detachment to the *Allibamons*, an Indian nation two hundred and fifty leagues from the capital. I take advantage of the opportunity of the King's ſhips, which will ſail for France at the end of the year; and I write to you by duplicates, that if one ſhip be taken, you may get the letter by the other. When I ſhall be informed of the manners of the nations which I ſhall paſs through, and which are ſituated to the eaſt of *New Orleans*, I ſhall deſcribe that country to you, which is reckoned very fine and very good.

At New Orleans, the 10th
of November 1758.

L E T T E R XIV.

To the same.

The Author departs from New Orleans *for the* Allibamons. *His Navigation on the Lake* Pontchartrain. *Short Description of* Mobile.

S I R,

I Left *New Orleans* on the fourteenth of December, according to M. *de Kerlerec*'s orders, and set out for the *Allibamons.* I sailed from the little creek of *St. Jean,* which is situated in the lake *Pontchartrain.* There is a portage of about a quarter of a mile from *New Orleans* to this creek *, which is about two leagues long; the winds were favourable to us, and on the twentieth of December I arrived

at

---

* *Bayouc,* a small inlet where the tide goes up.

at the bay and fort of *Mobile*, which is fifty leagues diſtant from the capital.

The *Mobile* was formerly the chief ſettlement in *Louſiana*, and the reſidence of the governor, *ordonnateur*, and of the chief officers. The ſuperior council held its ſittings there likewiſe.

There is a pretty regular fort, capable of reſiſting a whole army of Indians ; but European troops could ſoon take it. It is ſituated on a bay where the tide comes up ; and between two rivers, one of which is ſmall, and is called the river of the *Chaſtaws*, the other is more conſiderable than the *Seine* before *Rouen*, is called *Mobile* river, and riſes in the *Apalachian* mountains ; it is the rendez-vous of all the Indians who live to the eaſtward. They come there to receive the preſents which the King annually diſtributes to them by his governor. The ſoil about *Mobile* is gravelly ; however, the cattle ſucceeds exceedingly well there, and multiplies very much. The inhabitants are very laborious, and trade with the Spaniards ; they go to the fort of *Penſacola*, which is near *Mobile*, and get ſalt beef, wild fowl, maize, rice, and other eatables from thence. The inhabitants of *Mobile* likewiſe carry on a trade with tar. As to the

fur-

fur-trade with the Indians, the officers carry it on exclufively of all others, contrary to the King's intention.

About this place, there are white and red bays * and wild cherry-trees †. There are like-wife white and red cedars ‡ ; the latter is very fine, and very good for inlaid work ; its fmell expels infects, and the wood indeed is incorrup-tible. There are feveral forts of trees in the fo-refts hereabouts, which are unknown in Europe, and fome which abound with a gum like tur-pentine. There are likewife cypreffes § of fuch a fize, that the Indians make piraguas out of one piece, which can contain fixty men.

Before the French came into *Louifiana,* the Indians conftructed their boats in the following manner.

---

* The bays are probably the *Laurus æftivalis* Linn. which have white flowers ; and the *Laurus Borbonia* Linn. which has red flower-cups, and black or purple berries. F.

† The wild cherries of this country grow in clufters, and there are chiefly three kinds of them growing in America, viz. *Prunus Virginiana, Cænadenfis,* and *Lufitanica,* Linn.

‡ The red cedar is the *Juniperus Virginiana Linn.* and the white cedar is the *Cupreffus Thyoides Linn.*

§ Or *cedars.*

manner. They went to the banks of fome rivers, which are very numerous in this vaft re-
gion, and which by their rapidity tear up by
the roots the trees which ftand on their banks.
They took their dimenfions for length and
breadth, and accordingly chofe fuch a tree as
they wanted; after which they fet fire to it, and
as the tree burnt on they fcraped away the live
coals with a flint or an arrow; and having fufficiently hollowed it out, they fet it afloat. They
are very well fkilled in conducting thefe little
veffels upon their lakes and rivers. They employ them in time of war, and likewife load
them with the furs and dried flefh which they
bring back from their hunts.

Their inftruments and their weapons were
made in the following manner: they chofe a
young tree for that purpofe, in which they
made an incifion with a flint, or pebble as
fharp as a razor, and they put a ftone cut in
form of a hatchet into the incifion; therefore,
as the tree grew up, it enchafed the ftone, which
by that means became infeparable from it, and
they afterwards cut it off in order to make ufe
of it; their lances and their darts were made in
the fame manner. They had clubs of a very
hard wood.

As

As to their inftruments of agriculture, they only made ufe of the bones of animals, or of fpades of a very hard wood. The ground throughout *America* is very fruitful; the grafs there grows high and clofe; and after the froft has dried it up, the Indians fet fire to it; then they dig the ground with their fpades, fow it, and reap three months after their crops.

They plant maize, millet, beans, and other leguminous plants, potatoes, piftachios, and water-melons; gourds are likewife very common there, and the French inhabitants call them *gi-romonds*.

Their kitchen-utenfils were difhes and pots of earthen ware, and deep wooden difhes. They made cups of calebafhes, and fpoons * of the horns of wild oxen, which they cut through the middle, and form into the proper fhape by means of fire.

As foon as we fhall have got ready the provi-fions for our voyage, and for the garrifon of the fort, we fhall fet out, M. *Aubert* and myfelf in a boat armed with foldiers and *Mobile* Indians, whom

---

* Which they call *Micouens*.

whom we have hired to row during the voyage.

M. *Aubert*, though he is adjutant of the fort at *Mobile*, has been appointed, by M. *de Kerlerec*, to command Fort *Touloufe* at the *Allibamons*, which is contrary to the King's order, forbidding all majors and adjutants to do other functions than thofe of the place they belong to.

If any fhips arrive from Europe, I fhall perhaps receive letters from you. M. *de Velle*, who commands here, will be fo kind as to fend them to me with the firft convoy.

I am, S I R, &c.

At Mobile, the 6th of
  January 1759.

L E T T E R   XV.

To the same.

The Author sets out from Mobile *for the* Allibamons. *Description of the Manners of this Nation. Their Way of punishing Adultery.*

S I R,

I AM at last arrived at Fort *Toulouse* among the *Allibamons.* I have been fifty days a-coming; because, taking boat in the rainy season, the water in the river was often swelled to twelve or fifteen feet, this sudden increase was caused by the heavy rains, which are frequent hereabouts, and by the high hills that run along this river.

We have been obliged to work hard against the rapidity of the current, and there were days during which we scarcely advanced a league.

league. It is impoffible to fail, on account of the woods, the hills, and turnings of the river; and therefore we could do no otherwife than go alohg the fhores. One day I had the misfortune to fee my boat hemmed in by the branches of a tree * that was fet under water: we were be-nighted in this difagreeable fituation, and obli-ged to wait for the break of day. But as this river rifes and falls by the floods, I found my-felf now quite in the air in my boat. We were twenty-five leagues from the mouth of the river, and the *Mobilian* favages that accompanied me, comforted me by the hope that the next tide would fet me a-float again; and really the tide mounting up the river from *Mobile* bay delivered us from our uncomfortable fituation. You fee by this, dear Sir, what a difference it makes in navigating an *European* and an *American* river.

M. *Aubert* fell fick on the way, and I prevail-ed on him to ftay at *Mobile* for the recovery of his health; and fo he came from thence hither on horfeback, by croffing the fir-woods, which

Q 2 are

* There are hereabouts cedar-trees of fo prodigious a fize, that ten men can fcarcely clafp them; which eafily accounts for the goodnefs and fertility of the country, and befides this its climate is one of the moft healthy.

are very thin. M. *de Montberaut* is to give him
up the command of this poſt by order of the
governor, after having inſtructed him during
three months, of its ſituation, environs, and
many other articles. This latter gentleman *
has a high reputation among the Indians of this
country, who call him the *man of valour*, i. e.
the *hero*. He was remarkable for the ſpirited
ſpeeches which he delivered, in a manner analogous to the way of thinking of theſe nations.
This officer had a quarrel with the Jeſuits, and
therefore aſked to be recalled ; and was ſucceed-
ed by M. *Aubert*, the brother of Father *Aubert*,
a Jeſuit miſſionary in *Louiſiana*. M. *Montberaut*
is a declared enemy to theſe miſſionaries. Whilſt
Father *Le Roi* was at *Allibamons*, he wrote to the
governor to diſcredit this officer, to whom the
ſoldier who was to carry the letter delivered it.
The commander ſaw after this the Jeſuit, who
ſhewed him many civilities, according to the
political principles of theſe good fathers : The
officer aſked him, whether he had written ſomething againſt him. The Jeſuit, not ſuſpecting
his letter to be in the officer's hand, aſſured him
by all that was ſacred he had not. Then M.
Montberaut

---

* He is the brother of the Count *de Montaut*, who belonged to the houſehold of the Dauphin.

Montberaut called Father *Le Roi* an impoftor and a cheat, produced the letter, and fixed it at the gate of the fort, giving it in charge to the fentinel to take care of it; and fince that time there were no Jefuits among the *Allibamons*.

Whilft I am here going to fpeak of the *Allibamons*, I fhall have an opportunity to treat likewife of the *Tafkikis*, the *Oclafhepas*, the *Tonicas*, the *Kawuytas*, the *Abekas*, the *Talapoafhas*, the *Confhakis*, and the *Pakanas*, whofe manners are all nearly related to one another. All thefe nations put together can raife about four thoufand warriors. They are all well-fhaped men, live commonly along the river fides, and no fooner are you arrived among thefe well-behaved men, whofe women are of the fame character, and for the greater part beautiful, but they come to receive you at the landing-place, fhaking hands with you, and prefenting you with the calumet. After having fmoaked, they afk from you the caufe of your coming, and the time you fpent on the road; what ftay you intend to make among them, whether you have a wife and children *.

They-

---

* The politenefs of the Indians goes even fo far as to offer to the Europeans their girls, and for that purpofe the chiefs

fpeak

They likewife inquire the particulars of the war in *Canada*, and afk how the King their father does. They then bring you a difh made of maize or Indian corn, which they coarfely pound, and boil in water, generally together with fome venifon *. They likewife ferve up bread made of the flour of the fame corn, baked in hot afhes, roafted young turkies, broiled venifon, pan-cakes baked with nut-oil, chefnuts when in fea-fon, boiled with bears greafe or oil, roebucks tongues, together with hen and turtle † eggs.

The foil of *Louifiana* refembles, in the lower parts of the colony, that of *Egypt* after the Nile has overflown the country; it is excellent, and chiefly fo in the country of the nations I now fpeak of.

The melons are here prodigioufly large, full of juice, and in great plenty : the water-melons are

---

fpeak the next morning in the following manner in the vil-lage : Young men and warriors, do not be foolifh, love the matter of life; hunt for the fupport of the French, who bring us our wants : and you young girls, do not be hard-hearted, nor ungrateful with your body in refpeft to the white warriors, for to get their blood; by this alliance we fhall get wit like them, and be refpefted by our enemies.

* This is called *Sagamitè*.   † Sea-tortoife.

are fo delicious, that they are given to the fick to quench their thirft during the burning fits of the fever. Potatoes are plentiful here; and the Europeans are very fond of this kind of root, which taftes like chefnuts roafted in hot afhes.

The Indians are generally contented with one wife, of whom they are jealous to excefs. When an Indian lies at a village where he has no wife, he hires a girl for a night or two, as he pleafes, and her parents never have any objection to it; they concern themfelves very little about their girls, faying their bodies are free : the Indian girls do not abufe this liberty ; and they find it their intereft to keep up an appearance of modefty, in order to engage their lovers to afk them in marriage : but in regard to wives the Indians maintain, that they have fold their liberty by marrying, and that they muft not be ferved by other men than their hufbands. The men keep the privilege of having feveral wives, and they can leave them whenever they pleafe ; but this feldom happens. When a woman is caught in adultery, the leaft punifhment is being repudiated. The hufband then leaves the hut ; and if they have any children, he takes the boys, and the wife the girls ; fhe muft remain a widow for one year ; but he can marry again immediately.

He can likewife take his wife again, therefore
fhe muft not enter on a fecond marriage till a
whole year be paft.

The marriage of the Indians is quite fimple,
as I have already obferved ; the mutual confent
of the parties is the only tie which joins them.
The future hufband makes fome prefents of furs
and victuals in the hut of his bride's father ; if
they be received, a feftival is made, to which the
whole village is invited ; after the meal, the exploits of the new hufband's anceftors are fung,
and a dance enfues. The next day one of the
oldeft men in the village prefents the bride to
the relations of her hufband ; and thus the whole
ceremony of marriage is concluded. All the Indians deduce their lineage from the women, al-
ledging that they may be fure of their origin on
that fide, and accordingly of their having their
mother's blood in their veins ; but that claiming
their defcent from the men was uncertain. The
great warriors and the beft huntfmen chufe the
prettieft girls ; the others have only their refufe,
and all the ugly ones left. The girls, knowing that they cannot be miftreffes of their hearts
after they are married, know how to difpofe of
them to the greateft advantage : for when once
they have a hufband, all coquetry muft ceafe ;

they

they muſt apply themſelves to their duties in their houſes, ſuch as preparing their huſbands meals, dreſſing the ſkins, making ſhoes, ſpinning the wool of the wild oxen, and making little baſkets in which they are very well ſkilled and induſtrious.

The manner of puniſhing the infidelity of their wives is as follows: the huſband muſt firſt be perfectly convinced of his wife's miſbehaviour by his own eyes, and then ſhe is watched by his relations and her own. The huſband is then no longer allowed to keep his wife, though he ſhould wiſh it; becauſe the Indians ſay, that it is unworthy and beneath a true man to live with a wife who has failed ſo eſſentially in her duty to him. In this caſe, the huſband goes to the *Cacique*, and tells him his ſtory. The chief immediately orders ſome people to go and cut little ſwitches, and all keep a profound ſecret. The chief then gives orders for a grand dance, which every man, woman, boy, and girl in the village is obliged to attend, unleſs they will expoſe themſeves to be fined; but there are hardly ever any abſent: in the midſt of the dance the guilty woman is extended on the floor, and beaten on the back and ſtomach without mercy, and her ſeducer undergoes the ſame ceremony.

When

When thefe wretches have been well flogged, a relation on each fide comes and lays a ftick a crofs the criminals and the executioners. That moment they ceafe to beat; but then the hufband comes and cuts off all his wife's hair clofe to her head *, and reproaches her in prefence of all the people, that is, he reprefents to her how much fhe has done wrong to act as fhe had done with him, that he had let her want for nothing, but that fince fhe had however tranfgreffed, fhe might now go with her feducer; whofe hair they likewife cut on his forehead, and tell him, pointing to his paramour, There, that is thy wife. He is at liberty to marry her that inftant, but he muft go to fettle in another village.

When a married woman debauches a married man, the women meet together among themfelves each with a ftick of an arm's length, and go to the criminal woman, whom they beat without mercy, which creates great mirth and laughter amongft the young people; the women would kill the guilty wretch, if the men did not fnatch away the fticks.

Phyfic,

---

* The Indian women have long hair in treffes.

Phyfic, war, hunting and fifhing are the only arts which the Indians are ambitious of knowing. They educate their children very hardy, and make them bathe and fwim in winter time at day-break; which done the young men come of their own accord before their chief warrior, who holds a fpeech to them, telling them never to fear the water; that they may be purfued by their enemies; and that if they are taken they are burnt alive; that they muft on this occafion prove that they are true men, by uttering no complaints *.

When the harangue is finifhed, the chief fca-rifies their thighs, breaft and back, in order to ufe them to pain, and he then gives them great blows with leather ftraps †. The young men are then allowed to take place among the war-riors; and when they have done fome great ac-tion in the wars, they are marked with needles,

in

---

* The Indians are obliged to fupport bad luck with heroic conftancy, in order that their valour may defcend to their pofterity.

† Thefe leather ftraps are of the breadth of three fingers. The Indians ufe them for carrying their bundles when they fet out on a journey.

in the manner I have explained to you when I
fpoke of the *Illinois*.

Their children whilft they fuck their mother's
milk, are daily bathed in cold water during winter ; and when they grow up, the earth is their
bed. As the Indians love their children very
much, they accuftom them very early to fatigue ; and indeed as their whole body is naked,
it is no more fenfible to the cold than the face
and hands.

The old men, that cannot follow them,
whenever they make a retreat, defire to be killed
with clubs, both to fpare them the wretchednefs
of a decrepit condition, and to avoid falling
into the hands of their enemies, who would certainly burn or eat them ; for the Indians in their
wars kill men, women and infants at the breaft,
which together with the ravages of the fmall
pox, is a caufe of the depopulation of America.

It will not be amifs Sir, to obferve that
it is merely an act of humanity on certain occafions when a fon puts an end to his father's life. The Indians have a great veneration
for their old men ; they regulate their conduct
by their advice, for they undertake nothing
                                        with-

without their confent. They likewife take great
care of the old men, and I have feen their chiefs
on their return from a hunting party, before they
fhared the game, lay afide the fhare of the old
people, which is likewife appropriated to the ufe
of widows and orphans, whofe hufbands and fathers have been killed in defence of their country.
The Indians are very hofpitable towards ftrangers
with whom they are in peace, and kind to their
allies and friends, but cruel and unmerciful to
their enemies. They are furprifed and even
fcandalized to fee a number of Englifhmen at
New Orleans, drawn thither in time of war,
for the fake of trading under the fpecious pretence of coming to exchange prifoners *. A
cacique lately, returned from *New Orleans* freely
owned to me, that he had a great mind to
break their heads for killing the *French* in
the north, that is, during the fiege of Quebec,
and that he was tempted to take his revenge
upon thofe that were at *New Orleans*. He
added,

---

* Here our author inferts a long invective againft the Englifh who come in veffels to *New Orleans* with prifoners of
war on board, which they offer to exchange, and that under
this cloak, they get information of the ftrength and fituation of the colony, and buy up all the furs they can get.
Some allowance muft be made for national prejudice and
French pertnefs. F.

added, that in his country they spoke to their
enemies with the club in their hands, as soon as
the hatchet is dug up; a phrase which denotes,
that nobody ought to have any commerce or cor-
respondence with the enemy, directly or in-
directly, under any pretence whatsoever, after
war is declared, unless he will prove a traitor
to his country, and be punished accordingly.

When peace is concluded they bury the
hatchet or the club under ground, signifying
thereby that all their hatred towards their enemies is buried in oblivion, that the horrors of
war are at an end, and that friendship and
good understanding are growing again between
them and their friends, like the white flowers of
their tree of peace, (which is the white laurel),
that ought to spread its branches over the *white*
ground; which is a metaphorical expression
which means the ground of peace.

The cacique I mentioned before, is called
Tamathlemingo, and he is very warm in the
French interest. I know that he has scornfully
rejected the presents which some Englishmen
would have loaded him with, and he had a great
mind to break their heads for making him such
a proposition. He wears a silver medal fastened
round

round his neck by a leather thong. He often told me, he would be buried together with the image of his father (that is, the king's portrait) which he wears on his breaft; and having always been faithful to him he hoped to fhake hands with him in the land of the fouls, where he expected to fee him one day. After this worthy chief had fhewn me thefe fine fentiments which parted from his heart, I gave him a bottle of brandy to drink the health of his father and mine. Such little *douceurs* when given on proper occafions, have a great effect upon thefe people; thus they were greatly moved when I pulled off my fhirt and gave it them in the name of their father, telling them that he pitied them, becaufe he knew by means of the *fpeaking fub-flance* * that his children were naked.

Thefe nations have no idea of the political fyftems which are known among the European powers. In their opinion, the allies of a nation muft affift them, when they are in war, and have no correfpondence with their enemies. I have had a long and ferious conference with one *Allexi Mingo*, who is a juggler and likewife the chief of a diftrict among them, and pretends to have
been

* Paper, or letters.

been abufed by fome *Spanifh* foldiers of the garrifon of *Penfacola* : this Indian owned that he had
formed a defign in order to be revenged of them,
to make a general incurfion with his warriors
into *Florida*, to the very gates of *Penfacola*.
This Indian would pay me a compliment, and
make me approve of his defign, by telling me,
that he was partly drawn into it, becaufe the
Spaniards lay ftill upon their mats; i. e. they
were at peace with the Englifh, whom they received into their ports, though at that time, they
were our enemies.

I anfwered this difcourfe of the Cacique in
exprefs terms and fuch as were moft capable of
making him defift from his enterprize, as I was
willing to prevent a maffacre of the Spaniards
who were our allies and neighbours : accordingly I fpoke to him in a manner analogous to
the genius and character of the nation.

Alexi Mingo, faid I, prepare thy heart, open
thy ears to hear the force of my words, for it
will bring back to thee thy wits, which thou
haft loft to-day.

I tell thee, then that the grand chief fovereign of the *Spaniards*, who lives on the other
                                                            fide

fide of the great falt-water lake, in the old
world that fwarms with inhabitants. is the brother * of the father of the red men, i. e. of
the king of *France*, and accordingly, I muft
fay, I difapprove very much of thy bold
defign. I fairly declare to thee, that if thou
perfifteft in it, thou canft do no better than
to begin with breaking my head. The Cacique anfwered, " Thy blood is as dear to me
" as my own ; befides, the *French* have never done
" me any harm, and I am ready to give my
" life for them ; thou canft affure our father of
" that. Oh that I had the fpeaking fubftance
" which thou haft, to let him know my words,
" but no, I rather wifh I had a hundred mouths
" which he might hear †. "

After this proteftation of friendfhip he gave
me his *Calumet*, and when I had fmoked a little
I returned it to him, as having made peace for
the *Spaniards*, by whom he pretended to have been
ill-ufed ; and as a ratification I gave him a bot-

---

* The Indians call their allies brothers.

† Some time after the author's departure, the Indians of
thefe parts maffacred feveral Englifhmen, that were come
within two leagues of fort *Touloufe*, where *M. de Grand-Mai-
fon* then commanded, who is now Major of the troops at
New Orleans.

tle of the fiery water, that is of brandy, ſaying, this I give thee to clean thy mouth, that it may not utter any more bad words againſt the Spaniards our allies: and to ſtrengthen my diſcourſe I gave a great roll of tobacco, for his warriors to ſmoke out of the great *Calumet* of peace. After my harangue was at an end, the young people came one after another to ſqueeze me by the hand, as a mark of friendſhip, which is cuſtomary among them.

I wiſhed, however, to perſuade this Cacique, who was piqued at the *Spaniards*, who receive Engliſh veſſels at *Penſacola*, becauſe they are at peace: for he ſaid they came to inform themſelves of the ſituation and ſtrength of theſe coaſts.

By way of appeaſing the Indian, I told him, that the governor daily waited for the arrival of a great piragua *, which ſhould bring him ſome of the ſpeaking ſubſtance, wherein the great chief of the Spaniards ſhould order him to dig up the hatchet of war, and to lift up his club againſt the Engliſh.

This

---

* An European ſhip.

This difcourfe fatisfied my Cacique ; and as he had drank a good portion of brandy, he was very talkative, and I took the opportunity of queftioning him concerning the grudge he bore the *Spaniards* in *Florida*. He told me, that he had heard by tradition, that the firft *warriors of fire* * who came into this country had committed hof-tilities in it, and violated the law of nations ; and, that ever fince that period, the anceftors of his nation had always recommended it to their pofterity to revenge the blood which had been unjuftly fhed.   I told the juggling Cacique, that the Lord of life had revenged them fufficiently, by the death of *Ferdinand Soto*, and almoft all his warriors.

I added, that they had no further reafon to hate the *Spaniards* ; that *Philip* II. grand chief of the *Spaniards*, had difavowed all the mifchief which his generals had done in thefe climates, as being contrary to his intentions.

R 2   I told

---

* Hiftory inform us, that in 1544, *Ferdinand Soto* made incurfions into this country ; the Indians there, who had never feen any Europeans, called the Spaniards warriors of fire, becaufe they were armed with guns and piftols : they faid, that the cannon was thunder, and that it caufed the earth to tremble, by killing people at a great diftance.

I told this American prince part of the story of *Don Francis de Toledo*, viceroy of *Peru*, who publicly hanged the presumptive heir to the crown, and ordered all the princes of the royal family of the *Yncas* to be killed, not even excepting the Spaniards, who from their mother's side were descended from *Atahualipa*. Don *Francis*, after such an execution, expected to be raised to the greatest dignities of the state on his return to Spain; but he was very ill received by the grand chief of the nation, who ordered him with a harsh voice to get out of his presence, saying, I have not appointed thee to be the executioner of princes, but to serve me and assist the unhappy. These words struck the viceroy dumb, and caused him such an illness that he died a few days after. The same king caused the death of one of his ministers that had imposed upon him, merely by saying the word *Hoolabè*, which in the Indian language, signifies, *What, dost thou lye?* The Cacique very gravely replied, " But if the grand chief " of the men of fire, appeared, as thou " sayeft, so angry at the viceroy, on account " of the cruelties which he had com- " mitted against his will, why did he not put " him

" him in the frame * ? or why did he not cut off
" his head, and fend it back to *Peru?* This
" example of feverity and juftice would in part
" have fatisfied the people whom this general
" had ill-treated, by hanging on a gibbet, like
" a thief, the heir of a great empire, who de-
" pended only from the *Lord of life,* or the Su-
" preme Being. Thus we red men, whom the
" Europeans call favages and barbarians would
" act towards the wicked and the murderers,
" who ought to be treated like the fierceft beafts
" of the foreft."

I again replied to this Indian chief in the following terms, " Thou muft know that the
" grand chiefs of the white men that live in the
" old country, are defpotic and abfolute, and
" that when they drive from their prefence their
" generals or warriors, who have abufed their fub-
" jects without caufe, this affront is much more
" fenfibly felt by thofe proud chiefs, who are
" hated by the *Great Spirit,* or by God, on ac-
" count of their mifdeeds, than the punifhment

R 3   " of

---

* A punifhment which the Indians adjudge to thofe that
have committed cruelties, and are taken at war: they are put
into a kind of frame, compofed of two pofts, and a pole
laid acrofs them, and burnt alive.

" of the frame, or a hundred blows with the " club' upon the head, would be by a red " man."

At · laſt I ſuccceded in ſoftening the ha-tred which theſe people had conceived againſt the *Spaniards*, and I imagine every hoſtile inten-tion is ſuppreſſed now; for my explication was very ſatisfactory to my juggler.

I believe I have already obſerved to you, that the Indians are very ſenſible of injuries, and that they generally remember thoſe that have out-raged them when they are in liquor. I have of-ten been the mediator in order to terminate the quarrels between two Indians; I told them that they ought to live together as good bro-thers, forget the paſt, and employ their courage in the common defence of their country only. I further aſſured them that if they did not give ear to my words, the *Great Spirit* would be diſ-pleaſed with them, and make their crops of maize fail. The Indian women ran quickly to me, whenever any two were ready to fight, that I might judge between them, and I always did all I could to reconcile the parties; which pleaſed the women very much, who have nothing wild about them, but the name which people give

give them, and whofe features are very regular. In a word, in this new world, as well as in the old, that lovely fex is born to populate and not to deftroy.

What I have ftill to fay of this nation is fo ample, that I am obliged to divide it; I fhall, therefore referve their mourning and their funeral cuftoms for another letter.

I am, S I R, &c. &c.

Among the Allibamons the
28th of April 1759.

L E T T E R XVI.

To the same.

Mourning and Manner of burying the Dead among the Allibamons; *Juſtice done to the Chevalier* d'Er-neville, *for a Soldier killed by a young Indian: their Religion; their Means of catching the Roc-buck and the wild Turkies.*

S I R,

THE day before yeſterday I received one of your letters, which informs me that you are in good health, and that you continue to give me marks of your remembrance of me. In my preceding letter, I ſpoke to you of the marriage of the Indians; I ſhall now proceed to deſcribe their mourning. When a grand chief of the nation dies, this mourning conſiſts in not waſhing nor combing themſelves; the men daub their whole body with ſoot, mixed

up

up with bear's oil; and in a word, they re-
nounce all forts of diverfions.   When a woman
lofes her hufband, fhe is obliged to be in mourning for a whole year, and to lay afide all her
ornaments.

All the *Allibamons* drink the *Caffine* *; this is
the leaf of a little tree, which is very fhady;
the leaf is about the fize of a farthing, but den-
tated on its margins.   They toaft thefe leaves
as we do coffee, and drink the infufion of them,
with great ceremony.   When this direutic potion is prepared, the young people go to prefent
it in calebafhes formed into cups, to the chiefs
and warriors, that is the honourables, and afterwards to the other warriors, according to
their rank and degree.   The fame order is obferved when they prefent the Calumet to fmoke
out of: whilft you drink they howl as loud as
they can, and diminifh the found gradually;
when you have ceafed drinking, they take their
breath, and when you drink again, they fet up
their howls again.   Thefe forts of orgies fometimes laft from fix in the morning to two o'clock
in

---

* This is the *Prinos glaber* of Linnæus. Sp. pl. p. 471.
and *Caffena vera Floridanorum.*   Catefby's Carol. 2. t. 57.

in the afternoon. The Indians find no inconveniencies from this potion, to which they attribute many virtues, and return it without any effort.

The women never drink of this beverage, which is only made for the warriors. In such assemblies, where they are never admitted, the Indians tell their news and deliberate on political affairs, concerning peace or war. However the Chevalier *d'Erneville*, says that he saw a woman, who was the grand chief's wife, go in, because she was a female warrior, and had a quick, penetrating mind. Her opinion sometimes prevailed in the conclusion of treaties.

The *Allibamons* love the French very much; there is an agreement on both sides, that if a *Frenchman* kills one of the *Indians*, he must die, and the same if an *Indian* kills a *Frenchman*; the last accident happened whilst the Chevalier *d'Erneville* commanded the fort at the *Allibamons*; a young Indian shot a soldier of the garrison, and disappeared immediately. As the officer did not know where the criminal was, he applied to the chiefs of the nation, saying, they must do him justice. They answered, that the young man had taken refuge with another nation; the *Chevalier*

valier d'Ernville did not put up with this excufe ;
he told them that the dead man called for vengeance, and that blood ought to be avenged by
blood, as is their expreffion ; that the murderer
had a mother, and that fhe ought to fuffer in his
ftead. They anfwered, that fhe had not killed
the man ; but the officer replied, that he fpoke
like the red man, who when fomebody killed a
perfon of their nation, and they had not juftice
done them for it, were revenged upon fome
perfon of the nation of the murderer. He
laftly reprefented it to them, that in order to
keep the good underftanding between the white
and the red men, they ought not to oppofe the
punifhment of the criminal. They offered him
a great quantity of furs, and even horfes loaded
with booty. This officer who is known for his
zeal in preferring the king's intereft to his own,
and the honour of the nation to his fortune, refufed all thefe prefents. He added, that he had
not been able to fleep fince the death of his
warrior, who called every night to him, *avenge
my blood.* The poor Indians, feeing they could
not move him, held a council and fent out eight
men, conducted by a young chief of the warriors. He went immediately with his men to
the murderer's mother, and told her that fince
her fon was not to be found, fhe muft die in his
ftead.

ftead. The poor woman fuffered herfelf to be led away, and was all in tears; her relations followed her with very fad countenances; one of them feeing there was no pardon to be hoped for, faid to the chief of the troop, " *My mo-* " *ther-in-law dies through courage, as fhe has not* " *ftruck the blow.*" He propofed they fhould wait whilft he went to fetch the murderer; he actually brought him into the affembly, where the Chevalier *d'Erneville* was, and faid, See, there is the guilty man, do what you pleafe with him. The officer anfwered, that they ought to do him juftice; and they immediately killed him †.

Juftice

---

* Thus the Indians execute juftice; there is no need of drawing up cafes; all thefe forms are unknown; the law is, that he who has killed muft be killed again, unlefs it be by accident, as in a drunkennefs, in a fit of madnefs, or in their exercifes.

† The relation of this ftory, is by no means favourable to the French. They acted upon a barbarous and cruel principle, by bringing the mother of the guilty man to a punifhment which fhe did not deferve; and had not her fon on this occafion preferred filial duty to felf-prefervation, the French Chevalier would have committed an inhuman action, by inflicting death on an innocent perfon. The *In-*
dians

Juſtice being thus done, the chief harangued the young people, and recommended it very ſtrongly to them, to keep their hands from the

French,

---

dians act upon principle, by avenging the death of their countrymen upon any other perſon of the nation to which the murderer belongs ; for, on account of their confined ideas, and ignorance, they think the ſame conſtitution and manners take place among the Europeans, as are uſual among themſelves; and as they look upon their whole nation as a body of brethren, and a ſingle family, they are, therefore, of opinion that all the Europeans muſt be anſwerable for the death of one of their brethren. But as the Europeans boaſt to be civilized, inſtructed and Chriſtians, they ought to act according to the principles of their religion, the knowledge and inſtruction they enjoy, and their own conſtitution ; all theſe oblige them to ſhew the Indians, by their example, the ſuperiority of their religion, knowledge and conſtitution ; make them ſenſible, that if they acted like Indians they would commit an open injuſtice ; and to enforce the return of ſuch actions in ſimilar caſes. The Europeans inſtead of inſtilling principles of humanity into the minds of the poor Indians, very frequently ſcandalize them by their uncharitable and barbarous manners ; and thus the high refinements of our manners, our boaſted civilization, our pride, founded upon the ſuperiority of our knowledge, and that real great advantage of being inſtructed in a religion founded upon reaſon and charity, inſtead of bringing our immortal minds to that pitch of excellence they are capable of, according to the true intention of theſe advantages, prove only our deep corruption, and the wilful depravity of our hearts, and I may ſay, the barbarity of our manners. F.

French; and added, that as often as they fhould lofe their fenfes and kill our people, they would do us the fame juftice again.

The Chevalier *d'Erneville* held a fpeech to the affembly in his turn, and made the nation a prefent which the governor had fent him. The Indians gave him the great calumet of peace to fmoke, all the foldiers and *French* inhabitants likewife fmoked it, in fign of a general amnefty; afterwards they drank the *Caffine*, which is the potion of the *white word*, i. e. the potion of oblivion and peace.

Since that time this nation has never offended us. The *Allibamons* offered, in 1714, to build upon their ground, and at their expence, a fort, which was afterwards called Fort *Touloufe*, and they introduced the *French* into it. M. *de Bienville*, who was then governor, went to take poffeffion of it in the King's name *.

They

---

* This governor is in fuch great efteem with them, that they always mention him in their harangues. His name is fo deeply graved in the hearts of thefe good Indians, that his memory will always be dear to them. As foon as they faw me they inquired after him; I anfwered, that he was at the great village, or *Paris*, in good health, with which they were highly pleafed.

They never would permit the *Englifh* to do the like; they pay no regard to the menaces of the King of *England*; every Cacique or chief of a village thinks himfelf a fovereign, who only depends upon the *Mafter of life*, or the *Great Spirit*.

The *Allibamons* have called their country the *white country*, or land of peace; and repofe on their mats, that is, *they attack no body*; which is a kind of allegory by which they feem to tell all the nations on earth, that the murdering hatchet is buried, and that they may come to trade with them in fafety.

The following is an harangue which I heard one of the chiefs of this nation hold : " Young " men and warriors, do not difregard the *Ma-* " *fter of life*; the fky is blue, the fun is with- " out fpots, the weather is fair, the ground is " white, every thing is quiet on the face of the " earth, and the blood of men ought not to be " fpilt on it. We muft beg the fpirit of peace " to preferve it pure and fpotlefs among the na- " tions that furround us. We ought only to " fpend our time in making war with tygers, " bears, wolves, ftags, and roe-bucks, in order " to have their fkins, with which we may trade " with

" with the Europeans, who will bring us what
" we want, in order to maintain our women and
" children."

The Americans in general have no knowledge
of letters. The art of writing is unknown to
them. They are furprifed to fee that one can
converfe with another at a great diftance by a
paper; and they look upon the miffive letters
with admiration. When they are trufted with
letters, they bring them very exactly to the perfons they are directed to; and though it fhould
rain ever fo hard, and they had a great many
rivers to pafs, thofe letters are never wetted.
The *Allibamons* trade with the *French*, *Englifh*, and
Spaniards, but they do not love the latter much;
they make war upon them fooner than upon
any other nation, on account of their cruelties
towards the *Mexicans*; their memory is admirable, they always remember the wrong which is
done to them.

Thofe whom I fpeak of here acknowledge a
Supreme Being, whom they call *Soulbiechc*. I
afked them what they thought of the other
world; and they anfwered, that if they have
not taken another man's wife, or if they have
not robbed nor killed any one during their life,

they

they fhall go after their death into a very fertile
country, where they fhall want neither wives
nor proper places for hunting, and that every
thing will be eafy to them there; but that on the
contrary, if they have behaved themfelves fool-
ifhly, and difregarded the great Spirit, they will
come into a barren land full of thorns and
briars, where there will be no hunting, and no
wives. This is all I have been able to learn
concerning the belief of thefe people of another
life.

The *Allibamons* bury their dead in a fitting pofture; in order to juftify this cuftom they fay,
that man is upright, and has his head turned towards heaven, which is to be his habitation.
They give to them a calumet, and fome tobacco
to fmoke, that they may make peace with the
inhabitants of the other world. If the corpfe be
of a warrior, he is buried with his arms; which
are a mufket, fome powder and bullets; a quiver full of arrows, a bow, and an hatchet or club;
and befides thefe a mirror *, and fome vermilion
with which they may drefs themfelves in the
other world.

VOL. I.   S   When

---

* The young Indians are never without a little hatchet or
a mirror hung on their wrift.

When a man kills himfelf, either in defpair or in a ficknefs, he is deprived of burial, and thrown into the river, becaufe he is looked upon as a coward.

I have already faid, that the Indians muſt fupport misfortunes with heroic conftancy. Their enthufiafm prompts them to make fongs of death when they are taken prifoners, and deftined to be burnt; on fuch an occafion an Indian fays : " I fear neither death nor fire, make me fuffer " ever fo much, becaufe my nation will revenge " my death." This occafions his enemies either to accelerate his fate, or fometimes adopt him, faying he is a man of courage.

When there is a difturber of public peace amongft them, the old men fpeak to him thus : " Thou art at liberty to go away; but remem- " ber, that if thou art killed, the nation fhall " difown thee; we fhall not weep for thee, nor " avenge thy death." So irregular a life is punifhed with the greateft contempt among thefe people, as among all others *.

The

---

* The young Indians fometimes ramble into the neighbouring villages, and carry off the women; thefe kinds of

rapes

The Indians generally fet out a hunting to-wards the end of October. The *Allibamons* go fixty, eighty, and fometimes an hundred leagues from their villages, and they take their whole fa-milies with them into their piraguas: they do not return till March, which is the time of fow-ing their corn-grounds. They bring back many furs, and a great quantity of dried flefh. When they are returned into their villages, they regale their friends, and make prefents to the old men, who have not been able to go with them, and have kept in the huts during the time of the great hunt.

Thefe nations have fingular methods of catch-ing the roe-deer; an Indian takes the head of a roe-buck, and dries it; he then carries it with him into the woods, where he covers his back with the fkin of this animal, he puts his hand into the neck of the dried head, taking care to put little hoops under the fkin to keep it firm on the hand; he then kneels down, and in that at-titude,

S 2

titude, mimicking the voice of thefe creatures, he fhews the head; the roe-deer are deceived by it, and come very near the hunters, who are fure to kill them.

There are Indians who, by means of this ftratagem, have deftroyed four hundred roe-deer in one winter's hunting.   They employ very nigh the fame trick to get the wild turkies in the woods; fome of them put the fkins of thefe birds on their fhoulders, and on the heads a bit of fcarlet or other red cloth, which is agitated by the wind, and whilft the birds look at them, their comrades kill them with arrows; they do not ufe fire-arms, for fear of frightening them, and whilft there are any turkies on a tree, they continue to fhoot them with great dexterity; thefe birds are commonly foolifh enough to expect the return of their fellows who fell down; the Indians have often treated me with thefe birds, and I found them excellent during autumn.

The Indians are likewife very dextrous fifhermen; they neither employ hooks nor nets; they take reeds, which are very common along the fides of rivers, dry them near the fire, or in the fun-fhine, fharpen one end like a dart, and faft-

en

en a cord made of the bark of a tree, to the other end; when they are upon the lakes in their canoes, they throw this dart or harpoon into the water at the fifh, and draw it up again by means of the cord ; others fhoot the fifh with a bow and arrows, and when they have wounded a fifh, it comes to the furface of the water.

Before I have done with the *Allibamons*, I fhould not forget to tell you, that in July, when their harveft begins, they have a great feaft. That folemn day they pafs without eating; they light a new fire for phyfic, as they call it, or jug-gling, after which they take a purge, and offer to their *Manitou* the firftlings of their fruit : they finifh the day in religious dances.

This nation has likewife jugglers or quacks ; I fhall relate to you a very droll adventure which happened to me with one of them.   As I was going up the river of *Allibamons*, a quack and juggler came to fee me with feveral Indians, men and women.   He afked for fome brandy, I gave him a bottle full of it, which he drank with his companions.   He afked me for fome more, but I told him I had no more ; he would not believe me, and feeing that he could not get any thing, he thought he would intimidate

S 3   me,

me, by telling me he was a magician, and would *practife phyfic* * againft me, if I gave him no brandy; *i. e.* he would enchant my boat, fo that it could not proceed. I told him I feared him not; that I was a phyfician myfelf. This word aftonifhed my adverfary.

This pretended magician told me to fhew him the effects of my art; I anfwered, that he ought to begin, but he replied that I fhould do it being a ftranger; at laft, after many debates, I began to make ridiculous geftures, and looked into a book which the juggler underftood nothing of; I bid him retire, and leave me alone, it being the cuftom of the jugglers, by which means they conceal their impoftures from the other Indians. I had the fkin of a tyger-cat, the flefh and bones of which had been extracted through an incifion in the neck; I gave this fkin to the Indian quack, telling him to reftore its fight, and make the creature go about. He anfwered, that he could not do it; I fee, faid I, thou art a mere novice in this art, I fhall perform it.

I muft

---

* This is an expreffion which the Indians make ufe of, denoting the application of their flight-of-hand tricks, and grimaces intended for to make their countrymen believe that they are magicians or conjurors.

I muſt previouſly inform you, that, in my laſt voyage, I brought with me from France enamelled eyes, which perfectly imitated the natural eyes; a thing which the Indians here had never ſeen; I faſtened them with the reſin of firs, in the place of thoſe which were wanting in the ſkin, into which I afterwards put and confined a living ſquirrel, with its head towards the neck of the tyger-cat; a ſoldier whom I had inſtructed was quite ready with a club; every thing being thus prepared, I opened the door of the cabin, and the Indians advanced, with the juggler or quack doctor at their head. I held the cat in my arms, and the ſquirrel jumped about in it, which immediately ſurpriſed my pretended magician; he cried out that I was a true *phyſician* or ſorcerer, becauſe I had brought to life, reſtored to ſight, and made dead cats walk. When the other Indians had well conſidered it in my arms, I let it go on the ground, pricking the ſquirrel with a pin, which made it run with the cat's ſkin towards the ſpectators, who thought it would devour them; they went backwards, and the women, through a natural fear, ran from my boat, declaring that I was a ſorcerer. I then ran to my tyger-cat, ſeeming to be very angry with it, I quickly took out the ſquirrel and the glaſs-eyes, then preſſing the teeth in the

S 4   cat's

cat's head againſt my ſtomach, I cried out as if
the creature had bit me, flinging it on the ground
immediately; the ſoldier whom I had armed
with a club, ſtrikes at the revived tyger-cat, in
order to kill it for having revolted againſt its
maſter, and for having been willing to attack
red men, who were our friends and allies.

After this comic ſcene, I gave the ſkin to the
Indian juggler, and deſired him to make it re-
vive as I had done. He owned, that my art
was above the reach of his. I then bid him enchant my boat to prevent its going on; but he
anſwered, that one phyſician againſt another
could do nothing; that I was his maſter in the
art, and he an ignorant fellow *. All the ſavages

---

* The Indians repoſe a great confidence in their doctors;
the juggler's hut is covered with furs, with which he covers
and dreſſes himſelf. He goes in quite naked, and begins
with pronouncing ſome words which no body underſtands;
they are, as he ſays, to invoke the Spirit; after that he
riſes, cries, agitates himſelf, appears quite frantic, and
gets into a profound ſweat †.

The hut ſhakes, and the ſpectators believe it is done
through the preſence of the Spirit; the language which he
ſpeaks on this occaſion, has nothing in common with the ordinary Indian language; it is nothing but the ravings of a
hot

vages who were out upon the winter hunt along the river, brought me provifions of roe-deer and turkies, that I might begin again to play off my trick; but for fear of being difcovered, and to preferve my reputation, I faid I could

not

---

hot imagination, which thefe quacks have impofed upon their countrymen as a divine language; thus the moft cunning people have always deceived the reft.

† The heathen nations in the Ruffian empire have exactly fuch jugglers or conjurors as are here defcribed. In the government of *Cazan* are the *Tcheremiffes*, the *Tchuwafhes*, and the *Wotiaks*, three nations; the firft of which call their conjurors *Mufhan*, the fecond *Tommas* or *Tymmas*, and the third *Tona* or *Tuno*; they are of both fexes, and make the fame grimaces as thefe American jugglers. In *Siberia* the *Tungufi*, the *Yakuti*, and the *Byrati*, call their conjurors *Shamans*, and they perform the fame tricks, and make many antic geftures at their pretended conjurations. Their drefs is on thefe occafions likewife very remarkable, fometimes ornamented with the fangs and talons of beafts and birds of prey, fometimes hung with fuch a terrible quantity of feveral pieces of iron, as will both make the robe very heavy, and caufe a great rattling noife at the leaft motion of the conjuror's body. The more we go eaft in *Siberia*, the more common is this kind of conjurors, and the more ftriking is the likenefs between the favage inhabitants of *North America*, and the favage Nomadic nations of the north-eaft parts of *Afia*. Some more hints of this fimilarity are pointed out in a note to *Kalm's Travels into North America*, vol. III. p. 126. F.

not do it over again, left fome one of them
fhould be devoured by the revived creature, and
the better to convince them, I fhewed them the
marks of the animal's teeth on my ftomach.
They then approved very much of what I had
faid, and thanked me for interefting myfelf 'fo
much for them, as to expofe myfelf generoufly
to prevent the furious revived tyger-cat from
killing their women and children; they added,
that I had done well to reduce it to its lifelefs
ftate, in order to make it an example to others,
becaufe it was an evil fpirit; thefe poor people
regard the French as fupernatural men.

It is fometimes dangerous to be a doctor; for
if fome one dies among the Indians, they attribute his death to the phyfic, and not to the in-
curable difpofition of the patient; therefore I
would never advife any body to abufe the cre-
dulity of thefe people. I likewife told them, that
fince I had been bitten I had abjurated the office
of a magician, and that I knew no other phyfician than the *Mafter of life*, whofe aid they ought
to implore; that he was as much the father of
the red men as of the white men, who are their
elder brothers.

The

The pretended refurrection of my tyger-cat, however, gave me great reputation among the quacks or jugglers of this country, and even among thofe of Spanifh *Florida*, whofe natural curiofity led them to pay me a vifit ; they joined the *Allibamons* doctors, and begged me to perform the fame piece of legerdemain which I had done on my voyage : I told them, I was forry that I could not fatisfy their curiofity, becaufe I had ftruck the poft * ; however, that I might not fend them away difcontented, I told them, that their prefence was very agreeable to me, that the *Grand Chief* of the French and the father of the Indians was contented with their nation, and with them in particular ; that the doctors having more knowledge than the others, both in the art of curing the fick, and in their zeal towards infpiring their countrymen with fidelity and friendfhip for the French, it was on that confideration I come on purpofe to bring them a prefent, which was the word of their father, and that M. *Aubert* had orders from the governor to divide it among them.

I further told them, that as I was glad to get acquainted with them, and to converfe with them,

---

* The Indian manner of fwearing is to ftrike againft a poft with a club,

them, I wifhed they would tell me their proper
names.   As thefe people are neither baptifed
nor circumcifed, they commonly take the name
of fome animal, fuch as bear, wolf, fox, &c.
The gravity which I affeded, in order to command the refpect of thefe Indian doctors, made
them afk me, whether I wrote their names in order to give an account of them to their father,
by means of the fpeaking paper? to which I
anfwered, that it was for that very purpofe.

When I had written down their names, I
fometimes made ufe of them in order to pafs for
a fortune-teller.

I fhut myfelf up in the hut of one of the doctors, and a foldier, to whom I had told the
number of letters which compofed each name,
put his hand on the fhoulder of the juggler,
and with a little rod ftruck him as many times as
there were letters in his name; I being within
eafily guefled what man my foldier laid his hands
upon; and fo on with all the reft.   They could
not comprehend how I could guefs fo well without feeing them, and they owned that it went
beyond their imagination.

The

The Sieur *Godeau*, chief furgeon and keeper of the magazine at the fort of *Allibamons*, had already before me practifed phyfic in the prefence of the Indians,. who were looking at a little phial full of mercury ; after looking at it with attention, they told him they wifhed to have it. He faid he would give it them, but that he wanted the phial ; he poured out the quickfilver immediately on the ground, and bid them take it up ; they could never do it, for it rolled away on all fides ; the aftonifhed favages called it a fpirit which divided itfelf into feveral parts, which being collected together formed only one body ; but their aftonifhment was much greater when the Sieur *Godeau* took up all the mercury with a card, and put in the phial again, in their prefence, which none of them had been able to do. This furgeon did more, he poured *aqua-fortis* upon it, which diffolved it, and made it difappear entirely ; fince that time the Indians have revered him as a great doctor.

M. *de Montberaut* has put the command of the fort of the *Allibamons* into the hands of M. *Aü-bert*, who is adjutant of the fort *Mobile*. I take the liberty to write to the governor, in order to reprefent it to him with all refpect, that being the fenior officer of that gentleman, I could not

ftand

stand here under his orders; that he might not
be further obliged to do any services foreign to
his function *, the King's order concerning that
particular being very explicit; that as our insti-
tution is founded upon honour, I should think
I would derogate from that which I had acquired in the King's service, if I did not make the
observations of a soldier, whose zeal for the service he knows; that it was very natural for me
to think, that by this consideration he would
think himself obliged to let me enjoy the emolu-
ments annexed to my place, otherwise I should
beg him to recall me to *New Orleans*, that I
might seize the first opportunity of setting out
for Europe, where I should have the pleasure of
assuring you that I am, S I R, &c.

At the Allibamons, the 2d
of May 1759.

P. S. I

---

* I must, however, do M. *Aubert* justice; he has had
the command of the fort at the *Allibamons* to my prejudice,
but I must praise the regard he has had for me, in offering
to divide the authority, and to live upon the footing of a
friend with me,

P. S. I have forgot to mention to you a vifit which the emperor of the *Kawytas* has paid us fome time after M. *de Montberaut*'s departure. As we had advice of it by a courier, I went to meet his Indian majefty in order to receive him at fome diftance from the fort. I had pofted fome foldiers, who fired their mufkets by way of fignal to the gunners to fire the cannon at the moment, when the prince fhould put his hand in mine *: he was mounted on a Spanifh horfe, with an Englifh faddle, and with a houfing of a tyger's fkin †.

This emperor marched gravely at the head of his attendants; I could hardly keep from laughing, on feeing tall well made naked men, painted with all kinds of colours, follow each other in a file, according to their rank, like fo many Capuchin friars.

The Indian prince appeared enraptured with the honours that were fhewn him; he had

never

---

* The Indians are without compliments and ceremonies, they laugh at our bows, or method of faluting with the body bent, and the foot advanced forwards or retreated backwards.

† American leopard.

never feen cannons, and called them great
mufkets.

He wore on his head a creft of black plumes;
his coat was fcarlet, with *Englifh* cuffs on it;
and befet with tinfel lace; he had neither waift-
coat nor breeches, but only an apron made of a
bit of fcarlet cloth, which was taken up between the thighs and faftened to his girdle. Under his coat he had a white linen fhirt; his feet
were covered with a kind of bufkins, of tanned
roe-deer fkins, which were died yellow. As he
was a young man, of eighteen or nineteen years
old, his nation had appointed a noble and wife
old man as a regent; he held a fpeech in his fovereign's name; and he prefented the calumet of
peace to M. *Aubert*, who told him after the firft
compliments were over, that he fhould go to reft,
it being the cuftom among the Indians, not to
fpeak of political affairs till the next day, in order to have time to make reflections.

The Sieur *Laubérie*, the king's interpreter,
tranflated the difcourfe of the regent, who likewife acted as the emperor's chancellor,; he did
not fail to call to mind the great fervices which
his late father had done to the Frencli, and that
them;

the fon had always been willing to come to fee them, in order to renew the friendfhip, which had never ceafed to exift between his nation and ours, and to fmoke the fame calumet with them.

It is true, his predeceffor always was inviolably attached to M. *de Bienville*, and the latter granted that Cacique the title of emperor on that account.

The governor likewife defired to bring all the tribes of *Allibamons* to acknowledge the emperor as their grand chief; but they refufed it faying, that it was quite fufficient that every village was fubjected to a chief: in a word, they would change nothing in their form of government.

The emperor, his regent, his chief of war or general, his doctor or juggler, and his hired fervant appeared at ten o'clock in the morning before our commander, where we all were dreffed in our uniforms in order to compofe a kind of court for him. As to the emperor, his imperial habit was no better this day than that of his attendants, for they all were

dreſſed as Adam was in the terreſtrial para-
diſe *.

This young prince had a noble ſhape, and a
handſome appearance; he was ſprightly and
graceful; during his ſtay here he has been
treated at the king's expence. As he was of
my ſize, the governor of the fort begged me to
give him a blue coat, and a gold laced waiſt-
coat, a hat with plumes, and a ſhirt with laced
ruffles.

M. *Aubert* likewiſe made ſome trifling preſents
to this American prince, and to the officers of
his court, at the king's expence, and ſent them
home very well ſatisfied.

Their country is ſituated between *Carolina* and
Eaſt Florida, eaſtward of *Mobile*; theſe people
have never been conquered by the *Spaniards*, who
are become their declared enemies. The emperor always dined at M. *Aubert*'s table, with his
regent. The others had not the ſame honour
done

* The coat which the emperor had on when he arrived at
the Allibamons, had been given him by a captain in the
king of Great-Britain's army. He laid it by on this public
day, through political views, and in order to get one from
the French.

done them, in order to infpire them with a greater regard for the *French* officers. I muft tell you, that the fon of that noble *Kawytas* whom the French had honoured with the pompous title of emperor, was very much at a lofs the firft time he dined with us ; for he had never made ufe of a fork before; therefore he looked at us very attentively, in order to imitate our way of eating. His regent had not the fame patience, he took the breaft and back bone of a turkey and broke it with his fingers, faying, that the *Mafter of life* had made them before the knives and forks were made.

Towards the end of the repaft we had a little farce with the hired fervant of the Emperor, who ftood behind his Indian majefty during dinner; this fellow obferving that we eat muftard with our boiled meat, afked M. *de Boudin* what it was that we feemed to relifh fo much ; as this officer fpeaks the language of the nation, having lived forty years among them, he anfwered, that the French were by no means covetous of what they poffeffed ; the Indian immediately took a fpoonful of muftard, which being very ftrong, forced him to make many ridiculous contortions, which made his mafter burft out laughing; his fervant was far from

laughing

laughing ; for he thought he was poifoned ; M. *Aubert* ordered a bottle of brandy to be brought and bid him take a good draught, affuring him that he would be cured immediately.

The *Kawytas* are very referved towards ftrangers in matters of religion ; they never fpeak in public till they have reflected fufficiently on what they are going to fay.

Thefe people annually hold a general affembly in the principal village of their nation ; there is a great hut for that purpofe, in which every one takes place according to his rank, and has a right to fpeak in his turn *, according to his age, abilities, wifdom, and the fervices he has done his country.

The grand chief of the tribe opens the feffion by a fpeech, which concerns the hiftory or tradition of their country ; he tells the military exploits of his anceftors, who have diftinguifhed themfelves in defence of their country, exhorting his fubjects to imitate their virtues, in fupporting the wants and miferies of human life
with

---

* The Indians difapprove of the European habit of fpeaking all together in an affembly.

with patience, and above all, without complaining against the *Great Spirit, who is the Lord of the life of every being here on earth* ; and in enduring adverſity with courage, and laſtly in ſacrificing every thing to the love of their country and of liberty ; it being a thouſand times more glorious to die as a man, than to live as a vile ſlave.

The chief having ceaſed ſpeaking, the oldeſt among the nobles riſes, ſalutes his ſovereign, and harangues with his body naked to his girdle ; he is all over in a ſweat, on account of the heat which his action and declamation throws him into ; his geſtures are natural, and his metaphors explain his mind : he perſuades his audience into a belief of all that he ſays, by his eloquence, and the excellence of his diſcourſe. Nothing is more edifying than theſe aſſemblies ; you hear no prattling, no indecency, no ill-timed applauſe and no immoderate laughter there. The young men are very reſerved and attentive to hear the words of the old men, being perſuaded that it is for their good.

L E T T E R XVII,

To the fame.

The Author leaves the Allibamons. *His Navigation in the River of* Tombekbé. *How he ef-
capes the voracioufnefs of an Alligator. He meets
with a Party of revolted* Chactaws, *and brings
them to their Duty again. He returns to*
Mobile.

S I R,

INSTEAD of an anfwer to the letter
I which I had wrote to the governor, I
received an order at the *Allibamons* to
go to Mobile, and ferve there under the orders
of M. *de Velle*, the king's lieutenant in that
place ; thus in ftead of going to *France* as I had
told you, I have got orders to command a convoy of provifions and ammunition to the fort

Tom-

Tombekbé, which is fituated on a river of the fame name, this ftation is about ten legues from the nation of *Chaɛʈaws*, I have followed my inftructions with the greateft exaɛtnefs, and to the entire fatisfaɛtion of my fuperiors ; the letters and certificate which I can fhew up, are proofs of it.

I left *Mobile* on the 20th of Auguft 1759, with three boats, in which were foldiers and *Mobile* Indians : the latter offer themfelves to help the French in rowing, for fome trifle or other which is given them.

You embark in the river *Mobile*, and after going up about fifteen leagues, you come to a place called la *Fourche* (i. e. the fork) that is the juncture of two rivers which fall into the *Mobile*, viz. the river of *Allibamons* and the river *Tombekbé* ; I entered into the laft on the 27th of Auguft, in order to go up to the fort ; we were in the fine feafon, and I had chofen a very proper place for a camp on the banks of a river ; the Indians having had good fuccefs in fifhing thereabouts, made me a prefent of a *barbel*, a fifh of about four feet long, which they commonly dry. The weather being fair, I did not chufe to pitch my tent, but only fat down by myfelf

T 4   upon

upon a kind of plat-form covered with green
fods, which overlooked the river, thinking that
place the moft convenient for refting : I fpread
the bear's fkin taken in my pretended government, and wrapped myfelf up in my tent, covering my face with it, becaufe the vapours at night
are dangerous in this feafon; this little nicety
was near cofting very dear to me as you
fhall fee.

I had put my fifh at my feet, left it fhould
be ftolen; but it happened worfe. I had already flept for a whole hour very quietly, for
the inhabitants of thefe parts are our allies and
friends, when all of a fudden, I found myfelf
carried away by an extraordinary force, I awoke
immediately, believing fome one was playing me
a trick; I affure you I never was more frightened, and I believe that a thing of lefs confe-
quence will often have the fame effect; I
thought the devil was carrying me off. I called
for help, and the people believed that I was
dreaming, or a vifionary; but how great was
my furprife when I awoke. I faw an alligator
(crocodile) of above twenty feet long *; he was
come

---

* His fize frightened me, and I was likewife infected with
the bad fmell of mufk which that animal carries with it.

come out of the river in the calm of night, and voracious as these creatures are, being attracted by the barbel which lay at my feet, he greedily fell upon it, and carrying it to the river he took me along by the corner of the tent in which I had wrapt myself up. I had time enough left to get out of it, at the border of the precipice, and so escaped with the fright. I only saved the bear's skin, which I never leave now. This story, plain as it is, may pass for a prodigy among those who love the marvellous.

The *Collapissas* and *Wanchas*, two little Indian nations, which live above *New Orleans*, fight with the crocodiles, or alligators, in the water in the following manner.

One takes a piece of hard wood, or of iron, and sharpens it at both ends; he takes hold of it in the middle, and swims with that one arm extended. The alligator advances with his mouth open, in order to devour the arm of the Indian, who thrusts in his hand in which he holds the piece of wood, and the alligator pierces both his jaws through with it, can neither open nor shut his mouth again, and is brought on shore, by the Indian; they often take this diversion;

and

and the negroes of *Guinea* or of *Senegal* do the same.

After going up about fixty leagues between forefts and mountains which confine the river, we met with fuch low water, that we were obliged to unload all the goods, and hide them in the woods ; I only left the provifions and ammunition in the boat, and gave them all my attention.   I never was in a more difagreeable fituation ; we were obliged to draw the boats for upwards of fifteen leagues ; I put myfelf at the head of the foldiers and Indians, and drew at the cord, in order to fet them an example. You may judge of my uneafinefs, if you will confider that during this piece of work, it would have been eafy to defeat and to plunder us.   I met a party of revolted *Chaâaws*, going to the Englifh ; I exhorted them to return ; they croffed the river in a place, called in their language *Tafkalouffas*, which fignifies the white mountain * ; their chief, whofe name is *Mingo Houmas*, had the infolence to pretend he could oblige me to give him brandy ; he even was audacious enough to lift his hatchet over my head.
On

---

* It is a kind of marle or chalk which would be of great value in Europe.

On this occasion, I told him I was a *true man*, that I feared not death, that I had given up my body *, and was willing to die, being perfuaded that if he killed me and my warriors, who were but few, the grand chief of the French, beyond the great lake, would revenge my blood on their nation, by fending as many warriors there, as there are leaves on the trees.

Thefe men were furprifed at my refolution; they faid, " That I was a *man of valour* ; that I " made them recover their wits which they had " loft in forming the deteftable defign of leaving " their father's hand, but that they hoped I " would forget what was paft, becaufe I was " very good." At the end of this harangue, they prefented the calumet of peace to me, which I accepted on condition that I fhould fmoke with a new fire out of it, to fignify an eternal oblivion of what had paft, and a renovation of the alliance with the *Chaʃʃaws*, children of the grand chief of the French. To convince them that I would forget the paft, I told them that the fire would be produced of itfelf.

In

---

* That is, devoted myfelf to die for my country.

In my laſt voyage from France I took with me a little phial of phoſphorus; I put ſome of this powder into the calumet of peace, and looked up to the ſky in pronouncing ſome words addreſſed to the Great Spirit; in the mean time the phoſphorus being expoſed to the air, ſet fire to the tobacco, which ſurpriſed, not only the Indians, but even the Frenchmen who were with me, becauſe they had never ſeen the experiment tried with this powder.

After this myſterious ceremony, I made theſe people preſents of ſome European trifles, and gave their chief a bottle of brandy, for it is cuſtomary among the Indians, that when you treat with them, you muſt give ſomething to confirm your words. Then they all ſhook hands with me, and went back to their village. They told me, they were aſhamed of their fooliſh conduct, and we ſeparated, ſatisfied with each other.

Some time after this adventure, the rains were ſo frequent, that they ſwelled the water in the river very much,

As I had diſpatched an Indian to M. *de Chabert*, governor of Fort *Tombekbé*, he ſent me a

detachment

detachment commanded by M. *de Cabaret*, a very fkilful officer, who was of great fervice to me
on this occafion, by bringing me refrefhments
for my foldiers, who had hardly any provifions
left.

Our European coxcombs, who carry mirrors,
toilets, night-gowns, &c. with them, would be
looked upon as women by the Indians, and not
as chiefs of the warriors : they would not diftinguifh themfelves in thofe campaigns, where they
muft endure the exceffive heats of the fummer,
and the rigours of winter, lie on the bare ground,
and expofe themfelves to all the changes of weather, in order not to be furprifed by the Indians.
Mr. *Braddock*, general of *New England* in 1755,
made the fatal experiment, when he came to
take *Fort du Quêne*; he was maffacred with his
whole army at fome diftance from that place,
by a fmall number of French, and fome faithful
Indians, led by brave *Canadian* and European
officers, who did wonders of bravery in this
action.

At laft I happily arrived at Fort *Tombekbé* on
the 25th of September, after going a hundred
leagues by water, without feeing a fingle habitation. Every night we are obliged to camp in the
woods

woods upon the banks of the river; but the greateft inconvenience are the *Mufkitoes* or *Maringoins*, a kind of gnats which are infupportable in *Louifiana*. In order to be free from them, we put great reeds into the ground, and bent them over like arches; we then covered them with a linen cloth, and laid down a bear's fkin as a matrafs. All the voyages made by people of the colony are done in the fame manner by water.

After going on fhore to camp, the commanding officer fhould always take care to appoint a guard, and to place fentinels in the woods to prevent furprifes. The officer ought always to be very careful in chufing an advantageous fituation for his camp, fuch as an ifle or a cape.

If the Sieur *D* * * had taken thefe precautions, when he was fent to the *Illinois* by M. *de Bienville*, in 1735, with a boat laden with gunpowder, in order to carry on the war with the *Chickfaws*, he would not have been furprifed, as he was, by a party of warriors of that nation. It may be afferted, that the negleƈt of that officer has been no lefs fatal to us, than the meannefs, ignorance, and avidity of the governor of the fort of the *Natches*; this boat laden with powder,

powder, being taken by the *Chickſaws*, ſerved them to carry on the war againſt us for above thirty years, and cauſed the death of many brave men, and the loſs of many millions of money to the king.

The following is, in a few words, the manner in which M. *D* * * * was ſurpriſed and taken priſoner. One day when it blew a north wind, he was obliged to bring his boat to the ſhore, and ſo encamped thereon, in order to wait for better winds. He went out hunting, and his ſoldiers did the ſame in imitation of their chief; but the *Chickſaws*, who had followed and watched them for a long while, took the boat with the gun-powder, and made all the ſoldiers in it priſoners. When M. *D* * * returned from hunting, he was inveſted and taken as his ſoldiers had been; but the Indians, contented with their capture, and having loſt none of their people, granted them their lives; M. *D* * * had the good luck to eſcape, and returned to *New Orleans*.

When one is on a journey, he ſhould always have an Indian ſcout to go before him, both for the ſake of reconnoitring the enemy or preventing ſurpriſes, and likwiſe for finding out game.

It

It happened to me as I was going up the river of *Tombekbé*, that I was in want of provisions, but Providence supplied it visibly.   The Indians, who are like ferrets in the woods, came to give me advice that they had made a good discovery ; they found the nest of a great eagle, called the *royal eagle* * ; as the tree on which this

                                                        nest

----

* The eagle here called the *royal,* is called in Englifh the *Golden Eagle,* Penn. Br. Zool. p. 61. tab. A. and in 8vo vol. i. p. 121. Falco chryfaëtos, *Linn.* and Le grand aigle royal, *Planches. enluminées,* tab. 410.   Mr. Pennant relates, from *Smith*'s history of Kerry, " That a poor man in that county " got a comfortable subsistence for his family, during a sum- " mer of famine, out of an eagle's nest, by robbing the ea- " glets of the food the old ones brought."   This in some measure confirms our author's account.   M. *Buffon,* in his *Hist. naturelle des oiseaux,* 12mo. edit. vol. i. p. 117. attacks M. *Salerne,* for having related the account he got from a friend, *who found three strong eaglets of this kind in a nest, fixed between two rocks.*   M. *de Buffon,* though a great natural historian, is frequently subject to have his peculiar opinions, which he defends against all facts proving the contrary : and, by his eloquence, he explains away the strongest arguments ; and invalidates even facts, in so much, that their strength in proving against him dwindles quite away. Our author had no peculiar opinion to favour ; he must have known the bird, which is not uncommon in France, and may be seen in the menageries of the King and the nobility, and in various cabinets ; and therefore I think our author's

                                                        account

neſt was placed, was a very tall one, they came for hatchets to cut it down; they were indeed well paid for their trouble, for they found a great quantity of game of all kinds in the neſt, ſuch as fawns, rabbets, wild turkies, grous, partridges, and wood-pigeons, there were four eaglets in it, already pretty ſtrong; theſe the Indians took for themſelves, to the great ſorrow of their parents, who would have picked out their eyes, if the Indians had not been armed with muſkets; the poor birds were quite furious, and the eagle is very juſtly called the king of the birds on account of his intrepidity; but the balls did not ſpare their feathered majeſties, who

Vol. I.   U   fell

---

account a ſtrong proof againſt M. *Buffon's* opinion, that the golden eagle has no more than two eaglets, ſeldom three, never four. This will be a warning to all naturaliſts, not too much to rely upon the aſſertions of that French natural hiſtorian, who, with all his abilities, indulges too much his opinions, in ſpite of facts that are againſt him. I know and acknowledge the merit of this able zoologiſt, but as his fine language, the fine prints, the vanity of the French nation, and the preſent faſhionable taſte, have procured him a high reputation, it is no more than natural that his authority ſhould be deciſive with many, who like rather *light ſummer-reading*, than the heavineſs of a critical diſcuſſion in natural hiſtory. I therefore thought, that ſuch a hint might be ſerviceable to thoſe whom M. *de Buffon* would carry a-ſtray by his florid ſtyle. F.

fell the victims of parental love. The Indians told me, that the great Spirit sent us these provisions; indeed it was to be looked upon as a *manna* sent by Providence, which favoured us in these deserts.

I have received news here from *New Orleans*, from whence my friends write, that every thing is in great confusion there, on account of an English ship which is arrived from *Jamaica* as a smuggling vessel, commonly called there an *interloper*.

This ship is called the *Texel*, commanded by Captain *Dias-Arias*, a Jew, born an English subject. The *Ordonnateur* having found, that it ought to be confiscated according to the orders of the marine, has seized it for the King's account; M. *de Belleisle*, who is fort *major*, and the governor's *locum tenens*, has been requested to assist with the military for that purpose; but M. *de Kerlerec* returning from *Mobile*, has suspended M. *de Belleisle* in the performance of his functions; that governor afterwards has had M. *de Rochemore*'s secretary taken up at three o'clock in the morning, by a detachment of soldiers, who, after breaking the doors and windows, dragged him out of bed, and put him on board

a ves-

a veffel, the deftination of which remains unknown : upon this M. *de Rochemore* has fent to
the minifter, Monfieur *de Fontenelle*, counfellor
in the fuperior council.

When I fhall be better informed of all that
has happened there, I fhall impart it to you ; I
write to the governor to grant me my recall to
New Orleans.

I am, S I R, &c.

At Tombekbé, the 19*th of*
September 1759.

LET.

L E T T E R XVIII.

To the Same,

Description of the Country of the Chactaws. *Their Wars; their Way of treating their Sick; their Superstition; their Commerce; their Plays of Exercise. Country of the* Tchicachas *or* Chickfaws, *our Enemies.*

S I R,

I Thought of setting out from hence in two days, but the desire of knowing the most warlike and most numerous nation of *Louisiana* made me change my mind; I employ my leisure hours to describe what I have seen and heard of them. The *Chactaws* are entirely the friends of the *French*; they have given proofs of it under the government of M. *Perrier*, when they were made use of to punish the *Natches*

ches who maffacred the *French* that were fettled among them. The court likewife annually makes them prefents to keep them in our intereft. This nation can bring four thoufand warriors into the field, who would march with pleafure. It would be very eafy, if it was managed as carefully as it ought to be, to make them fing their fongs of war, and ftir them up to revenge us againft the *Englifh*, who are committing hoftilities in our poffeffions in *Canada*; thefe people might on occafion ferve us to great advantage, if they made incurfions into the Britifh colonies, efpecially the provinces of *Georgia* and *Carolina*, which are quite empty, all their troops and the national militia having been fent to the fiege of *Quebec*. Many brave officers of this colony, who fpeak the language of the Indians, fuch as M. *de Rouville*, *du Tiffenet*, and others, are eager to head fome parties of this nation, who could deftroy the crops of our enemies, would pillage and burn their habitations, and give the alarm even to the walls of *Charles-town*, which might make a diverfion in favour of *Canada*.

The *Chaƈaws* love war, and are acquainted with ftratagems. They never fight in order, or ftand their ground, they only harrafs and teaze their enemies much, without being cowards;

U 3　　　　　　　　　for

for when they come to clofe engagement, they
fight very coolly. Some of their women are fo
fond of their hufbands as to go into the wars
with them. They ftand by their fides in the
battle, with a quiver full of arrows, and encourage them continually by telling them, they
ought not to fear their enemies, but die as *true
men.*

The *Chaflaws* are very fuperftitious; when
they go to war they confult their *Manitou*, who
is carried by the chief. They always expofe him
to that fide where they are to go towards the. enemy, and place fome warriors as fentinels round
him. They have fuch a veneration for him, that
they do not eat till the chief has given him firft
his fhare.

During the continuance of the war, they obey
their chief very exactly; but as foon as they return, they only confider him according to the
liberality with which he difpofes of his property.

It is a cuftom among ■■■ that when the
chief of a party of warriors has got booty from
the enemy, he muft diftribute it to the warriors,
and to the relations of thofe who have been killed

ed in battle, in order, as they fay, *to dry up their tears.* The chief keeps nothing for himfelf, except the honour of being the fupport of the nation.

Intereft, which is the caufe of fo many crimes in the old world, is unknown in the new world; it is not without reafon that the *Cuba* Indians faid, Gold is the true God of the Spaniards, and we muft give it them in order to have peace. In *America* we do not fee any of thofe men, whom we call *favages*, kill their brothers in cool blood, or make ufe of falfe witneffes to undo them, in order to get their eftates. Thofe intrigues are unknown there, which are made ufe of to acquire riches, by means unworthy of a human being. No wife poifons her hufband there, as is done in Europe, in order to marry again. There are no women lafcivious or audacious enough publicly to declare the impotence of their hufbands, as the European women do; nor does any Cacique's wife get her hufband ftrangled, as that Neapolitan princefs did with her's, becaufe he would not fatisfy her brutal paffion; no girls there deftroy their own off-fpring, in order to appear chafte in the eyes of men. The Indian women abhor the Chriftian girls who fall into that cafe; they oppofe the

U 4   fierceft

fierceft wild beafts to them, becaufe they take
great care of their young.

If the chief of a party of *Chaftaws* does not
fucceed in the war which he has undertaken, he
lofes all his credit; nobody has any truft in his
command, and he is obliged to come down to
the rank of a mere warrior. However, admire
the variety of opinions among the different nations. It is no fhame, if, among thefe warlike
people, a man turns his back upon the enemy.
This defertion is attributed to a bad dream; if
the chief of a great party, having dreamt that
he will lofe fome men, tells his warriors that he
has had a bad dream, they return immediately
to their village; as foon as they arrive there,
they have recourfe to phyfic, *i. e.* to juggler's
tricks, which they employ on all occafions;
then they march towards the enemy; and if they
meet him, they kill five or fix of his men, and
come home as content as if they had fubdued a
great empire.

A general who fhould gain a victory with the
lofs of many of his men, would be ill received
by them; becaufe they do not value a victory
when it is bought with the blood of their friends
and relations; their chiefs are always careful to
preferve

preferve their warriors, and never attack the enemy unlefs they are fure of an eafy victory, either
on account of their numbers, or their advantageous fituation; but as their adverfaries are likewife cunning, and evade all the fnares that are
laid for them, it depends then upon fuperior
fineffe; therefore they hide themfelves in the
woods in day-time, and only walk at night; if
they are not difcovered, they attack by break
of day. As they are generally in a woody country, he that goes firft fometimes carries a very
thick bufh before him, and as they all follow
each other in a file, the laft hides the marks of
their feet, by putting the leaves on the ground
on which they went in order again, fo as to
leave no veftiges that might betray them.

The chief things by which they difcover their
enemies are the fmoke of their fires, which
they can fmell to a very great diftance, and their
tracks or footfteps, which they can diftinguifh
in an incredible manner. One day an Indian
fhewed me, in a place where I had feen nothing,
the footfteps of fome *Frenchmen*, *Indians*, and
Negroes, and the time when they had gone that
way; I own that this knowledge is amazing: it
may well be faid, that when the *Indians* apply
to any fingle thing, they excel in it.

Their

Their art of war confifts, as you fee, in vigilance, attention to prevent furprife, and to attack the enemy unprepared, in patience and ftrength to fupport hunger, thirft, the rigours of the weather, and the labours and fatigues infeparable from war.

He that has done a fine action carries the fcalp of his dead enemy as a trophy, and gets the mark of it made on his body, then he mourns for him, and during that time, which lafts a month, he muft not comb himfelf; and when his head itches, he is only allowed to fcratch it with a little rod, which he ties to his wrift for that purpofe.

The *Choctaws* and their wives are very uncleanly, living chiefly in places at a diftance from rivers. They have no kind of religious fervice, they live without troubling their heads with futurity, and however believe that they have an immortal foul. They have a great veneration for their dead, whom they do not bury. When a *Choctaw* dies, his corpfe is expofed upon a bier, made on purpofe, of cyprefs bark, and placed on four pofts fifteen feet high. When the worms have confumed all the flefh, the whole family affembles; fome one difmembers the fkeleton,

leton, and plucks off all the mufcles, nerves and tendons that ftill remain ; they bury them and depofit the bones in a cheft, after colouring the head with vermillion. The relations weep during this ceremony, which is followed by a feaft, with which thofe friends are treated who come to pay their compliments of condolence; after that, the remains of their late relation are brought to the common burying ground, and put in the place where his anceftor's bones were depofited. During the performance of thefe fad ceremonies, a deep filence is obferved, they neither fing nor dance, and every one goes home weeping.

In the firft days of November they celebrate a great feaft, which they call the feaft of the dead, or of the fouls ; all the families then go to the burying-ground, and with tears in their eyes vifit the chefts which contain the relics of relations, and when they return, they give a great treat, which finifhes the feaft.

It may be faid in praife of thefe *Americans*, that the friendfhip fubfifting among the relations, a thing uncommon in *Europe*, is worthy of imitation. I have mentioned fome inftances of it which exceed thofe of antiquity. The mutual
love

love of the *Indians* towards each other, inclines them to affift each other when they are infirm. This fincere love particularly fhews itfelf in the laft duties which they pay to their friends and relations by their tears and grief, even then, when they exift no more.

The *Indians* in general have a great veneration for their doctors or jugglers, who are real quacks, that impofe upon the people, and live handfomely at their expence. They have a great authority among the *Indians*, and the latter go to them upon every occafion for their advice; they confult them as oracles. When a *Chactaw* is fick, he gives all he has in order to be cured by them; but if the patient dies, his relations attribute his death to the phyfic, and not to his indifpofition; and can confequently kill the doctor if they have a mind to do it *; however, this cafe fcarce ever happens, as they generally have an excufe at hand. Thefe doctors are, however, acquainted with feveral excellent plants for curing the difeafes common in their country;

---

* There are, likewife, people in *France*, who lay the death of their relations to the charge of the phyfician, and refemble the Indians very much in their thoughts on this fubject.

country; they know a certain remedy for the bite of rattle fnakes, and other poifonous animals.

When the *Indians* are wounded with a bullet or an arrow, the doctors or jugglers begin with fucking the wound of the patient, and fpitting out the blood : they never employ lint, or tents, in their chirugical operations; but they have the powder of a root, which they blow into the wound, to accelerate its fuppuration, and they make ufe of another which dries and heals it; they preferve wounds from mortification, by bathing them with a decoction of fome roots, which they know *.

When they are tired and exceffively fatigued, after returning from a war, or from a hunt, they ufe fweating in ftoves †, as a reftorative.

In

---

* M. *de Boffu* would have very much obliged all the world, by making ufe of his influence over the Indians, which he repeatedly mentions, in order to get from them the knowledge of fuch plants as they employ in their feveral difeafes and aliments : this would have been really ufeful, and a proof of his humanity and curious inquiries.   F.

† Thefe ftoves are round huts, built like ovens in the middle

In thefe baths they boil all forts of medicinal
and odoriferous herbs, whofe effences and falts
rifing with the fteam of the water, enter into
the body of the afflicted perfon, and reftores his
loft forces. This remedy is equally good for
abating and deftroying all kinds of pains; of
courfe you fee no Indian affected with the gout,
the gravel, and other diftempers which we are
fubject to in Europe; but this may likewife be
attributed to their frequent bodily exercifes.
You fee no great Dutch bellies there, nor any
great tumours under the chin, fuch as the Pied-
montefe wens.

The Chactaws put a firm belief in enchanters
and magicians, and when they meet with one
fuch pretended forcerer, they cut off his head
* without any ceremony.

I faw an Indian of the nation of *Chactaws*,
who had lately been baptized: as he had no
luck

---

middle of the villages; they are kept in order by an *Alexi,*
or public doctor.

* In 1752, when I was at *Mobile*, I faw an Indian whom
the others killed with a hatchet, becaufe he pretended to be
a forcerer. The other Indians attributed to him all the
misfortunes that happen to their nation.

luck in hunting like his companions, he imagined he was bewitched; he went immediately
to Father *Lefévre* the Jefuit * who had converted
him, and told him that his *medicine* or trick was
good for nothing, becaufe fince he had practifed
it upon him, he could kill no ftags or roe-deer;
he therefore defired he would take off his enchantment again. The Jefuit, in order to avoid
the refentment of this Indian, did as if he anni-
hilated the baptifmal ceremony. Some time after, this Indian killed a roe-deer, either by accident, or by his own fkill, and thus thought
himfelf freed from the enchantment, and was
content.

The mind of this nation in general, is very
rough and unpolifhed. Though one tells them
ever fo much of the myfteries of our religion,
they always anfwer, that what we fay is above
their underftanding. They have, befides, very bad
morals, moft of them being addicted to fodomy.
Thofe defiled men, wear long hair, and a little
petticoat like the women, who defpife them very
much.

The

---

* The Indians call the Jefuits the men with the black
robe; they fay that they are not like other men, and call
them women, in derifion.

The *Chactaws* are very active and merry; they have a play at ball, at which they are very expert; they invite the inhabitants of the neigh-bouring villages to it, exciting them by many fmart fayings. The men and women affemble in their beft ornaments, they pafs the whole day in finging and dancing; they even dance all the night to the found of the drum and *chichikois.*

The inhabitants of each village are diftin-guifhed by a feparate fire, which they light in the middle of a great meadow. The next day is that appointed for the match; they agree upon a mark or aim about fixty yards off, and diftin-guifhed by two great poles, between which, the ball is to pafs. They generally count fixteen till the game is up. They are forty on each fide, and every one has a battledoor in his hand, about two feet and a half long, made very nearly in the form of ours, of walnut or chef-nut wood, and covered with roe-fkins.

An old man ftands in the middle of the place appropriated to the play, and throws up into the air a ball of roe-fkins, rolled about each other. The players then run, and endeavour to ftrike the ball with their battledoors; it is a pleafure to
fee

fee them run naked, painted with various colours, having a tyger's tail faftened behind, and
feathers on their heads and arms, which move
as they run, and have a very odd effect: they
pufh and throw each other down; he that has
been expert enough to get the ball, fends it to
his party; thofe of the oppofite party run at
him who has feized the ball, and fend it back to
their fide; and thus they difpute it to each
other reciprocally, with fuch an ardour, that
they fometimes diflocate their fhoulders by it.
The players are never difpleafed; fome old men,
who affift at the play, become mediators, and
determine, that the play is only intended as a
recreation, and not as an opportunity of quar-
relling. The wagers are confiderable; the women bet among themfelves.

When the players have given over, the women affemble among themfelves to revenge their
hufbands who have loft the game. The battledoor they make ufe of, differs from that of the
men, in being bent; they all are very active,
and run againft each other with extreme fwift-
nefs, pufhing each other like the men, they having the fame drefs, except on thofe parts which
modefty teaches them to cover. They only put

rouge on their cheeks, and vermillion, inſtead of powder, in their hair.

After playing well on both ſides all the day long, every one retires with his glory or ſhame, but without rancour, promiſing to play again another time as well as they can : thus the Indians both men and women, exerciſe themſelves in running ; they are likewiſe very ſwift, for I have ſeen ſome run as faſt as ſtags.

The children exerciſe themſelves in ſhooting with a bow and arrows for prizes ; he that ſhoots beſt, gets the prize of praiſe from an old man, who calls him an apprentice warrior ; thus they are formed by emulation, without corporal puniſhment ; they are very expert in ſhooting with an inſtrument made of reeds about ſeven feet long, into which they put a little arrow, feathered with the wool of a thiſtle, and in aiming at an object, they blow into the tube, and often hit the aim, and frequently kill little birds with it.

Almoſt all the aſſemblies of the *Chaɛtaws* are held in night-time. Though they are barbarous and ferocious, it is neceſſary, in order to gain their confidence, to take great care to keep your

promiſes

promifes to them, without which, they treat you
with the greateft contempt, proudly telling you
that you are a liar, an epithet which the *Indians*
have given to the prefent governor, whom
they call *Oulabé Mingo*, i. e. the lying
chief.

When the women are with child, their hufbands abftain from falt, and from pork, for fear
thofe aliments might do harm to their children.
The women never lie-in in their huts; they go
into the woods to be delivered, without receiving any affiftance.

As foon as they are delivered, they wafh their
infants. The mothers apply a mafs of earth
to the foreheads of their children, to make
them have flat heads, and as they get more
ftrength they increafe the bulk, it being a beauty
among thefe people to have a flat head. They
never fwaddle their children.

They never wean their children till they are
difgufted with their mother's milk. I have feen
fome children grown up fo as to be able to tell
the mother, *fet down, that I may fuckle,* and the
mother immediately fat down. Their cradle is
made of reeds, they put their children into it fo

that

that their head lies three or four inches lower than the reft of the body, therefore you never fee any contracted or hump-backed people amongft them. The women leave the huts in their catamenia, which the Indians call marks of valour. During that time, they are obliged to prepare their own meat and drink, and they do not return among men, till they are thoroughly purified. The Indians believe, that if they come near a woman in that ftate, they would fall fick, and that if they went to war after it, they would have bad luck.

Though the *Indians* only value themfelves upon their origin from the fide of the women, yet the latter are not allowed to correct the boys; they have only an authority over their daughters. If a mother fhould ftrike her fon, fhe would be reprimanded and ftruck again; but if the boy difobeys her, fhe muft bring him to an old man, who inflicts a punifhment on him, and then throws fome frefh water over his body.

If a woman commits an infidelity, fhe muft *pafs through the meadow*, i. e. all the young men, and fometimes even the old ones, fatisfy their brutality on her, by turns. Such is the punifhment

ment of adultery among the *Chactaws.* Sometimes the guilty woman, has the good luck, after this infamy, to find a mean fellow, who takes her as his wife, under the pretence that she must be disgusted with a criminal conduct, that has drawn such a punishment on her, and that she will consequently behave better for the future. Be this as it will, she is always looked upon as a depraved and immoral woman.

Before I finish my letter I must say a word of the *Tchicachas,* or *Chicksaws.* This nation is not so numerous as the *Chactaws,* but more terrible, on account of their intrepidity. All the northern and southern *Indian nations,* and even the *French,* have attacked them, without ever being able to drive them out of their country, which is the finest and most fruitful on the continent. The *Chicksaws* are tall, well made, and of an unparalleled courage. In 1752 and 1753, they attacked Mess, *Benoist* and *de Reggio,* who commanded the convoys from the *Illinois* station, descending the river *Missisippi*: these *Indians* always choose some advantageous situation, to make an attack in, their most common post is at the rocks of *Prudhomme,* the river being

ing

ing narrow there, they can annoy the boats, which have no decks.

It is believed that the *Chickſaws* killed Meſſ. *Bouſſelet* and *de la Morliere*; theſe two officers, though they were very brave, fell into an ambuſcade for want of experience, not knowing the topography of the country they were in any more than general *Braddock*. An officer ought, therefore, always to apply to that, in order to avoid ſurpriſes, or elſe he ſhould always be on the defenſive and prepared.

The *Engliſh* have always been in alliance with theſe valiant warriors; they have always traded with them, and ſupplied all their wants.

The *Indians* of this nation ride well on horſe-back : they leave the care of cultivating and ſowing their grounds to their women, who are handſome and cleanly. When a *Chickſaw* has killed a roe-deer, he tells his wife whereabouts it lies ; ſhe goes to fetch it, dreſſes it, and ſerves it up to her huſband : the women never eat with the men, who ſeem very indifferent about them, but really love them better than any other nation.

The

The *Tchicachas*, or *Chickfaws*, only punifh adultery with whipping the two offenders who have been caught in the fact, making them run naked through the village ; after which the hufband repudiates his wife.

As thefe *Indians* gave fhelter to the *Natches*, after the maffacre of the *French*, the latter armed in 1736 againft, and attacked them, with the united forces of the whole colony, but without fuccefs.

M. *d'Artaguette* major and governor for the king, in the country of the *Illinois*, came to join M. *de Bienville* the governor of *Louifiana* ; he brought him the troops of the *Illinois*, and from the frontiers of *Canada*, but the army which that officer commanded, was furprifed and defeated, becaufe he had been abandoned by the *Indians*, who were our allies. M. *d'Artaguette* was taken, with feven officers, and about twentyfix foldiers and inhabitants, by the *Chickfaws*, who burnt them alive ; among them was the Father *Senat* à Jefuit, who went with M. *d'Artaguette* in the quality of chaplain. The detail of this tragic feene has been related by a ferjeant, called *Louis Gamot*, who was a fpectator of the fad fate which his companions underwent ; he

X 4

was

referved to be burnt laft, but he efcaped by an odd ftratagem. As he was acquainted with the language of the *Indians*, he employed it on this occafion to utter invectives againft them ; and getting loofe, he threw all he found near him at their heads, faying, you are dogs, becaufe you have burnt my chiefs ; I will be burnt too, I fear neither fire nor death, for I am a true man, make me fuffer much, becaufe I defire it. The *Chickfaws*, feeing his refolution, looked upon him as an extraordinary fellow, and granted him his life ; he was afterwards ranfomed by an *Englishman* from *Carolina*, and is now at *Charlestown* the capital of that colony.

In another expedition againft the *Tchicachas*, which was undertaken on the 26th of May in the fame year, and commanded by M. *de Bienville*, we had not any more fuccefs ; many brave officers loft their lives in it, and the major-general of the army, and the adjutant received fuch dangerous wounds, that the laft died of them. I have heard from the Chevalier *de Lucer*, who is of a Swifs offspring, that his father, who ferved as captain in our troops, had been in this unlucky expedition ; this officer has likewife told me the ftory of the Chevalier *de Grondel*, who now belongs to the garrifon of *Mobile*, and commands

commands the Swifs troop of the regiment of
Halwill, belonging to the fervice of the marines;
he had then the command of a detachment of
grenadiers of the regiment of *Karrer*, in M. *de
Bienville*'s army againft the *Chickfaws*.

In order to abridge the account of this affair,
I fhall only fay, that this officer, joining fidelity
and bravery natural to his nation, to the impe-
tuofity of youth, received five fhot in his body
during the attack.   As he remained on the field
of battle after the retreat, he was juft going to
become the objeċt of the enemy's vengeance and
fury, if feveral foldiers of his troop had not generoufly expofed their lives to fave his, notwithftanding the balls and arrows which were
fent at them from the fort of the *Chickfaws*,
killed five of them one after another.

However, one, without fearing the danger,
returned to the field, and happily arrived in his
troop carrying his officer on his fhoulders.   The
chief furgeon of the army tried all he knew to
cure him, and the general, who values military
merit, did not fail to give in an account of the
officer's behaviour at court; and M. *de Maure-
pas*, in confideration of the wounds M. *de Grondel* had received, granted him an extraordinary
grati-

gratification, till he could get the crofs of *St. Louis.*

The foldier * who faved him at the peril of his life, was immediately made ferjeant at the head of his troop. You fee, Sir, by this fhort account, how worthy of admiration that well-eftablifhed fubordination is, among the troops of the *Helvetic* body, that are fo inviolably attached to the fervice of our King, and how much thofe that keep it in force feel the happy effects of it.

The action of thefe foldiers, which was really an heroic one, well deferves that their names fhould be tranfmitted to pofterity.

In 1754, the Baron *de Porneuf* imparted to me his intention of going upon a difcovery into the weft of *Louifiana*, up the *Miffifippi* and the river *Miffouris*, the fources of which are unknown to us. This officer, who is a *Canadian*, has the proper qualities for undertaking fuch an expedition ; but the war which arofe between *France* and *England*, on account of the boundaries

---

* His name was *Regniffe.*

ries of thefe countries, has been an obftacle to the execution of this projeĉt.

I can affure you, that I fhould have been very happy to accompany him, both for the honour of my King and for my own fatisfaĉtion ; for, notwithftanding the fatigues and dangers I have undergone in my voyages, I have never been difgufted or tired out of patience. Misfortunes pafs like dreams, and I fee nothing fo happy as the life of a traveller; he conftantly fees new objeĉts, which inftruĉt and amufe him at the fame time. His mind is cultivated in an agreeable manner, he learns to read the great book of the univerfe, which cannot be read in a library, where there are as many fyftems, opinions, and contradiĉtions, as authors. If you were in my place, you would have room to make philofophical refleĉtions. I am, S I R, &c.

*At the fort of Tombekbé, the
30th of September* 1759.

P. S. As I may perhaps not meet with an opportunity of writing to you this good while, on account of the war, I fhall add here an abftraĉt concerning the differences which have arifen between

tween us and the *Chaktaws*. Some time after the war with the *Tchikachas* or *Chickfaws*, the *French* had fome quarrels with a party of *Chaclaws*, who followed the intereft of a prince of their nation called the *Red Shoe*, who was infolent, and committed feveral hoftilities againft the *French*. M. *de Vaudreuil*, then governor of *Louifiana*, having heard of this action, and what gave occafion to it, immediately forbid all the *French* to go to that nation, and commanded them not to fell them any arms or ammunition, in order to ftop thefe commotions foon, and without bloodfhed.

The Marquis *de Vaudreuil*, after thefe precautions, fent to the fovereign of the nation, to inquire whether he was angry with the *French*, as the *Red Shoe*; the fovereign anfwered, by means of the interpreter, that he was the friend of the *French*; that his general, meaning Prince *Red Shoe*, had loft his fenfes.

After this anfwer, he got a prefent, but was much furprifed to find neither arms nor powder and fhot in it, at a time when he was our friend as before. This proceeding, together with the prohibition of felling them arms, which they knew had been iffued out, redoubled their aftonifhment, niſhment, and brought them to an explication with the governor, who told them, that our people would not treat with them concerning arms and ammunition, as long as the *Red Shoe* had not found his wits again ; becauſe, if they got powder, they could not help, being all brothers, to give a ſhare of it to the warriors of captain or chief *Red Shoe*. This anſwer determined them to ſpeak to the tribes that inſulted us ; they told them, if they did not ſoon go with the calumet to the *French*, they themſelves would go to war againſt them as rebels. This threat made them aſk peace, and offer a reparation to the *French*, who were not in a condition to ſuſtain a war againſt ſo numerous a nation.

Thus M. *de Vaudreuil*, as a wiſe politician, put a ſtop to this war, without expences to the ſtate, and without expoſing a ſingle man ; it was M. *de Grand-pré*, a captain of our troops, who was charged with this important negociation ; the Marquis could not pitch upon a fitter perſon. M. *de Grand-pré* is a *Canadian*, and ſerves the King with zeal, bravery, and diſintereſtedneſs. I was upon the point of going to ſerve under him at Fort *Tombekbé* among the *Chaɛ́taws*, when I firſt arrived here in 1751.

L E T-

L E T T E R   XIX.

To the fame.

The Author returns to Mobile. *Remarkable Events
which happened in the* Cat's Ifle. *Tragic Death
of the Sieur* Duroux *governor of that ifle.*

S I R,

I AM now returned from my voyage
up the river of *Tombekbé.* I have fulfilled this important and troublefome
miffion, to the fatisfaction of my fuperiors. In
waiting for my recal to *New Orleans,* my curiofity led me to vifit the little ifles on the coaft of
Louifiana.

The ifle of *Maffacre* was the firft where the
French made any fettlements. It got its name
becaufe the *French,* when they landed there,
found a great quantity of human fkeletons
but

but could not diftinguifh whether they were of *Spaniards* or *Indians*.

It has fince been called the *Dauphin* ifle*. It was peopled by degrees; they built magazines, a fort, and barracks there.

In

---

* 'It muft not be confounded with that which is mentioned in the relation of the firft voyage of the Eaft India company to the ifle of *Madagafcar*, which they called too precipitately the *Dauphin*'s ifland.

The author of this relation, who wrote in 1665, and had done that fame voyage, agrees that the *Englifh* and *Dutch*, who were already eftablifhed in *India*, were the models which M, *de Colbert* propofed to imitate, and afterwards to furpafs; but all the projects of that worthy minifter proved abortive, both by the imprudence and vanity peculiar to the nation, and by the mifmanagement of thofe who were at the head of affairs.

The fame author adds, that he only found there " violent " and unfkilful men, ill chofen officers, incapable of the oc- " cupation they were intended for; whereas they ought to " have been men above the coarfer paffions, with no other " inclinations than for the good of their country, which " ought to be the rule by which every one fhould be guided " who wifhes to acquit himfelf with honour."

It feems to me, that this ufeful leffon fhould be graved into the hearts of all thofe who go to our colonies with fome authority.

I have

In 1717, the entrance of the harbour was stopped up by a prodigious quantity of sand, collected together by a hurricane; the whole isle was almost overflowed, and great numbers of cattle were drowned; it was neceffary to seek another port, and they chose the isle *Surgere*, which has since been called *Ship Ifland*; it has a pretty good harbour. In 1722 M. *de Bienville* transported every one from thence to *New Orleans*, and that place became the capital of *Louifiana*.

Six leagues from the *Ship Ifland* is the *Cats Ifle*, so called on account of the number of wild cats which have been found there. This isle is only remarkable on account of the murders and robberies which have been committed there during the command of two officers, who were fent thither by M. *de Kerlerec*, governor of *Louifiana*.

In 1757, he appointed the Sieur *Duroux* chief commander of this isle, and gave him a detachment

---

I have chosen this piece of history as an example, which has a particular fimilarity with what is seen every day in our colonies. There are, however, governors and intendants, that must not be confounded with those who have got fortunes with rapidity, and in an odious manner, from the public miseries, and from the blood of many unhappy people.

ment of troops from the marines, and from the Swifs regiment of *Halwyl*.

The Sieur *Duroux* was no fooner come thither, than he looked upon himfelf as abfolute; he immediately affumed the right of having a garden made by the foldiers of the garrifon; he likewife employed them to make for him lime from fhells, and charcoal, but he never paid them; and thofe who refufed to fubmit to thefe vexations, were faftened quite naked to a tree, and expofed to the infupportable attacks of the *maringoins* or gnats. This was the punifhment which the officer made the foldiers of his garrifon undergo; an unworthy treatment, unexampled even among barbarians.

The Sieur *Duroux* obliged them to make their bread of the flour faved from the wreck of a Spanifh fhip, which was loft on the coaft; and fold for his own account the King's flour, intended for the ufe of the garrifon. This repeated bad ufage from this commander, determined fome foldiers to go to *New Orleans*, in order to complain to the governor, to whom they fhewed fome of the bad bread they were forced to eat; but M. *de Kerlerec* paid no regard to their juft remonftrances, and fent them back at the

difçretion

discretion of their commander. Then these wretches, fearing his resentment, resolved to make an example of him, which they executed in ceremony.

One day, when that officer was gone out a hunting in a neighbouring little isle, the revolted troop took their measures for executing their plot, which was to murder the Sieur *Duroux*. So strange a resolution could only be occasioned by their not having obtained the desired justice from the governor. If an officer superior to M. *Duroux* had been sent in his place, and the latter left to command as the second officer, this misfortune would have been avoided.

As he returned from hunting, the sentinel, perceiving the boat at sea, hoisted the *French* flag, upon which the garrison took to arms, and went out into the field. The rebellious soldiers advancing to the shore with their corporal at their head, called to the boat by means of a speaking trumpet, according to custom; the Sieur *Duroux* answered, "*Commander*;" he lands, and as he sets his foot on shore, the corporal gives the signal, and at the same instant the soldiers fire, and their commander falls, pierced with wounds;

wounds; the foldiers then ftripped him, and threw his corpfe into the fea. Such was the burial and the punifhment of this petty tyrant, who was regretted by nobody, for he had no other recommendation than that of the Sieur *Thiton*, the governor's firft fecretary. The foldiers, become mafters of the ifle, fet at liberty an inhabitant whofe name was *Beaudrot*, who had been unjuftly imprifoned by the late commander. The Sieur *Duroux* had affumed the privileges of an admiral of France, and pretended to fhare with the foldiers and inhabitants all that they fhould fave of any veffel wrecked upon the *Cats Ifland*; and all that refufed to pay him his fhare were feverely punifhed, as if they had committed fome great crime. This was the crime of *Beaudrot*; he was put in irons becaufe he would not fhare fome goods with the commander, which he had faved from the wreck of a *Spanifh* fhip called the *Situart*, which was wrecked on the ifle in 1758.

- The foldiers who had killed M. *Duroux*, having afterwards pillaged the effects belonging to the King in the *Cats Ifle*, took the inhabitant whom they had fet free, and obliged him to bring them into the road to the Englifh colony of *Carolina*. When they arrived in the country

of

of a great Indian chief, whom the Europeans
have ftiled Emperor of the *Kawytas*, they fent
back *Beaudrot* with a certificate, which proved
that he had been obliged to ferve them as a
guide. Part of this troop went towards the
Englifh ; but thofe who remained among the Indians, were foon feized by order of M. *de Montberaut*, then governor of the fort at the *Allibamons* ; among this laft party was a corporal of
the regiment of *Halwyl*, who, in order to avoid
being fawed afunder, as is ufual among the
Swifs, killed himfelf with a knife, which he
wore hung from his neck, as the Indians do.

M. *de Beaudin*, an officer of the garrifon, was
fent with a detachment, in order to conduct the
criminals to *Mobile*. During this interval, the
two fons of *Beaudrot* arrived at *Mobile* from *New
Orleans*, and brought, without knowing it, an
order from the governor to M. *de Velle*, who
commanded at *Mobile*, for arrefting their father;
who was in his habitation with great fecurity; he
returned to prifon without reluctance, not knowing that the deferters whom he had guided were
taken. M. *de Velle* tranfmitted the criminals to
New Orleans, where a court-martial was held to
judge them.

Beaudrot

Beaudrot the inhabitant, for guiding the murderers of the governor of *Cats Iſle*, was ſenten-
ced to be broke upon the wheel, and his .corpſe
to be thrown into the river; which was accordingly executed; a ſoldier ſuffered the ſame puniſhment, and a Swiſs was ſawed alive through
the middle of his body.

When one reflects upon the fate of the unhappy *Beaudrot*, it is eaſily perceived that he was
judged contrary to form, and by military men,
who were ignorant of civil and criminal laws, as
he could not have deſerved the cruel puniſhment
which he underwent. If politics require that
for preſerving public ſafety, no crime ſhould be
left untuniſhed, juſtice demands in favour of
humanity, that the judge ſhould always be more
afraid of puniſhing too much than too little,
according to the axiom, *It is better to let an hundred guilty men eſcape, than to puniſh one ſingle innocent man.*

If the man ought to be puniſhed in order to
ſerve as an example, according to this law, the
puniſhment might have been mitigated in favour of his wife and four children, whom his
death threw into the greateſt deſolation; among
the four children was a girl of an admirable
Y 3   figure,

figure, who was admired in the whole colony for her beauty, and ſtill more for her virtue ; this charming Creole, and the reſt of the family, are retired into an habitation far from the commerce of men, to lament the death of their unhappy father.

This unhappy man had been ſuccefsfully employed in ſome important negociations with the *Indians*, with whom he was in high eſteem. He ſpoke their language, and, from experience, he knew the ſituation of the country as well as themſelves. He had likewiſe an extraordinary bodily ſtrength. All theſe qualities had ſo far gained him the eſteem and friendſhip of the *Chaꞔaws*, who had adopted him into their nation, that they would certainly have revolted on his account, had not M. *de Velle* * wiſely taken care to keep his impriſonment and execution from coming to their knowledge.

After the tragic death of the Sieur *Duroux*, M. *de Kerlerec* fixed upon the Sieur *de Cha——* to ſucceed to the command of the *Cats Iſland*.

That

* This officer knows that nation perfectly well, having been governor of *Tombekbé* for ſeveral years ; the *Indians* eſteemed him much on account of his bravery and diſintereſted behaviour.

That officer fet out from *New Orleans* in 1758, with a garrifon compofed of foldiers and inhabitants of the capital ; but the inhabitants were all vagrants, whom the magiftrates fent in their own ftead, with the governor's confent, for the fervice of the place.

Thefe vagabonds ftayed in the *Cats Ifle* as long as thofe citizens paid them, whofe bufinefs it was to guard the place. You may well imagine, that a body of fuch troops, who are not alternately relieved in their pofts, according to the rule of fervice, take opportunities to lay fchemes for deferting, as it has happened in many ftations of *Louifiana*.

In March 1759 there appeared, in fight of this ifland, a three-mafted fhip, belonging to M. *St. Criq*, a merchant, who had bought her at the *Havannah* ; her cargo confifted in fugar, coffee, taffias, cables, and fome warlike ftores. The crew were merely Spanifh failors, who abandoned Captain *St. Criq* upon the coaft of *Louifiana* near *Balife* ; this obliged him to embark in his long-boat, with a few men who remained with him. He arrived at *New Orleans*, and addreffed himfelf to M. *de Belle-Ifle*, fort-major and commander during the governor's

abfence ;

abfence; he begged this officer to give him people, in order to go out in fearch of his fhip,
which could only be loft on the coaft of the *Cats
Ifland*.

M. *de Belle-Ifle* gave the Sieur *St. Criq* an intelligent ferjeant and ten foldiers, to navigate
his fhip ; at the fame time he wrote to the Sieur
C——: " That if this fhip were loft near his
" ftation, he fhould immediately place a guard
" on her, and forbid, under pain of death, that
" nothing fhould be unloaded out of her, with-
" out the confent of the Sieur *St. Criq*, the pro-
" prietor ; and laftly, that he fhould not fail
" to conform to the orders of the King's marine,
" fpecified under the title *Shipwreck*," &c.   Unhappily for the Sieur *St. Criq* the advice of M. *de
Belle-Ifle* came too late ; the Sieur *de C——* had
already taken care to have the cargo of the fhip
unloaded by the foldiers and inhabitants, who
hid it in the neighbouring fands ; they took all
the neceffary precautions to cover this trick.
The Sieur *St. Criq* arrived at the *Cats Ifle*, put
the major's letter into the commander's hands,
and then went into his fhip with his people in order to fearch her ; but perceiving that he had
forgotten his pocket-book, in which he had the
bill of lading, he left her immediately, and
went

went on fhore to fetch it : a happy accident of
Providence ! he was but juft come on fhore,
when his fhip fuddenly took fire, and burnt with
fuch fiercenefs, that three men who were in the
hold were burnt to death : the others only efcaped by throwing themfelves into the fea, and
fwimming on fhore *.

The Sieur *St. Criq* complained to M. *de Kerle-*
rec; but after a long delay, the governor *obliged*
the captain to terminate his quarrel with the
Sieur *de C—*, the latter giving the former the
fum of 1500 livres. This commander being recalled to *New Orleans*, gave himfelf up to fuch
debaucheries, that he fcandalized the whole colony.

---

* At the time when the Sieur *St. Criq* reclaimed his fhip
with M. *de Bell-Ifle*, and received his orders addreffed to M.
de C—, to take care of the prefervation of the cargo, the
governor of the *Cats Ifle* wrote to M. *de Belle-Ifle* himfelf:
" That, on fuch a day, a fhip with three mafts was loft in
" fight of his ftation, and he having made figns without re-
" ceiving any anfwer, he took it to belong to the enemy,
" who kept his men in clofe quarters ; that he having arm-
" ed the boat belonging to his ftation, and going into it
" with all his people, after getting no anfwer upon a re-
" peated fignal, came on board the fhip, but found no living
" foul in her, and the cargo taken out of her ; he only
" found a cut cable upon the deck, and faw that the fhip
" was bored for twenty-fix guns.

ny. When he had confumed all that he had
gained by his iniquitous practices, he went on
board a Dutch ship from *Curaçao*, a colony belonging to that republic. The opinions are divided upon the clandeftine evafion of this officer; fome believe, that he efcaped in order to
avoid the punifhments which his crimes deferved; others think he was charged with papers
to court from the governor: the event will determine this.

It is fufficiently proved by this reftitution of
1500 livres on the part of the Sieur *de C----*,
that this commander had pillaged the fhip of
Captain *St. Criq*, getting 60,000 livres by it,
according to his own confeffion to the Sieur *la
Perliere*, who fucceeded him in the government
of *Cats Ifland*. He has however efcaped the capital punifhment which this piracy deferved *.
For the quoted order fays, " That all who fhall
" endanger the life of fhipwrecked perfons, and
" lay hands upon their goods, fhall be punifhed
" with death." This crime is fo enormous,
that, though one were not a Chriftian, natural
religion

---

* The Sieur *de C----*, hoping to enjoy the fruits of his
iniquity in France, died there as he had lived, that is, in
a debauch, by a decree of Providence.

religion engages us to affift the unhappy in time of danger. Such were the officers in whom the governor of *Louifiana* put confidence.

We have juft received advice, that a party of warriors of the nation of *Cherokees*, commanded by their chief of war called *Wolf*, have taken the fort *London* belonging to Great Britain, and that the Englifh governor of it, M. *Damery*, has been killed by the Indians, who have put earth in his mouth, faying, You dog, fince you are fo very greedy of earth, be fatisfied and gorged with it; they have done the fame to others.

If I do not fet out for *France*, I fhall write to you from *New Orleans*, concerning the difcord between the two chiefs of the colony, M. *de Kerlerec* the governor, and M. *de Rochemore* the *ordonnateur*. I am, S I R, &c.

At Fort Mobile, the 10*th*
of January 1760.

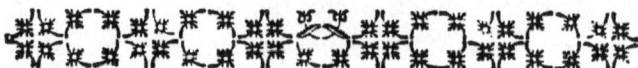

L E T T E R XX.

To the fame.

The Author goes to New Orleans. *Caufe of the Troubles which agitate that Place. Moving Relation of M.* de Belle-Ifle's *Captivity among the* Attakapas. *Curious Animals and falutary Simples to be met with in* Louifiana.

S I R,

I HAVE fo much news to communicate to you, that I know not where to begin : I wrote to you from *Tombekbé,* that every thing was in confufion in the capital ; indeed every body talks of quarrels and divifions ; avidity and intereft are every where lighting the torch of difcord. As I neither have, nor will have, any part in all thefe quarrels, and as I cannot fatisfy my zeal for the king's fervice in this colony, where every thing is in diforder,

I have

I have not ceafed to demand leave to return to
France. The moft faithful fubjects, who will
do their duty, are contradicted and difgraced,
and their zeal is rewarded with the moft cruel
perfecutions. But without enquiring minutely
into the fufferings of a number of brave officers,
moft of them ftill alive, I fhall only fpeak of
thofe which M. *de Belle-Ifle* has undergone. This
worthy officer, whofe probity and unqueftionable
conduct have gained him the good will and efteem of all worthy men, and efpecially of the
general officers, fuch as M. *de Perier*, M. *de Bienville*, and the Marquis *de Vaudreuil*, &c. well deferves that I fhould tell his ftory to you, having
heard it from himfelf with all its circumftances.

I fhall give you an account of what has happened during the forty-five years which he ferved
the king in this colony *. I fhall fay nothing but
truth,

---

* The hiftory of M. *de Belle-Ifle*, Chevalier of the royal
military order of *St. Louis*, Major of *New Orleans*, and who
has formerly ferved as Major General of the troops of the
marine in *Louifiana*, has been inferted in a *Relation of Louifiana* printed at Paris in 1758. The author of it left the colony in 1733, has forgotten the moft interefting circumftances,
and the facts he has mentioned, have been difowned by M..

de

truth, though fome circumftances may appear very wondrous.

As I know the goodnefs of your heart, I am fure you will pity the unhappy fate of this poor officer; great fouls are not afhamed to fhew that they are touched by the misfortunes of others: even the *Indians* fay, that he who is not fenfible to the fufferings of his brothers, is unworthy of bearing the name of a man, and that he ought to be avoided as the peft of fociety.

In 1719, M. *de Crozat* put *Louifiana* into the hands of the Weft India company, who fent a thoufand men to people it. M. *de Belle-Ifle* embarked in one of their fhips at port *l'Orient,* with fome other officers and volunteers, for the new colony. The winds and currents carried the fhip to the bay of *St. Bernard* in the Mexican gulph The captain fent his boat on fhore in order to fetch water. M. *de Belle-Ifle* and four of his companions went into the boat with the captains confent. Whilft the boat returned to the fhip, the officers went a hunting: the boat came on fhore again, and having taken

in

---

de Belle-Ifle himfelf: my relation is an abftract of a manufcript memoir, written by that officer's own hand.

in the neceffary provifion of frefh water, returned on board without the young officers, who
were not yet returned.

The captain is impatient, weighs anchor and
fets fail, leaving the five paffengers on fhore.
Their agitation and anxiety, when they returned to the fhore and found the boat and fhip
gone, may well be imagined. Thus being abandoned in an unknown country, they erred for a
long time upon the defart coaft, having the fea
on one fide, and a country inhabited by a nation
of cannibals on the other. They did not venture to quit the marfhy fhores of the fea ; they
were in fuch defpair of finding a remedy for
their misfortunes that they knew not what to
do : this alone was capable to make them lofe
their fenfes ; and then the thought of falling
into the hands of cannibals, troubled the imagination of thefe young Europeans. They went
along the fhore in the miflaken opinion, that the
fhip was gone to the weft, imploring divine
mercy, and complaining of their unhappy fate.
They lived upon infects and herbs, not knowing
whether they were good or bad ; what was moft
troublefome to them was the abundance of gnats
in that place, as they had nothing to defend
themfelves againft them. They continued feveral

veral days in this fituation. M. *de Belle-Ifle* had taken a young dog from the fhip, which was very fond of him. His companions were often tempted to kill him; their hunger was extreme : M. *de Belle-Ifle* gave the dog up to them, but would not kill it himfelf; one of his companions feized the dog; but he was fo weak, that as. he was going to ftrike with the knife, the dog efcaped, ran into the woods, and was not feen again. The four unhappy officers died with hunger one after another, in fight of M. *de Belle-Ifle*, who did all he could to dig them graves in the earth, or rather in the fand, with his own hands, to preferve their fad remains from the voracioufnefs of wild beafts : he paid this tribute to human nature in fighing over its miferies, nothing but the ftrength of his conftitution could make him furvive them. He was refolute enough, in order to fubfift, to eat the worms which he found in rotten wood. Some days after the death of his comrades, he faw at a diftance his dog holding fomething in his mouth; he called him, the creature came to him fawning, and with great demonftrations of joy, threw at his feet an *opoffum*; the dog howled, as if he would fay, I bring thee fomething to fupport life. The opoffums are good eating, and of the fize of a fucking pig. M.

de

de Belle-Iſle, having no other company than his dog, looked about for food every where. At night he always made a little intrenchment at the foot of a tree, in order to ſhelter himſelf againſt the wild beaſts. One day a tyger * came near the place, where he ſlept; his dog watched by his ſide, he ſaw the tyger, and ran at it with a prodigious howl. M. *de Belle-Iſle* awoke, and haſtened to his aſſiſtance; the tyger let the dog looſe, but had wounded him: his maſter was obliged to kill him, left he ſhould turn mad, and afterwards he eat him. Then being left alone in this deſart place, he fell on his knees, lifted up his hands to heaven, and thanked the Almighty for preſerving him till now; and reſigning himſelf to Providence he went into the country in order to ſeek for men. He ſoon found foot-ſteps, and followed them to the banks of a river, where finding a *piragua*, he croſſes the river in it. On the oppoſite ſhore were ſome *Indians*, drying human fleſh and fiſh; they were of the nation of the *Attakapas* †;

VOL. I.　　　Z　　　they

---

* By this muſt always be underſtood the *American* tyger, i. e. the *brown cat* of P. *Synopſis of Quad.* p. 179, and the *Cugucuara* of *Piſo* and *Margrave* in their *Nat. Hiſt. Braſil.*

† This name ſignifies men-eaters among the *American* nations.

they went towards M. *de Belle-Ifle*, whom they took for a ghoft, becaufe he was lean; he pointed to his mouth, and made figns of being hungry. The Indians would not kill him becaufe he was exceffively lean; they offered him fome human flefh, but he preferred fifh, of which he eat greedily. The *Indians* looked at this cloathed man, ftripped him naked and divided his cloaths among themfelves; they then carried him to their village in order to fatten him. There he had the good fortune to become the *dog* * of an old widow. He recovered his ftrength gradually; but was extremely fad, conftantly apprehending, that his hofts would facrifice him to their falfe deities, and afterwards make a feaft of his flefh; his imagination was always ftruck with the terrible fight of the feafts which thofe barbarians made of the flefh of their fatteft prifoners of war, which I cannot help fhuddering at, whilft I relate it. He always expected to receive a blow with the club, as foon as he fhould be fat. The Indians held a council,

---

tions. When they take an enemy in the wars, they make a great feaft and eat his flefh. They commonly live upon fifh and drink the *Caffine*. They can fpeak by figns, and hold long pantomime converfations.

* An expreffion which fignifies *flave*.

cil, in which they refolved that it would be fhameful and cowardly to kill a man, that did not come to them to do any harm, but to demand their hofpitality ; in confequence of this refolution, he remained a flave of the widow. The firft days of his flavery, though it was not a heavy one, were very difagreeable to him, becaufe he was obliged to take care of the little children of thefe men-eaters, and to carry them on his fhoulders, which was very troublefome to him ; for he was naked like them, having no more cloaths than were fufficient to make his nakednefs lefs indecent ; but the widow abovementioned, having taken him under her protection, he was better treated in the fequel.

As M. *de Bell-Ifle* was young and ftrong, he acquitted himfelf very well of his functions as a flave, and even gained the good graces of his miftrefs fo much, that fhe adopted him, and he was then fet at liberty, and looked upon as one belonging to the nation. He foon learnt the manner of converfing in pantomimes, and the art of ufing the bow and arrows as well as they could do it. They took him into the wars, where he fhewed them his dexterity, by killing one of their enemies with an arrow in their prefence, he was then acknowledged a true warrior.

Z 2

An-

Another *Indian* having killed a roebuck, they dried the flesh of the man and the roe, to make use of it as provisions on their expeditions. One day as they were walking, M. *de Belle-Isle* being hungry, asked for something to eat. An *Indian* gave him some human flesh, saying it was of the roe-buck. M. *de Belle-Isle* eat of it without knowing the cheat; and the Indian afterwards said to him : *Formerly thou didst make difficulty, but now thou canst eat man's flesh as well as ourselves :* at these words M. *de Belle-Isle* threw up all he had eaten.

About two years after his captivity, some deputies arrived at the *Attakapas*, from a nation who sent them the calumet of peace. A kind providential care ! This nation lived in *New Mexico*, and were the neighbours of the *Natchitoches*, where M. *de Hucheros de Saint Denis* commanded, who was beloved and respected by the deputies of this nation, though they lived on Spanish ground. After attentively considering M. *de Belle-Isle*, they told the *Attakapas*, that in the country from whence they came, there were white men like him : the *Attakapas* said he was a *dog*, whom they had found towards the great lake, where his comrades were starved to death; that they had brought him to their habitations,

where

where a woman had made him her slave; that they had taken him to war against a nation which they conquered in a battle, and that he had distinguished himself on that occasion, and shewed them his skill in sending an arrow, which killed one of their adversaries; that they had for that reason adopted him, and received him as a warrior.

This officer, who heard their conversation, did as if he took no notice of it; and immediately conceived the idea of returning to his country: he took one of the Indian deputies apart; and questioned him much about the white men he had seen. M. *de Belle-Isle* had luckily preserved his commission in a box; he made some ink with soot, and wrote with a crow-quill the following words: " *To the first chief of the* " *white men.* I am such and such a person, aban-". doned at the bay of *St. Bernard*; my comrades " died of hunger and wretchedness before my " face, and I am captive at the *Attakapas.*" This unhappy officer gave his commission to the *Indian*, telling him it was some speaking paper; that, by presenting it to the chief of the *French* in his country, he would be well received. The *Indian* believed, that this letter had something divine in it, because it was to speak for him to

the

the *French*. His countrymen wanted to take it
from him ; but he efcaped by fwimming acrofs
a river ; and left he fhould wet the letter, he
held it up in the air. This *Indian*, after a journey of one hundred and fifty leagues, arrived
at the *Natchitoches* *, an Indian nation. The
French commander there at that time being M.
Hucheros de St. Denis, an officer of diftinction,
known for having made the firft journey over
land from *Louifiana* to *Mexico*, where he married
the *Spanifh* governor's niece. The Indian gave
him M. *de Belle-Ifle*'s letter, and M. *de St. Denis*
received him very well, and made him many
prefents ; after which, this officer began to cry
after the manner of the Indians, who afked what
ailed him ? He anfwered, he wept for his brother who was a captive among the *Attakapas*.
As M. *de Saint Denis* was in great efteem with
the nations about him, the *Indian* who brought
the letter promifed to fetch M. *de Belle-Ifle*, and
fome other Indians joined him.

M. *de Saint Denis* gave them fome fhirts and a,
hat for M. *de Belle-Ifle*, and they fet out immediately, ten in number, on horfeback, and armed

---

* A ftation near *Mexico*. There is a fettlement of Indians
on the *Riviere Rouge*, or *Red-river*.

ed with guns; promifing to M. *de Saint Denis* to return in two *moons* time with his brother upon a horfe, which they led with them.

On arriving at the *Attakapas*, they difcharged their fire-arms feveral times, the explofion of which the other Indians took to be thunder: they gave M. *de Belle Ifle* the letter of M. *de Saint Denis*, which mentioned, that he had nothing to fear with thofe Indians, and that he rejoiced beforehand that he fhould fee him. The joy which this letter gave to the officer is inexpreffible; however he feared that the *Attakapas* would oppofe his departure. But the chief of the deputation made him get quickly on horfeback, and went off with his whole troop. The *Attakapas* being frightened with the report of the mufkets, did not venture to fay any thing, and the woman who had adopted M. *de Belle-Ifle* fhed tears. Thus this officer efcaped from a captivity, which might otherwife have lafted as long as his life.

The *Indian* who carried off M. *de Belle-Ifle* was as proud as *Hernando Cortez* when he conquered *Montezuma*, the laft emperor of *Mexico*. They arrived at the *Natchitoches*, but did not find M. *de Saint Denis* there; for he was gone to *Biloxis*,

Z 4   which

which was then the chief place of *Louiſiana*, *New Orleans* being not yet built.

M. *d'Orvilliers*, who commanded at the *Natchitoches* in M. *Saint Denis*'s abſence, ſent M. *de Belle-Iſle* and his eſcort to M. *de Bienville*, then governor of *Louiſiana*. That general embraced him, being happy to ſee him, and liberally rewarded his deliverers. Every one complimented him on his eſcape from this captivity; M. *de Bienville* gave him a ſuit of cloaths.

This officer has ſince been very uſeful to the governor, by his knowledge of the cuſtoms of the *Attakapas*, whom the Spaniards of *New Mexico* could never ſubdue, as they have done with the other nations of their empire.

M. *de Bienville* ſent a preſent to the *Attakapas*, and another to the widow who had adopted and protected M. *de Belle-Iſle*.

Theſe people, who did not expect this generoſity from the governor, ſent ambaſſadors * to him to thank him, and to make an alliance with the *French*.

---

* The chief of the embaſſy addreſſed the following ſpeech to M. de *Bienville*, which M. de *Belle-Iſle* interpreted; " My
" father,

French. M. *de Belle-Iſle*'s miſtreſs attended in perſon ; ſince this period the *French* have always been humanely treated by the *Attakapas*, who have at their deſire left off the barbarous cuſtom of eating human fleſh.

When the *Attakapas* came to *New Orleans*, they were well received by all the *French*, in gratitude of the reception M. *de Belle-Iſle* had met with among them ; for without them, he would have undergone the unhappy fate of his companions.

M. *de Bienville* ſometimes procured himſelf the diverſion of a pantomime with theſe cannibals, by means of M. *de Belle-Iſle*, who, as their pupil, converſed with them by geſtures. The *Attakapas* are armed with bows and very great arrows ; they cultivate maize, as the other *North American*

" father, the white man, whom thou ſeeſt here, is thy fleſh
" and blood, he was united to us by adoption. His brothers
" were ſtarved to death, if my nation had found them ſooner,
" they would live ſtill and enjoy the ſame prerogative."

The hoſpitality ſhewn to M. *de Belle-Iſle* by the *Attakapas*, convinced us, that we muſt regard their cruelty only as a fault of education, and that nature has planted ſentiments of humanity in their breaſt.

American nations do.   This part of the world is
of fuch an extent, that it has not yet been poffible to become acquainted with all the nations
in it, nor with its limits.

In 1759, M. *de Marigni de Mandeville**, an
officer of diftinction, formed the defign, with
the confent of the governor of *Louifiana*, of making new difcoveries towards the ifle of *Barata-
ria*, of which we know the coafts but very im-
perfectly: with this intent he made a general
map of the colony.   This officer has difcovered
this unknown country at his own expence, with
indefatigable zeal, which characterizes a worthy
citizen, who is always occupied for the glory of
his prince, and the enlargement of his poffeffions.

I have endeavoured, in my preceding letters,
to give you an abridgment of the hiftory of the
country, from the time of its difcovery till now,
and an idea of the fituation of its commerce, and
likewife of every thing that feemed inftructive
and amufing to me.   I do not believe I have
omitted any thing material, I fhall now finifh
                                                    our

---

* See the Memoirs of this officer, printed at Paris, by
Guillaume Defprès, in the ruë S. *Jacques* 1765.

our correfpondence by fome obfervations on the natural hiftory of this colony, of which you could learn nothing from the fpecial relations that are publifhed. You muft know then, Sir, that all the fruit-trees which have been tranf-ported thither from *Europe* fucceed very well there. M. *Fazende,* one of the fuperior council of *Louifiana,* has brought a fig-tree from *Provence,* the figs of which are excellent; as this tree is propagated by layers, it richly fupplies all the habitations with them. Among the fruit peculiar to this country, there is one called a battledoe, it has the figure and tafte of a pickled cucumber. This fruit is very common about *Mobile,* and it is very refrefhing.

The *piakmine* is a kind of medlar, called *ou-goufié* by the Indians; this fruit, which is no bigger than the European medlar, is yellow and red like an apricot; it is a very good aftringent, and an excellent remedy to ftop the dyfentery and bloody flux. The Indians make bread of it, in the form of ginger-bread, and dry it for their long voyages *.

The

---

* The piakmine has yet another virtue: take a quantity of its feeds, pound them, then infufe frefh water upon them,
which

The *Jafmine* fruit has the form and colour of a lemon; it is odoriferous, and taftes like Banian figs; it feeds refemble. beans; they are a poifon to hogs ‡.

Here are a number of orange and peach trees; and both the oranges and peaches are fo common in this colony, that they are left under the trees to rot.

There are apple-trees and plum-trees; and whole forefts of walnut-trees; of which there is a white kind or the *hiccory*, and another black; both kinds bear nuts; they are as in Europe of different goodnefs for eating; there are likewife fome walnuts as big as the fift, but they are bitter, having very thick and hard fhells. There is a tree which bears a fruit called *pacannes*; they are oblong like almonds, and more delicious:

the

---

which muft ftand upon them twenty-four hours: ftrain the water through a cloth and keep it in a bottle. When you are attacked with the gravel, drink a glafs full of the infufion fafting, and continue to do it till you are cured †.

† This is perhaps the perfimon, *diofpyros Virginiana* Linn. F.

‡ This plant feems to be one of the various kinds of *anora*, which grow over all the warmer parts of *North-America*. F;

the Indians make an oil of it, to feafon their *fa-gamitty* with.

It is a circumftance worthy of admiration, to fee the providence of the Creator, who has planted fuch a number of fruit-trees of various kinds in this part of the new world. There are thoufands of curious animals, known before neither by their fhape nor by their name, and of which men of the preceding ages have not even had an idea.

There are red and likewife white bays ; the latter bears a white flower like a tulip ; it is an exceeding bufhy tree, and would be an ornament to the gardens of European monarchs : the Indians call it the tree of peace *.

Near the banks of rivers there are vines, which climb fo high along the trees, that when the grapes are taken off, they can often make a whole barrel full of wine from a fingle ftock. Thefe vines grow without cultivation, and the wine that is made of them is very harfh

---

* This is probably either the *tuliptree*, *liriodendron tulipifera*. Linn. or the *laurus æftivalis*. Linn.   F.

harſh *. There are many mulberry-trees † in the woods, and their berries are very ſweet; there are likewiſe ſome that always keep the figure of ſhrubs, and their berries are made uſe of for jellies.

There is a tree in the woods full of ſpines of ſix inches in length; its wood is ſo hard, that it makes the edge of the hatchets' blunt, and ſometimes breaks them. The Indians, by means of fire, make mortars of it to cruſh their maize in. This tree bears pods about a foot long like *caſſia*; the fruit they contain is gummy and ſticking, having ſeveral ſeeds like beans. It is an excellent laxative, and the Indians take it as a purge.

There are reſinous trees (ſuch as pines, &c.) in the woods, which produce reſin and tar; there are likewiſe many trees, from which a kind of gum like turpentine runs down.

There

---

* The American foreſts have three kinds of vines; the *vitis labruſca, vulpina,* and *arborea,* Linn. And this, here mentioned, ſeems to be the laſt. F.

† The *morus rubra* Linn. is the mulberry-tree, known to grow in *North America.* F.

There is a fhrub which we call *cirier*, or the wax-tree, and it refembles an olive-tree. It bears little berries like juniper, they are melted in water *, and give a kind of wax for candles ; this wax is of a fine green, and has an aromatic fmell. The Sieur *Alexandre*, a furgeon and che-mift, is the firft that difcovered it here. The academy of fciences gave him a penfion for this difcovery. He has likewife found the method of bleaching it, as we do bees wax in *Europe*.

Whilft I was in *Louifiana*, the inhabitants got from *St. Domingo* plants of fugar-canes, in order to make plantations of them. M. *Dubreuil*, who commands the militia of citizens, was the firft planter that built a fugar-mill at *New Orleans*.

It is known, that fugar is made of the juice of a reed or cane, which is propagated by lay-ers ; it grows tall and thick, in proportion to the goodnefs of the foil. The canes have joints at certain diftances ; when thefe are ripe, which is eafily known by the yellow hue which they get, they are cut above the firft joint, which has no juice ; the leaves on both fides are plucked off;
the

* Boiling water. The tree is the candleberry myrtle, *myrica cerifera*. Linn. F.

the canes are made up into bundles, and brought to the mill, where they are crufhed between two wooden cylinders, covered with fteel. A negro puts the canes between the cylinders, which prefs all the juice out, which is received in a great hollow, from whence it goes through a leaden pipe into a refervoir, which leads it into the place where the ovens are, which are defti-ned to boil it in great boilers. When the juice is refined, it is poured into another boiler; it muft be continually ftirred, and boiled till it has a proper confiftency; and when the fugar is got to the firft ftate of perfection, it is put into forms of earthen ware, in order to be refined; it acquires the fecond degree of perfection by the opening being covered with clay to prevent the air from acting upon the fugar, and that it may not harden too much before it is refined by the feparation of fyrups and melaffes.

It is with the fcum of fugar that they make taffia or kill-devil. This liquor is prepared as brandy is in *France*; and goes through the ftill. The *Europeans* in *America* prefer it to brandy for curing of wounds. They likewife make rum with it.

In

In the country of the *Illinois* there is a little
fhrub, about three feet high, which bears a
fruit of the fize of a fmall apple, and of the
tafte of citrons. The woods there likewife contain chefnuts, and hazel-nuts of the fame kind
as in *France*.

Louifiana abounds with good fimples; among
them is the *ginfeng*, the root cf which is an
excellent reftorative, *jalap*, *rhubarb*, *fnake-
root*, *farfaparilla*, and *St. John's wort* *, of
which they make an excellent oil for healing
of wounds. The following is the Indian doctor's method of making the oil. They take an
earthen pot, and put the flowers of St. John's
wort in it, and fome bear's oil above it; the
pot or vafe is well ftopped up, and expofed to

VoL. I.   A a   the

---

* *Ginfeng* is the plant fo much in requeft in China; it is
Panax quinquefolium, Linn. See Oibeck's Voy. to China,
vol. i. p. 222. and Kalm's Travels into North America, vol.
iii. p. 114. and Catefby's Nat. Hift. of Carolina, app. t. 16.
——*Jalap* is the *Mirabilis* of Linnæus, there are feveral fpecies of it.——*Rhubarb* is the *Rheum* Linn. but probably not
the true one.——*Snake-root*; perhaps the *Polygala Senega*,
Linn. or elfe an *Ariftolochia*.——Sarfaparilla, *Smilax farfaparilla*, Linn.——St. John's wort, *Hypericum*, Linn. there
are many plants of this genus in *North America*; and it is
among the *defiderata* of the botanift to know what fpecies are
employed for medicinal ufes. F.

the morning fun; the heat concentrated in the vafe turns the oil of a red colour, and gives it an agreeable fmell, which cures and purifies all kinds of wounds. There are even plants which have the virtue of ferving as counter-poifons; but it is a rare and precious gift to man to know them, and to know how to make a proper ufe of them; the Creator has not granted this knowledge to all men. There are numerous fimples proper for cleanfing the mals of blood, and of which the Indians have a peculiar knowledge.

There are forefts of *faffafras* trees *, the wood of which is ufed in phyfic, and for dying; there is likewife the *copal* tree †, whofe gum is an excellent balfam, equal in goodnefs to the balfam of Peru; the animals which are wounded by hunters, cure themfelves by rubbing againft the tree from which this balfam exfudes, which has an aromatic fmell. The *Indians* have in their huts bitter gourds and calabafhes, of which latter they make a pectoral fyrup; *maiden-hair,* which is a good pectoral medicine, and the *caf-fine,*

---

* Saffafras-tree grows all over North America, it is *Laurus faffafras,* Linn.

† *Copal* tree grows only in the fouthern part of North America, *Rhus copallinum,* Linn.

fine, which is a good diuretic *. When the dose is strong, it excites a kind of convulsions; which, however, cease immediately. The *Allibamon* Indians call it the *liquor of valour.* The natives of *America* value their simples more than all the gold of *Mexico* and *Peru.*

You find several sorts of curious animals in *Louisiana*, which are unknown in *Europe.*

The wild ox is very large and strong; the French and the Indians make various uses of it; they eat its flesh, which they salt or dry; they make coverings of its hide. The wild bull is covered with a very fine wool, with which they make good matrasses; of its tallow they make candles, and its pizzles afford cords to the Indian bows. The Indians work its horns, and make them into *micouens* or spoons, and into powder-horns.

A a 2

The

---

* Bitter gourds, *Coloquintes, Cucumis colocynthis,* Linn.— Calabashes, *Cucurbita lagenaria,* Linn.—Maiden-hair, *Adiantum pedatum,* Linn. grows all over *North America,* from *Canada* down to *Virginia,* and is much esteemed as a medicinal herb. See *Kalm*'s Trav. to North Amer. vol. iii. p. 113.—Cassine is the *Prinos glaber,* Linn. mentioned in Letter XVI. p. 249. F.

The wild ox has a bunch or hump on its back * like a camel. It has long hair on the head like a goat, and wool on its body like ſheep, which the Indian women ſpin into ˙ threads.

On going towards the head of the river *Miſ-ſouris*, you find all ſorts of wild beaſts. The wild goats and their young ones are very common at certain ſeaſons †. Theſe animals are very lively and pretty ; the females have double furrows or ringlets to their horns, and are not ſo ˊ big as ours : the French that eat of them have aſſured me, that the young veniſon was as good

as

---

* The hump is ſituated on the ſhoulders. The animal has been deſcribed by *Linnæus* under the name of *Bos bijon*, and drawn by *Cateſby* in his *Nat. Hiſt. of Carolina*, app. t. 20. and in Mr. *Pennant's Synopſis of Quadrupeds*, p. 8. t. II. f. 2. F.

† This animal ſeems to be of the antelope kind, perhaps the *Temamaſama* of *Hernandez*, an animal which hitherto has not been noticed by our zoologiſts. It ſeems not to be an animal belonging to the goat kind, on account of the double ringlets or *cornichons* mentioned by the author. This would be perhaps a new animal ; and however it be, it will deſerve the attention of our natural hiſtorians. And as the Engliſh dominions now extend to the river Miſſiſippi, it would certainly be worth while to deſcribe the animals upon that river, and thoſe that fall into it. F.

as the beft mutton. As the *Indians* of thefe parts do not ufe our mufkets, they kill them with arrows; for thefe animals feed in the mountains, and when they are wounded they cannot climb fo eafily, and by that means the *Indians* catch them.

The hunters have likewife told me, that they had found a large kind of eagle in the woods, of the fpecies called the *royal eagle* *.

I think it my duty to mention to you the fingular manner in which the Indians hunt and take thefe birds, which the northern nations efteem very much, becaufe they adorn their calumets of peace with eagle's feathers, which they call *feathers of valour.*

This kind of hunting is referved for the diverfioh of old warriors, as it requires no exercife. The old man who intends to take eagles, firft of all examines the places which are moft frequented by them; after that, he brings flefh, the entrails of animals or dead fnakes to thofe fpots, and faftens thefe baits to fome fixed wood. The

A a 3   firft

---

* The royal eagle is the *Falco Chryfaëtos*, Linn. or *golden eagle*, Penn. Br. Zool. fol. 61. tab. A. & in 8vo vol. i. p. 121. F.

firſt eagle that comes there eats of it, grows familiar with the place, and attracts others of his
ſpecies thither, that greedily diſpute the prey
with each other. Then the old man digs a kind
of *niche* or hollow at the top of the hill; he
makes a chimney or vent to it which he ſtops
up with a bundle of fagots, on which he places
the baits: he ſuffers the bird to eat its fill; then
he puts his hands, which he has wrapt in a little
ſack of leather through ſome ſtraw under the
faggots; takes hold of the eagle's legs, pulls it
down, wraps it in his ox-hide, and ſo kills it.
If he is lucky enough to take five or ſix of them,
he is content, becauſe the feathers are an article
of trade throughout *North-America*. This way
of hunting is not very troubleſome: the baits
are taken together by the old man's children,
and the women ſend him victuals.

You likewiſe ſee hares* and white bears whoſe
ſkin is very fine and ſoft.† The *tygers* of Louiſiana differ from thoſe of Africa and South America,

---

* The American hares are already declared by *Prof. Kalm*,
vol. p. 105. to differ from the European ones; ſo that is im-
proper to think the American ones to be the ſame F.

† The white bear here mentioned, cannot be the great *Po-*
lar

rica, becaufe they have no fpots.‡ They take the roe-deer as cats do mice. As to the *tyger-cats*.§ they kill the wild oxen in the following manner. They get upon a tree, in a little path where the oxen are ufed to go to the river; and as they come by, the tyger-cats fall upon the necks of the oxen, bite through their throats and

A a 4   kill

---

lar bear, Penn. Synn. Quad. p. 192. to 20. f. 1. as this latter is only to be met with in the moft frigid parts of our globe; and the foft hair here mentioned will not admit to think of the polar bear, whofe hair is like briftles. The common black bear is fometimes found quite white in Siberia, and therefore it is not improbable that fome of thefe white bears are found in the interior parts of *North America*. Befides this, I find it neceffary, here to obferve, that the *black Virginia bear* feems to me to be a fpecies different from our European bears, my reafons for this opinion are thefe : *firft*, the European bear has never fo black a coat as the Virginian, *fecondly*, the fnout of the Virginian is longer, and the head fmaller than in our European ones ; *thirdly*, the European bear is more clumfy than the Virginian. F.

‡ The North American tyger is the *Caguacara* of Marggrave, or the *brown Cat*. Penn. Syn. quad. p. 179. In South America it is immenfely fierce on account of the heat of the climate, and miftakenly called a lion. F.

§ The American tyger-cat is the *pichou du fud* mentioned in *Kalm's Travels*, vol. 3. p. 275, and *Penn. Syn. quad. Cayenne Cat*. p. 182.

kill them; their ftrength and their horns are
rendered ufclefs by this treachery.

The *wood rat* or *Indian-rat* is of the fize of an
European cat; its head is like the head of a fox,
it has feet like a monkey, and the tail of a rat.*
This animal is very curious; I once killed a female that had feven young ones; what is moft
furprifing is to fee them all ftick faft to the teats,
where they grow, and continue till they are able
to run about; then they drop into a membrane
that forms a pouch: thofe young ones which I
faw were as big as new-born mice; nature has
furnifhed the female with this pouch under the
belly, which is covered with hair, as a retreat for
her young ones, when they are purfued, by
means of which the mother can fave them and
carry them off. Their flefh taftes like that of a
fucking pig; their hair is whitifh, and they have
likewife a down or wool like the beaver. This
pretended rat, lives in the woods upon the feeds
of beech-trees, upon chefnuts, walnuts, and
acorns. I have often eaten of them on my
voyages: their fat is very white and fine; a fine
pomatum or unguent is made of it for the He-
morrhoids.

Here

* This is the Virginian *Opoffum. Penn. Syn. quad.* p.
294. and *Didelphis marfupialis.* Linn.

Here is likewife an animal, which they call the *wood-cat*; it is of the fize of a fox, and nothing but its tail is like that of a cat. This creature is very fond of oyfters; it refembles a marmot in its figure; and may be tamed like a dog, licking and fawning upon its mafter, whom it follows every where; it takes its food with its paws, like a monkey. I believe thefe were the *dumb dogs* which the Spaniards found, when they difcovered the Antilles or Caribee iflands.*

There are four forts of fquirrels in Louifiana; large, black, red, grey, and little ones of the fize of little rats; the latter are called flying fquirrels, on account of a membrane which joins their four legs, and which they extend in jumping from one tree to another.†

The *French* and the *Indians* have often told me that the fnakes have the power of fafcinating fquir-

---

* This animal here called *wood-cat* is common all over the Britifh colonies in America, and known by the name of *Raccoon*, fee Penn Syn. quad, p. 199. *Urfus lufcus*. Linn. and Kalm's Travels into North America, vol. i. t. 2. p. 96, 208. F.

† Black fquirrel, *fciurus niger*. Linn.—red fquirrel *fciurus ftriatus*. Linn.—grey fquirrel, *fciurus cinereus*. Linn.—flying fquirrel, *fciurus volans*. Linn. F.

squirrels; this I wished to see with my own eyes. I cannot avoid communicating my observations on this subject to you. I was once hunting at the *Illinois*, in a wood which abounded with hazelnuts, which is a very nice food for squirrels; they were likewise very plentiful there; I heard upon a tree, under which I stood, the sad cry of a squirrel which seemed frightened; I did not know what ailed it; at last I perceived a snake hung over a branch of the tree, looking upwards, waiting for its prey; and the unhappy squirrel, after leaping from branch to branch, fell into the mouth of the snake, which swallowed it.

Without entering into a physical detail, I imagine the squirrel was fascinated by the snake in the following manner. The antipathy of the squirrel, makes it look upon the snake as fastened to the tree, when it sees it thus immoveable, and hung upon a branch; therefore instead of remarking that it is only a snare, laid by its adversary, it jumps from branch to branch, as it were to insult the snake; when by jumping round the reptile, the latter sees it near enough to dart upon, seize and swallow it.† Many authors pretend

---

† This is a very ingenious explication, but it supposes, that we must attribute to the squirrel nicer feelings, than animals

pretend that the fnakes have an attractive power.

The cunnnig of fnakes is admirable; I have feen fome, which perceiving that I looked at them, did not ftir at all, in order to make me believe they were not there, and always conti-nued in the fame attitude; but as foon as I went afide to get a ftick or ftone to crufh their heads, the fnakes made off and I did not find them again when I returned. This is an experiment I have often made in the defarts which I have gone through, and where thefe animals are common.

There are many forts of them, of which the moft remarkable is the *rattle-fnake*, having four or five round bones, at the end of the tail, which make a kind of noife by rubbing againft one ano-ther, fimilar to the noife of a child's rattle. The Indian women pound this rattle and fwallow it when they are going to lye-in, becaufe they pre-tend that they can by its affiftance bring forth without pain. The fat of the rattle-fnake makes

an

mals in general and fquirrels in particular have; another me-thod to account for this pretended fafcination, fee in *Kalm's Travels* I. p. 319. note. F

an excellent unguent for the rheumatic pains; this unguent penetrates into the body, to the very bones.

It is generally believed that the number of *vertebræ* in the rattle encreafes with the age of the fnake; I have feen fome rattle-fnakes fo big, as to be able to eat a whole roe-deer, by fucking it little by little.

There is another kind of ferpent, which they call the whipper, *fouetteur*; it is red on the belly and black on the back; it is fometimes about twenty feet long, and when it finds any body in the water, it twines round him fo violently as to take away his breath, and drown him.*

That fnake which is called the *whiftler* is about two feet long, but is fo much more dangerous, becaufe it is not fo eafily feen, being very little; fo that the Indians and negroes often tread upon and are bitten by it: it has a prodigious wide mouth and when angry, it whiftles at a terrible rate,

_____

* This fnake is reprefented by *Catefby nat. hift. of Carol.* II. 46. It might be called *coluber erythrogafter*, for Catefby calls it the *copper-bellied-fnake*. The circumftance here mentioned, relative to its twifting round people in the water, and its enormous fize are both new. F.

rate, and therefore the Indians call him *ho-huy*, that is, *whiftler*. During my voyage to *Tombek-bé*, a whiftler hidden under the leaves, bit a foldier of my detachment, who trod upon its tail; the foldier was barefoot, and the fnake was fo angry that it got hold of his big toe and would not let go its hold. I was very uneafy and forry to fee this foldier expofed to perifh he being my interpreter; I applied to an Indian doctor who accidentally went by the place, where we were. He took a powder out of a little fack, and blew it through a tube upon the fnake's head, which died inftantly; he put another powder upon the wound, which prevented the poifon from taking its effect; he likewife gave fome of it in water to the patient, who was quite well after. I re-compenfed this juggler very handfomely; I wifh-ed likewife to know his fecret, but he would not teach it me, and acted like a quack telling me haughtily that the mafter of life had communi-cated it to him alone.*

The

---

* It is highly probable that this powder, was of the root or whole plant of the *ariftolochia anguicida* a Mexican plant, which probably grows likewife in *Louifiana*, and according to Dr. *Jacquin* is an infallible remedy againft the fnakes, for thefe animals are actually fafcinated and even killed by it. In

Car-

There are very large and long *crocodiles* or *alliga-tors* in some parts of the river *Miſſiſippi*; they are so carnivorous, that if they find a man aſleep on the land, they carry him into the water and de-vour him, though they are elſe very cowardly, and run off as ſoon as one walks towards them; it ſeldom happens that they eat a man, becauſe it is ſo eaſy to eſcape from them; they purſue thoſe that fly from them, and are very formi-dable in the water. The alligator is the moſt horrid animal in nature and I cannot without horror remember that which had almoſt carried me into the river of *Tombekbé*; I thought I ſaw the devil juſt come out of hell, and I believe he could not be better repreſented than under that hideous form; its back is covered with impenetra-ble

Carthagena the Indians chew the root of this *Ariſtolochia*, and mix its juice with the ſaliva; if one drop of this mix-ture is put into the ſnake's mouth, it inebriates it, and you may handle the ſnake as you pleaſe; if two or three drops are forced in; and they reach the ſnake's ſtomach, convul-ſions immediatly enſue, and the reptile dies. The Indian who ſhewed Dr. Jacquin this method, likewiſe informed him that he had been thrice bit by ſnakes, and had always cured the wound by uſing the *Ariſtolochia* both internally and ex-ternally. The plant itſelf has ſo nauſeous a ſmell, that it is always avoided by ſnakes, and cauſes, when chewed, vomiting even to men. See Jacquin's Hiſt. Select. Stirp. American. p. 232. t. 144. F.

ble fcales, almoft as ftrong as oyfter-fhells, refifting the force of a ball from a mufket. It is difficult to hurt an alligator any where except in the eye. They are numerous in the *red river*: they are torpid during the cold weather, and lie in the mud* with their mouths open, into which the fifh enter as into a funnel, and can neither advance nor go back. The Indians then get upon their backs and kill them by ftriking their heads with hatchets, and this is a kind of diverfion for them.

Here are likewife frogs of an extraordinary fize, whofe croaking exceeds the roaring of a bull. On my voyage from Mobile to New Orleans, I touched at the Horn Ifland and found a fhell fifh there, which the Indians call *Naninatelé*, which means *Sea Spider*; it was petrified. Its outward covering confifted of a more fhining varnifh than the Chinefe; its eyes were petrified and hard as diamonds. This fhell fifh is of the

fize

---

* This circumftance of the allegator's being torpid during winter, is quite new, and very remarkable for natural hiftorians. It feems almoft all the clafs of animals called *amphibia* by Dr. *Linnæus*, when found in cold climates, grow torpid during winter. F.

size and figure of a barber's bason turned upside
down, and has a very sharp tail about ten inches
long, and they say it is dangerous to be stung
by it *.

The higher parts of *Louisiana* contain beavers
and others; the Indians say that these beavers
have been expelled by their brethren from *Canada*, because they were too lazy to join with
them in constructing the habitations which those
animals make in common, and the dikes, to alter the bed of rivers, all which they contrive and
execute with great art and industry.

The *Karancro*, a bird of prey, is of the shape
and size of a turkey †, and the most voracious

bird

---

* This shell-fish is now in the Marquis *de Marigny's* cabinet of Natural Curiosities.

This *rare* animal is nothing else than the king's crab,
common in the seas all round *America* and the *West-Indies*;
monoculus Polyphemus. Linn. These animals are employed in
New-York to feed pigs with, and the ingenious gentleman,
who communicated this remark, adds, sometimes it is eaten
even by the two legged pigs. F.

† Hence it is called *Turkey Buzzard* by Catesby, Carol.
I. t. 6.----It is the *Carrion Vulture*, Forster's N. Amer. Animals, p. 8. and *Vultur Aura*, Linn.

bird that ever was known; it follows the hunters and likewife the convoys that travel to their different ftations. They wait in flights, like ravens, for the decampment; and then they come and eat greedily all that has been left there, after which they go on, towards the new camp. They eat dead corpfes; their feathers are black, and the foft downy feathers under the wings, have the quality of ftopping the blood.

The *Flamingo* is of the fame fize, the end of its wings is black, the back white, and the belly flame-coloured *.

There are ftares of two kinds; the leaft are of the fize of the European ones: they are fo common that a hundred of them are often killed at one fhot; they are very good to eat but the inhabitants are obliged to guard their crops of maize and rice, which otherwife would be entirely eaten up by thefe birds; they are as black as jet, and have the tip of the wing of a fine bright red; their feathers are very fine, and the ladies

VOL. I.   B b   wear

---

* Flamingo, *Phœnicopterus ruber*. Linn.

wear muffs, and linings to their dreffes of them *.

Here are parrots and parrokeets, and fine jays in great abundance: in the country of the *Miſſouris* there are magpies, only different from the European ones by their plumage, their black and white colours being ſhaded; the Indians make ornaments for their hair of them.

The eyes are taken with the beauty of nature unaſſiſted by art; here ſhe appears as ſhe came from the hands of the Creator, before the fall of man. The ear of the traveller is enchanted by the ſongs of the birds, and eſpecially thoſe of the *mocking* birds, which are fond of being in his company, and ſeem formed on purpoſe to make him forget the fatigues and tedioufneſs of the journey. Indeed as ſoon as the mocking bird perceives a man, he perches near him, and ſings very agreeably, flying from place to place; and in a word, this bird is inimitable; it ſettles at the top of a tree, and mocks or mimics all

the

---

* Theſe are the *red-winged ſtares* or *maize thieves* mentioned and drawn in *Kalm's Travels*, Vol. II. p. 74. *Oriolus phœniceus*. Linn.

the other birds; he likewife imitates the mewing of a cat. The mocking bird fometimes comes to the towns and houfes, and appears enchanted and pleafed when one plays on any inftrument and even joins the concert; it is of the fize of a ftare, and of a bluifh grey colour: it is eafily tamed, if taken young *.

The *Pope* is of a bright blue round the head; on the throat it is of a fine red, and on the back of a gold green colour, it fings very finely and is of the fize of a canary bird †.

The *Cardinal bird* is quite red, having the throat black, and a creft of feathers on its head, its bill is ftrong and red; it is a kind of fparrow, which is very fond of men, and comes to the fize of a lark, but whiftles during fummer like a black-bird ‡.

B b 2   The

---

* Mocking bird, *Turdus Orpheus* Linn. Kalm's Travels, Vol. II. p. 90. F.

† *Pope* is the male of the *Emberiza Ciris* Linn. known by the name of painted Finch. F.

‡ Cardinal bird is the *Loxia Cardinalis*, Linn. F.

The *Bishop* is blue mixed with purple and of the size of a linnet *.

The gold-finch is quite yellow, with the tips of the wings black †.

There is a bird they call the *Harlequin*, because it is varied with many colours, and another called the *Swiss*, becaufe it is red and blue; the laft three fpecies only come to the *Illinois* in fummer.

The *humming bird* is no bigger than a large beetle, and painted with many bright and changing colours; it lives upon the fweet juice of flowers as bees do; its neft is made of a very fine cotton or woolly fubftance, and fufpended on the branch of a tree ‡. There are numberlefs unknown birds, which would make the account too long.

I have feen butterflies of great beauty; I found two on my voyages (that have been eaten

up

---

* Bifhop, *Tanagra Epifcopus* Linn.

† Goldfinch, *Fringilla triftis*, Linn.

‡ Humming bird, *Trochilus Colubris*, Linn.

up by worms) the like of which I never faw;
I never beheld any thing more magnificent! it
feemed as if the author of nature had been
pleafed to throw upon their wings the fineft and
moft vivid colours; the fineft and pureft gold
appeared mixed among the other colours with
admirable fymmetry.

Thefe butterflies were probably carried to the
Akanzas by a fudden ftorm, for in the whole
fpace of a thoufand leagues which I have gone
through, I have never found their equals. I
defired fome Indians, of the *Ofages* nation, who
live near the mines of *St. Barbe*, to bring me
fome of thefe butterflies: they anfwered, that
in the country where they were to be found, the
inhabitants were very ferocious, and had merely
the forms of men.

Here are various forts of ducks, but the
moft curious are thofe which perch on trees, having pretty ftrong claws at the end of their
palmated toes; they build their nefts upon thofe
trees which lean over rivers or lakes, and when
their young ones are hatched, they go into the
water immediately. As to their feathers, they
are fhaded with the fineft colours: the male has
a creft upon its head. Thefe ducks are the beft

to

to eat, they feed in the woods on acorns and beech feeds *.

On the banks of rivers there are birds called Egrets, they are exceeding white and the ladies employ their feathers as *aigrettes* †.

The *Pelican*, which the inhabitants of the country call great throat, on account of a pouch he has under his throat, is as white and as large as a fwan, its bill is about twelve inches long; they make muffs of its fkin, and precipitate the pafte of indigo with its fat. This pafte is made from a plant, the grain of which comes from the Eaft Indies, for dying blue ‡.

The fpoon-bill §, having a bill like a *Spatula*, an apothecary's inftrument fo called. There is likewife a bird called *Lancet-bill*, whofe beak is
actually

---

* This is the *Anas arborea*, Linn.

† Egrets, *Ardea alba?* Linn. the great white heron ? Forft. North. Am. Animals, p. 14.

‡ Pelican, *Pelecanus Onocrotalus*, β. Linn.

§ Spoon-bill, *Platalea Leucorodia*, Linn.

actually like a lancet. It is impossible to finish this matter, it would require whole volumes; I leave this detail to our learned countrymen, M. *de Buffon* and *Daubenton*, who have undertaken this vast work. I wish you may be content with this short account.

I am, S I R, &c.

At New Orleans the 1*st*
of June, 1762.

P. S. Before I conclude my letter I shall speak to you of two precious plants in Louisiana; which are the *Indigo* and the *Cotton*.

Indigo is a plant resembling the *Broom* or *Genista* very much. A kind of it is growing in Louisiana spontaneously, and commonly upon hills and near woods. That which is cultivated is brought from the West India isles. There are two crops of it every year. It grows to the height of two feet and a half. When it is ripe, it is cut, and brought into the place where it is to rot; this is a building twenty feet high, without walls; but only supported by posts. In it they make three troughs, one above an-

B b 4 other

other, the loweſt is made ſo, that the water
it contains, may run out of it, and out of the
building. The ſecond ſtands on the edge of
this, ſo that the water it contains falls into the
firſt, and the third is diſpoſed in the ſame manner with regard to the ſecond. The indigo
leaves are put into the uppermoſt trough; with
a certain quantity of water, and muſt putrify in
it. The man who is at the head of the manu-
facture examines the indigo from time to time,
and when he ſees it is time to empty this trough,
he turns the cock, and the water runs into the
ſecond trough; there is a proper time which
muſt be well obſerved for doing this operation,
for if the plant remains too long in this putrefy-
ing place, the Indigo becomes black.

As ſoon as the water is in the ſecond trough,
it is beaten till the overſeer thinks it ſufficient;
it is uſe and habit by which one learns to ſeize
upon the true moment. When the water has
been well beaten, it is left to ſettle : the indigo
forms a kind of ſediment at the bottom of the
trough; the water above it muſt have time to
become clear, and is afterwards drawn off
by means of ſeveral cocks placed above each
other.

The

The indigo is then taken off likewise, and put into facks made of common fackcloth, where the remaining water may run off. After this it is fpread upon boards, and when dry it is cut into little fquare pieces, put into barrels, and fo fent to *Europe*.

In order to have feeds, it is neceffary only to let fo many plants grow up as are wanted; it grows more or lefs tall according to the nature of the foil, which ought to be light; in the Weft India iflands they have four crops a-year, on account of the great heat, but in *Louifiana* they cannot have above three; the indigo in the latter place is likewife not fo good *.

The cotton-fhrub is no bigger than a rofe-bufh, but fpreads more. It does not fucceed fo well in ftrong or rich grounds as in others; therefore that which grows in Lower *Louifiana* is inferior in goodnefs to that which is cultivated in the higher parts of that province.

The

* The indigo plant is, with Dr. *Linnæus*, the *Indigofera tinctoria*, and the indigo mentioned to grow fpontaneoufly in *Louifiana* is the *Sophora tinctoria*, Linn.; which, with a proper management, is faid to afford as good indigo as the celebrated *Anil* of the Indies and Egypt. F.

The cotton of this country is of the species called white cotton of Siam. It is neither so fine nor so long as the silky cotton, but it is however very white and very fine. Its leaves are of a lively green, and resemble spinage very much; the flower is of a pale yellow, the seed contained in the capsule is black, and oval like a kidney-bean: it is commonly planted in such grounds as are not yet fit for tobacco or for indigo; for the latter requires the greatest care.

The shrub is cut down to the ground every two or three years, because they say it bears more after it. The pistil of the flower changes into an acuminated capsule, of the size of a pigeon's egg, green at first, then brown, and at last almost black, dry and brittle.

When the cotton is ripe, the heat of the sun makes it expand; the capsule that contained it opens in three or four places with a little noise. Then it must be gathered quickly, lest it should be lost. Each capsule contains five, six, or seven seeds, of the size of pease; the cotton sticks to them, and it is therefore difficult to get the seeds out, except in time and with patience; for

this

this reafon, however, many planters have been difgufted with the culture of cotton *.

I have not mentioned tobacco to you; it is likely that it is a native of the country, becaufe the tradition of the Indians, or their *ancient word*, tells us, that they have always employed it to fmoke in their calumets of peace. I fhall conclude with an obfervation that has already been made, and which it is good to repeat, till fomebody tries the experiment. The climate of *Louifiana*, and the hilly parts of that country, give reafon to believe, that it would not be difficult to plant faffron there; the colonifts would reap great advantages from it, and the neighbourhood of *Mexico* would procure them a quick and certainly an ufeful confumption.

---

* The people in the Englifh colonies, and in China, employ an inftrument which feparates the pods from the cotton with great eafe. F.

L E T T E R XXI.

To the .same.

Reflections on the Population of America *; that Continent has not been unknown to the Ancients; it seems that it is connected with* Asia *on the Side of* Tartary, *from whence the People that first settled it must naturally be supposed to have come. A Digression upon the Way of preserving one's Health in* America.

S I R,

I Expect to set out for *France* very soon; and I take advantage of an opportunity that offers to write to you, before I leave this part of the world. After giving you an idea of the manners, customs, and of the history of the people with whom I have been during my voyages, I do not believe I could better conclude my narrative, than by some reflections

tions on the population of this immenfe continent; but this matter is fo obfcure, that we
cannot now flatter ourfelves to clear it up: many learned writers have already attempted to
throw light upon it, but they have not fucceeded; modern philofophy has endeavoured, with
as little fuccefs, to draw advantages from it,
and its reafonings and opinions have not even
been able to feduce weak geniufes.

By reflecting attentively upon the old writers,
every thing feems to convince us, that *America*
was not entirely unknown to them. *Diodorus
Siculus* feems to have fpoken of it with precifion
enough: Father *Laffiteau* quotes a paffage from
that hiftorian, and adds his reflections to clear
it up. The *Phœnicians*, if we may believe the
Greek author, after fending feveral colonies upon the coaft of the Mediterranean, being enriched by their trade, did not go far beyond the co-
lumns of Hercules; that vaft and unknown
ocean, which they difcovered on coming through
the ftreights of *Gibraltar*, infpired them with a
kind of horror, which they furmounted only by
degrees: fome bold navigators ventured out upon the ocean afterwards; but failing along the
coaft of *Africa*, a violent tempeft, of feveral
days duration, carried them to an ifle of very

great

great extent, at a great diftance to the weftward. At their return they were very ready to fpeak of their difcovery, they embellifhed their accounts, with all the fictions familiar to travellers of all countries, and at all times. When the *Tyrrhenians* became the mafters of the fea, they were willing to make a fettlement there; but the *Carthagenians* oppofed it, fearing that their countrymen, attracted by what was faid of this land, fhould leave their country in order to fettle there; they likewife confidered this new-difcovered country as a laft refource for themfelves, in cafe fome difafter fhould have overturned their empire.

To this paffage of *Diodorus Siculus*, Father *Laffiteau* adds one of *Paufanias*. This writer was inquiring, whether there were any fatyrs; one *Euphemus*, who was born in *Caria*, told him, that, in a voyage of his, he had been carried by a ftorm to the extremities of the ocean, where he had feen feveral ifles, which the failors called *Satyrides*. The people that inhabited them were of a red colour, and had tails; the failors trembled, and endeavoured to avoid them; but the contrary winds forced them to come near the fhore; the favages invefted the veffel, and the crew,

crew, in order to get rid of them, were obliged to deliver a woman to them.

Father *Laffiteau*'s reflection will appear very juft to you. " The defcription of thefe ifland-
" ers," fays he, " perfectly fits to the *Caraïbes*,
" who were mafters of the Antilles, commonly
" called the *Caribee* iflands, out of moft of
" which they have been expelled by the Euro-
" peans in thefe latter times. The complexion
" of thefe people is very red, and it is naturally
" fo; it being lefs the effect of the climate,
" than of the imagination of the mothers, who,
" finding the red colour beautiful, tranfmit it
" to their children * ; their flefh is likewife arti-
" ficially red, for they paint themfelves every
" day with *rocou*, which ferves inftead of vermi-
" lion to them, and appear as red as blood by
" it. As to what concerns the imagination of
" the failors, who thought they beheld fatyrs,
" it only was the effect of fear, that made them
" take

* Every one will not agree with the Jefuit upon the effect of the mother's imagination on their children : the different colours of men from the feveral parts of the world, offer
many more difficulties. All that has been written on the
fubject has not explained this phenomenon ; men who were
originally white, muft have become black, red, and brown,
(bronzed), by the union of feveral caufes.

" take falfe tails for real ones; almoft all the
" barbarous nations of *America* wore this orna-
" ment, efpecially when they went to war."

The fimilarity which has been obferved to exift between the manners of feveral *American* nations, and thofe of fome of the oldeft nations on
our continent, feems to demonftrate that this
country was not unknown in ancient times, and
chiefly proves that the known or old parts furnifhed the new one with men; how could that
fimilarity be explained, if this had not happened? How great a refemblance is there in the
religion, manners, and cuftoms of the *Indians,*
with thofe of fome ancient nations. Thefe details will always deftroy moft of the bold fyftems
which have been ftarted on the population of
America. If they were a colony of people efcaped from the deluge, the univerfality of which
is in vain contefted, they would have brought
anti-diluvian cuftoms into America. Thofe nations that were born after this dreadful punifhment, do they refemble their anceftors that were
buried under the floods? We have not yet light
enough upon this fubject to make a juft comparifon; we can anfwer nothing to thofe who fay,
*That the Almighty hand, which fowed plants and
fruits in all parts of the world, could likewife place*
                                               men

men there. An ingenious phrase is not always a reason : no one disputes this power of the Creator; but he has been pleased to teach us himself, that it was not his will to people the world so, and that he gave existence to two creatures, who were the origin of the whole human race.

All these opinions rest upon the course that men must have taken, in order to come from the old world to the new; and it is upon this difficulty that most authors found their writings. A more exact and extensive knowledge of our globe would annihilate all these difficulties. It is very probable, that there is a passage which unites *Asia* to *America*; I have already said something of it to you, in speaking of the elephants bones found in one of the countries I have gone through : this is not a new opinion : this conjecture has been made long ago. " *America*," says Father *Laffiteau*, " can be come at " in different places, and accordingly it may " have been peopled from all sides; this is be- " yond a doubt; it is but at a little distance " from the southern unknown countries; and " in the north, *Greenland*, which is *perhaps* con- " tiguous to this new continent, is not far from " *Lapland*. Those parts of *Asia* which bound it " towards the land of *Yeso*, probably make but

" one continent with, or are only at a little di-
" ftance from *America*, if the ftreights that are
" fuppofed to be there go to the Tatarian fea:
" the ocean which furrounds *America* almoft en-
" tirely, is ftrewed with ifles, both in the nor-
" thern and fouthern feas. Men may have gone
" from ifle to ifle, either by fhipwreck or by
" mere chance."

This author alledges many reafons to prove,
that *North America* joins to *Tartary*, or to fome
country contiguous to it ; the following is a very
fingular one : You know that *ginfeng* is originally a native of the *Mantchcoux Tartary*, the *Chinefe*
or *Tartarian* name of it fignifies, the *thighs of a
man*. The *Americans*, who were long acquainted with it, and made ufe of it, called it *garel-
oguen*, which has the fame fignification. If *A-
merica* did not join to *Tartary*, or if the latter
had not peopled the firft, how could their refpective inhabitants give names of the fame fignification to the fame plant ? I do not fpeak
here of etymologies of words that have been
corrupted, and which are only found by forcing
them ; their fignification is here in queftion.

Captain *William Rogers* looks upon it as very
probable, that fome *Tartarians* paffed over into
America:

America: he obferves, that the fhips which annually go from the *Philippines* to *Mexico,* are obliged to fteer to the northward, in order to meet
with favourable winds, thofe which rife between
the tropics being always contrary to them. He
adds, that after paffing forty-two degrees of
north latitude, failors often meet with fands and
fhallows, which feem to indicate that they are
near fome coafts. He imagines, that thefe coafts
might well be fome continent unknown to *Euro-*
peans, and uniting *California* with *Japan*; but
fhould they not rather be the coafts of *Kamtchat-*
ka, or of that new country to the eaft difcovered
by Captain *Bering?*

To thefe obfervations I fhall add an abftract
of a relation, publifhed in the *Mercure Galant*
for November 1711. I fhall quote the fact,
without making any reflections to confirm or con-
tradict it; the author pretends to have got it out
of a manufcript found in *Canada.*

Ten men refolved to go out upon difcoveries,
with a view to get riches; they embarked in
three canoes, and went up the river *Miffifippi.*
After a long voyage, they found another river
which flowed to the fouth-fouth-weft; they carried their canoes to it, and continued their na-

vigation ; fome time after, they arrived in x
country which extended two hundred leagues,
and was inhabited by a nation who called themfelves *Efcaaniba.*

The Frenchmen (for the ten travellers were
of that nation) found much gold with thefe
people. Their king pretended to deduce his
origin from *Montezuma* ; his name was *Agau-
zan,* and he kept a ftanding army of an hundred
thoufand men in time of peace. The *Efcaaniba*
women were white as the *European* women ; they
and the men of that nation had long ears, to
which they faftened gold rings. One of their
diftinctions was, to let their nails grow : polygamy was permitted among them ; they did not
pay any attention to their daughters, who lived
in the greateft liberty, without any one to watch
over their conduct. Their country produced tobacco, various fruits, fome common to *Europe*
and *India,* and fome that were peculiar to it ;
the rivers abounded with fifh ; their forefts were
full of game of every kind, and contained above
all a great number of parrots. The capital was
fituated at fix leagues from the river, which they
called *Miffi, Golden river.* They valued gold
fo little, that they permitted the *French* to take
as much as they pleafed with them : you may
con-

conceive, that they made a good ufe of this per-
miffion; each of them took for his fhare two
hundred and forty pounds weight of gold. Their
mines were in the mountains, from whence they
brought the gold upon rivulets, which were dry
during one feafon of the year.

Thefe people traded with a nation very diftant
from them; and in order to make the *French*
fenfible of it, they told them, that it required
fix months to make the voyage. The adventurers happened to be with the *Efcaanibas* at the
time when their caravan fet out to trade with
thofe ftrangers; it confifted of three hundred
oxen loaded with gold; an equal number of
men, armed with lances, bows, arrows, and a
kind of daggers, conducted and watched them:
they brought back, in exchange for their gold,
fome iron, fteel, lances, and other weapons.

I cannot afcertain in what degree we may
truft this account; the adventurers conjectured,
that the diftant country whither the *Efcaanibas*
went, was *Japan*; in that cafe, there muft be a
communication between *Afia* and *America*; fome
Englifh writers, without attempting to difpute
the authenticity of this account, believe, that
the favages went to trade with the inhabitants of

C c 3

Kamt-

Kamptchatka, or of fome ifle or continent near that peninfula. This communication will never be well afcertained whilft it remains undifcover- ed *. Conjectures explain nothing; they give probabilities, but go no further: however, be it as it will, it is very probable that fuch a com- munication exifts: fuppofing there are ftreights that divide thefe two great parts of the world, they cannot have prevented men from penetra- ting out of one into the other, by croffing thofe ftreights. We muft hope, that the ignorance in which we are at prefent will not laft for ever; the difcoveries which men fhall endeavour to make in the great fouthern or Pacific ocean, will give us more light on this fubject †. If, after

making

---

* The modern geographical difcoveries, and efpecially thofe made by the Ruffians, fufficiently evince, that the fea entirely divides *Afia* from *America*; there can be no doubt neither of *Japan*'s being an ifle, and unconnected with the continent of *America*; it is true, however, that the fea which divides *Afia* from *America* near Cape *Tchukfhi*, is very nar- row, and not a fufficient obftacle to the migration of the na- tions that inhabit the north-eaft parts of *Siberia* into *Ameri- ca*; for a further hint concerning the population of that vaft continent, fee *Kalm's Travels to North America*, vol. iii. p. 125. &c. F.

† When thefe letters were gone to prefs, I heard that the Englifh had difcovered ten iflands in that ocean. There is

an

making voyages that way, fome ftreights be really found, it is no reafon why they fhould always have been there: earthquakes may have divided the ifthmus or neck of land which combined the two continents; many authors attribute the ftreights of *Gibraltar* to the fame kind of event: the Mediterranean, they fay, had formerly no communication with the Atlantic; many pretend, that *Great Britain* was joined to *France*; now the fea feparates *Dover* and *Calais*: why cannot this be the cafe with *Afia* and *America* likewife?

The time in which the population of *America* was commenced, is as obfcure and indeterminate as the manner in which it was peopled; every thing which is difficult to penetrate excites the curiofity of men; they wifh to fee fomething new, and to fpeak of it, and frequently they

C c 4

give

an account of it in the voyage of Commodore *Byron*, who has been fo much talked of, and has proved the exiftence of giants, which was blindly believed by the ancients, rejected as chimerical by the moderns, and now confirmed by new difcoveries. The next voyage which the Englifh will make that way, will furnifh us with more minute accounts; others will be encouraged to imitate them, and a perfect knowledge of the South Sea will clear up the difficulties concerning the junction of *Afia* and *America*.

give us their own chimerical imaginations as
fomething real. Among the fingular opinions
which this fubject has given rife to, I fhall mention that of *Marc Lefcarbot*, in his Hiftory of
New France; Father *Laffiteau* fhall ftill be my
guide on this occafion, and from his work on
the manners of the favage *Americans*, I fhall
take what I have to fay on this matter. " *Lef-*
" *carbot* has not fcrupled to advance very pofi-
" tively, and in a manner that goes beyond con-
" jecture, that *Noah* was not unacquainted with
" the weftern continent, (where *Lefcarbot* was
" born); and that at leaft he knew it by fame.
" That, having lived three hundred and fifty
" years after the deluge, he himfelf had taken
" care to people, or rather to re-people that
" country: that, being a good workman, and
" an excellent pilot, and being charged to re-
" pair the defolation of the earth, he may be
" fuppofed to have conducted his children thi-
" ther; and it may have been as eafy to him to
" have gone through the ftreights of *Gibraltar* to
" *New France*, *Cape Verd*, and *Brazil*, as it was
" to his children to go and fettle in *Japan*, or
" as it was to himfelf to come from the moun-
" tains of *Armenia* into *Italy*, where he founded
" the *Janiculum* upon the banks of the *Tiber*, if
" we

" we may credit the accounts given by profane
" writers."

I doubt whether it is neceſſary to go back to
Noah, to find the period of the population of
America; if, as is very probable, the *Tartars*
went over into that continent, it muſt have happened in the following times : a ſet of people,
who are not numerous, do not eaſily leave the
vaſt country they inhabit; they do not ſo ſoon
endeavour to ſeparate from each other; they
continue together, till, by having multiplied too
much, they ſpread more, or till ſome other cir-
cumſtances force them to leave their native
country : ſuch reſearches are of little importance;
they are mere matters of curioſity, and the difficulty of ſatifying that ought to prevent men
from employing their time in them. All that
can be aſſerted with certainty is, that *America*
ſeems to have been inhabited only of late.

Powell, an Engliſh writer, mentions, in his
Hiſtory of *Wales*, that, in the year 1170, there
was a war in that country for the ſucceſſion to
the throne, after the death of Prince *Owen Gwin-
neth*. A baſtard took the crown from the legitimate children ; one of the latter, whoſe name
was *Madoc*, embarked in order to make new diſ-
coveries;

coveries; directing his courfe to the weftward, he came to a country the fertility and beauty of which were amazing. As this country, was without inhabitants, *Madoc* fettled in it; *Hakluit* affures us, that he made two or three voyages to *England* to fetch inhabitants, who, upon the account he gave them of that fine country, went to fettle with him.

The Englifh believe, that this prince difcovered *Virginia*. *Peter Martyr* feems to give a proof of it, when he fays, that the nations of *Virginia*, and thofe of *Guatimala*, celebrate the memory of one of their ancient heroes, whom they call *Madoc*. Several modern travellers have found ancient Britifh words ufed by the *North American* nations. The celebrated Englifh Bifhop *Nicholfon* believes, that the Welch language has formed a confiderable part of the languages of the *American* nations; there are antiquaries who pretend, that the Spaniards got their double or guttural *l (ll)* from the *Americans*, who, according to the Englifh, muft have got it from the *Welch*. I fhould never have done, if I were to mention all their reafonings to prove the voyage of the *Welch* Prince *Madoc*. The Dutch brought a bird, with a white head, from the ftreights of *Magellan*, which the natives called

Penguin;

Penguin; this word is an old Welch one, and fignifies *white head*; from hence they conclude, that the natives originall came from *Wales* *.

The *Englifh* are not the only people, who, according to our hiftorical romances, went to *America* and fettled there : *Bayer* pretends, that the *Normans* were the firft Europeans who ventured to fail to that country.

Doctor *Lochner* afferts that a *Bohemian* of a diftinguifhed family went to *Brafil*, and difcovered the ftraights of *Magellan*, before *Columbus* went to the New World ; this Bohemian was called *Martin* †. Many German writers who
feem

---

* This, however, is a wrong fuppofition ; for it appears, that the bird in queftion has a black and not a white head ; but its name is Spanifh, and fignifies a fat bird, the *Penguin* or rather *Pinguin* being very fat.   F.

† Our author miftakes the name of this man for that of his country : he was called *Martin Behaim*, a native of *Nurenberg* in Germany ; his father was a noble fenator of that city : after ftudying mathematics, and efpecially aftronomy and geography, under the great mathematician *Joannes Regiomontanus*, he went to the *Netherlands*, then governed by the Princefs *Ifabella*, daughter to *John* I. of Portugal ; he there obtained the command of a fhip, fitted out for the purpofe of making difcoveries : he fet fail in 1460, and, failing

.feem to wifh that America fhould bear his name preferably to that of *Americo Vefpucci*, have followed this opinion.

Whether thefe traditions are adopted or rejected, whether they are fabulous or true, it remains inconteftible that the *Americans* have the fame origin with us; among all their errors, they have preferved fome ideas that have a great fimilarity with thofe, which have been tranfmitted to us by writing: I fhall mention to you a piece of an Englifh differtation on the population of *America,*

. failing to the weftward firft met with the ifle of *Fayal* one of the *Azores*, all which iflands were afterwards called the *Flemifh* ifles from the firft inhabitants, which *Martin Behaim* brought thither. He then returned, and obtained two fhips, with which he cruized in the atlantic for fome time, and at laft difcovered the fourth part of the world, and even went as far as the ftraights, now called *Straights of Magellan*; he laid down all his difcoveries in a fea chart, which he prefented to king *Alphonfus* the fifth, of *Portugal*. This fketch afterwards fell into the hands of *Chriftopher Columbus*, a Genoefe who was at *Lisbon*, and firft infpired him with a defire of vifiting thofe unknown countries. When he undertook the voyage, he always followed the fame courfe which *Martin Behaim* had laid down on his chart, and performed the voyage in as fhort a time as is done now. In the noble family of *Behaim* at Nurenberg, they ftill preferve among other curiofities a globe drawn with a pen, and coloured by that able navigator, in which all his difcoveries are marked. F.

America, in which many *American* opinions are
collected, which owe their origin to the truths
preferved by *Mofes*. " The *Peruvians* believe,
" that there formerly was a deluge, by which
" all the inhabitants of their continent perifhed,
" a few excepted, who retired into caverns at
" the top of the higheft mountains, and whofe
" defcendants filled the earth with inhabitants
" again.   Some ideas, little different from
" thefe have been received by the natives of
" *Hifpaniola*, according to what *Gemelli Carreri*
" relates.   The old hiftories of *Mexico* likewife
" mention an univerfal deluge, by which all
" men, one man and woman excepted, perifhed.
" Thefe two people, according to the *Mexicans*,
" had numerous defcendants ; but all their chil-
" dren were dumb, till a pigeon endowed them
" with the power of fpeech ; they add, that the
" primitive language of the immediate de-
" fcendants of the couple who furvived the de-
" luge, was fplit into fo many dialects, that it
" was impoffible for them to underftand each
" other ; which after obliging them to feparate,
" contributed to make them people the different
" countries of the earth.   Some *American* na-
" tions have a tradition, that all men derive
" their origin from four women, which agrees
" pretty well with the *Mofaic* hiftory, which
" makes

" makes all the nations defcend from *Noah* and
" his three fons. All thefe traditions manifeftly
" fhew, that the *Americans* are defcendants of
" *Noah*, and that various accounts of the *Mo-*
" *faic* hiftory are even come down to them.
" This is fufficient to overthrow the ftrange fyf-
" tem which attributes anceftors to the *Americans*
" anterior to *Adam.*"

Does not this quotation anfwer all the arguments of thofe fyftematic writers, who will give
us the fruits of their abfurd imagination as
truths? Where could the *Americans* get thefe
notions, if they were not all pofterior to the deluge, and defcended from nations that had preferved the tradition? It is eafy to explain, that
by length of time, by the ignorance and the
mutability of the *Indians*, they have immerfed
true facts, which were committed to their memory, in fables. The want of monuments,
characters or letters to write down thofe events,
certainly impairs the purity of tradition; as
foon as it is tranfmitted by word of mouth from
father to fon, it muft be much changed after
paffing through fo many generations.

The wars which the *Indians* ever carried on
among themfelves, have contributed greatly to
hinder

hinder population; their fmall number has certainly been the caufe of the nomadic life they
lead; they ran through the woods in order to
fearch for game, and fettled in all the places
where they found food in abundance, leaving
them again in order to go further, whenever it
began to fail them.

If they were more numerous their wants
would increafe; it would become more difficult
to provide food for them all; this difficulty
would open their minds, give them new ideas:
they would feel that it was neceffary to provide
a fubfiftence more independent from mere
chance; the fruits which the earth produces,
would teach them to multiply them by cultivation; they would fee all the ufes of thefe pro-
ductions, think of appropriating them to themfelves, and fucceed in it; in fome places we fee
them already cultivate maize, they would foon
cultivate other corn; one kind of knowledge
would lead to another: they would fettle in the
country which they had cultivated, and be no
longer fuch vagabonds as there are now.

The fettlement of the *Europeans* in the northern parts has engaged many of thefe nations
to come and fettle in their neighbourhood in
order

order to get that affistance from them which they want; the defire which the *Europeans* fhew of poffeffing their furs and the eafe with which they can obtain brandy and fire-arms in exchange for them, often excite them to go through the woods and hunt in the extent of two hundred leagues around, in order to get thofe things, which become real wants to them; thus they are only apparently fixed; they preferve their love for a rambling life, and the period of their civilization feems as yet very diftant; perhaps they will deftroy each other before they come to it.

This is all that can be afferted with probability on the population of *America*; my letter would be too long, if I would only mention a hundredth part of what has been faid on this fubject. The fyftems and contrary opinions which have been long publifhed, would make confiderable volumes; I have endeavoured to confine myfelf to curious obfervations; thofe who think the *Tartars* have chiefly furnifhed *America* with inhabitants, feem to have hit the true opinion; you cannot believe how great the refemblance of the *Indian* manners is to thofe of the ancient Scythians; it is found in their religious ceremonies, their cuftoms and in their food.

food. *Hornius* is full of characteristics, that may satisfy your curiosity in this respect, and I desire you to read him.

I shall now quit all these discussions which ought to finish the account of my voyages, and shall speak of another subject, more useful to the human race, in regard to which observation and experience suffice to instruct us.

As it is the natural desire of man to live long, I hope it will not be foreign to my purpose, to shew in a few words, how one may preserve life and live long in *America.*

I shall therefore finish my letter by a small dissertation on the method of managing one's health. I remember to have read, in the *Holland Gazette* of the 3d of April 1687, that *Frederick Gualdus*, a noble Venetian, has preserved his life to the age of four hundred years; it is pretended, that he was possessed of the universal medicine. He left *Venice* the 7th of March 1686; having his picture with him painted by *Titian*, who was then already dead an hundred and thirty years. I am sure you will agree with me in saying, that exercise and sobriety procure a perfect health. The nations of *America* knew neither wine nor brandy two hundred and fixty years ago, when the *Europeans* came to them; they lived, as I have already faid, on the flefh of wild beafts dried, roafted, or boiled with maize pounded in a mortar made of fome hard wood. This food is wholefome, and makes a very good *chyle*. I have lived about two months upon thefe victuals, going up the river *Mobile* with the *Indians*, and can affirm, that I never enjoyed my health better in my life than at that time. Of all Latin proverbs, this is the beft:

Plures gula occidit, quam gladius.

Voluptuoufnefs and intemperance in eating and drinking, deftroy more men than the fword. Therefore one ought to prefcribe to himfelf a proper regimen of life, efpecially in the hot countries of *America*.

First of all, great care muft be taken to be accuftomed to the climate by degrees, and to abftain from eating all kinds of fruit, and drinking all forts of liquors, till the body is ufed to it. People who are very replete with blood, may be bled from time to time, to prevent an apoplexy. A gentle purge will fometimes do well; the
burning

burning heat of the fun muft be avoided, and the air at night likewife.

When one has drunk too much wine, it is neceffary to take four things; fuch as lemon, which is very common there ; by this means you will neither find yourfelves ill, nor be overcome by the vapours which commonly follow. If the quantity of liquor which has been drank heats the body, fome refrefhing aliments muft be ta-taken, but every thing that increafes heat muft be avoided : fpirituous liquors fhould be drank as little as poffible, for they burn the blood, and eafily caufe a hot fever.

When you have eaten too much, ftrong liquors are good to ftrengthen the ftomach, and help digeftion ; but if, on the contrary, it happens that you are heated by drinking too much *, they would prove very dangerous. Thofe who are too much addicted to debauchery are almoft always tormented with bad dreams, which fatigue them fo much as almoft to trouble their

D d 2

mind,

---

* It ought to be remarked, that, fince the *Americans* have drank wine and brandy, they have like us fhortened their days.

mind, becaufe the fumes of the wine, with which their body is filled, fucceffively excite their imagination. It is known by experience, that fober perfons, and thofe efpecially who drink water, fleep quietly, their fleep being neither too flight nor too heavy. It appears, from the fecond chapter of the Life of *Apollonius*, written by *Philoftratus*, that at Athens thofe who were afflicted with bad dreams applied to the priefts of the falfe deities, in order to be rid of them; they ordered them to abftain from wine for three or four days; this cleared their imagination, and produced a cure, which they attributed to their gods.

If, after taking too much food, you are heavy, and your members fatigued, fo that too great an abundance of nutritive juice occafions a plenitude in the whole body, and makes you tired; I believe that, in imitation of the *Indians*, fweating is an infallible remedy, when the natural heat is affifted with an exterior one; this remedy is infallible, provided it be applied at the firft appearance of the diftemper; the *Europeans*, in order to perfpire well, get between two blankets, and remain there covered up, the face excepted; they do not get up till they have

fweated

fweated well, and about an hour after the whole perfpiration is performed. If this method of fweating is continued during fome days, you find yourfelf fo much eafed, that your ftrength and appetite return, and you are furprifed to fee yourfelf fo light and fo nimble; for by the perfpiration all the *vifcera* are perfectly cleared of all their fuperfluities, without pain or any violence done to nature, which the ordinary medicines cannot do. In order to be healthy, this ought to be done thrice in the year, *viz.* in fpring, autumn, and in winter.

My conclufion is, that diet, perfpiration, and fweating compofe an univerfal medicine.

Therefore I fay, that nature fhould direct us in all things; from her we muft learn the true means of preferving health, which fhe orders us to do upon pain of the greateft evils, and even of death. I have already told you, that the frequent exercifes of the Indians of *North America*, fuch as dancing, playing at ball, hunting, fifhing, and fighting, increafe their natural heat fo much, that it drives all the fuperfluities out of their bodies by perfpiration. Why do the peafants

fants live long, and are healthy, without the affiftance of phyficians! The perpetual labour they are employed in keeps them fo; exercife prevents their knowing the gout, gravel, and other infirmities, to which the richer people in *Europe* are fubject, on account of the refined tafte of their tables, and becaufe they make no more ufe of their legs than old infirm men. I have known fome, who, like Moliere's *Malade imaginaire*, fillèd their ftomach with as many drugs as an apothecary's fhop.

It has been obferved, in the hot countries of *America*, that the young *Europeans* die fooner there than the old ones; becaufe the former imprudently eat all forts of fruit, which caufe them a dyfentery; therefore it is neceffary to eat very little of them, till the body is accuftomed to the climate, after which, at the expiration of a year, this will caufe no further inconveniencies.

By obferving thefe precautions, I will warrant, that people will live longer in this part of the world than in the old one. There are now many people alive in *Louifiana*, who have been there ever fince its firft fettlement. I faw
a planter

a planter called *Graveline*, aged one hundred and eighteen years, who came hither with M. *d'Iberville*, in 1698; he ferved in *Canada* as a foldier for about thirty years, in the reign of *Lewis* the Fourteenth.

I am, S I R, &c.

End of the FIRST VOLUME.

www.ingramcontent.com/pod-product-compliance
Lightning Source LLC
Chambersburg PA
CBHW032314280326
41932CB00009B/811